HELL YEAH™

VOLUME ONE: LAST DAY ON EARTHS

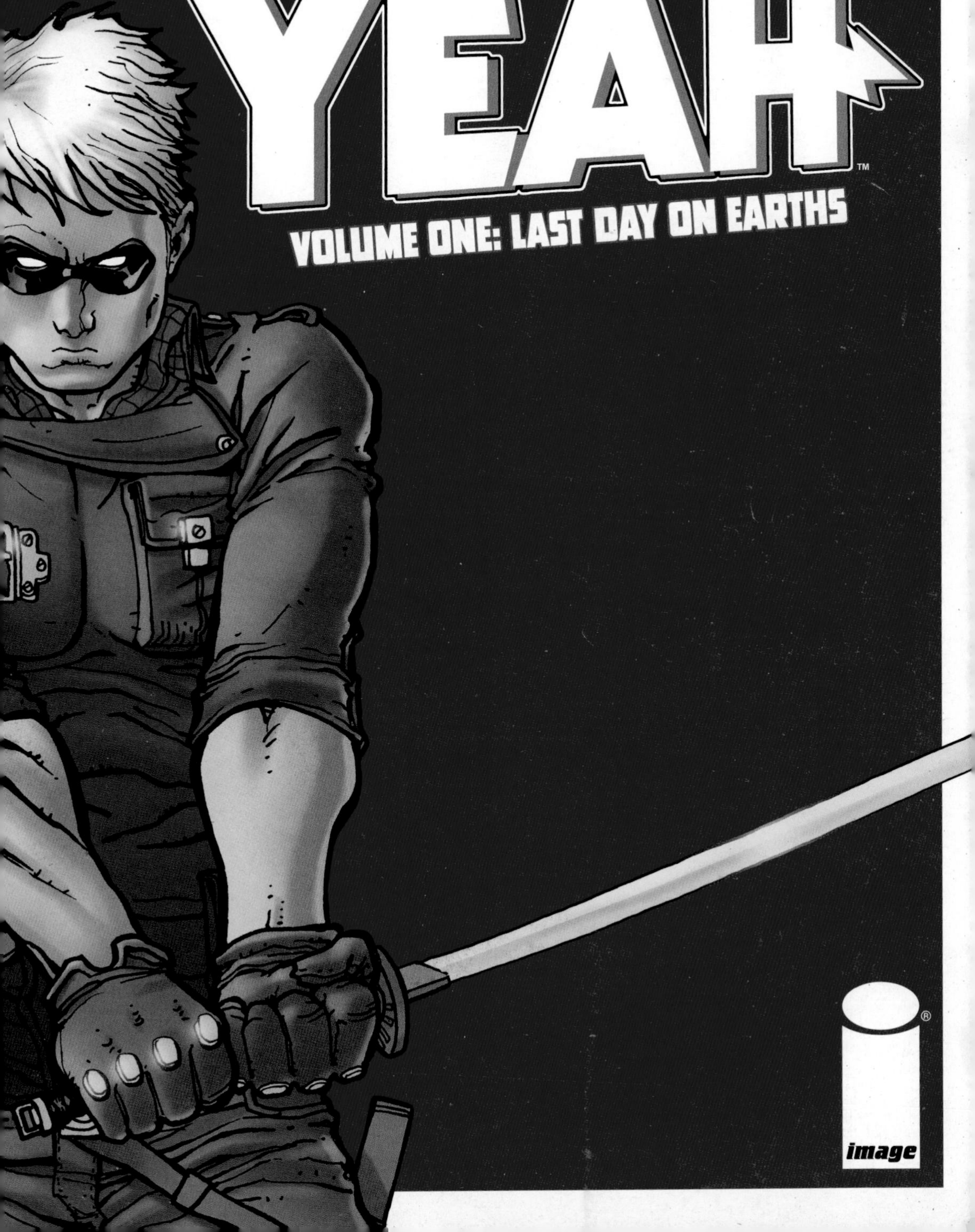

image

HELL YEAH

VOLUME ONE: LAST DAY ON EARTHS

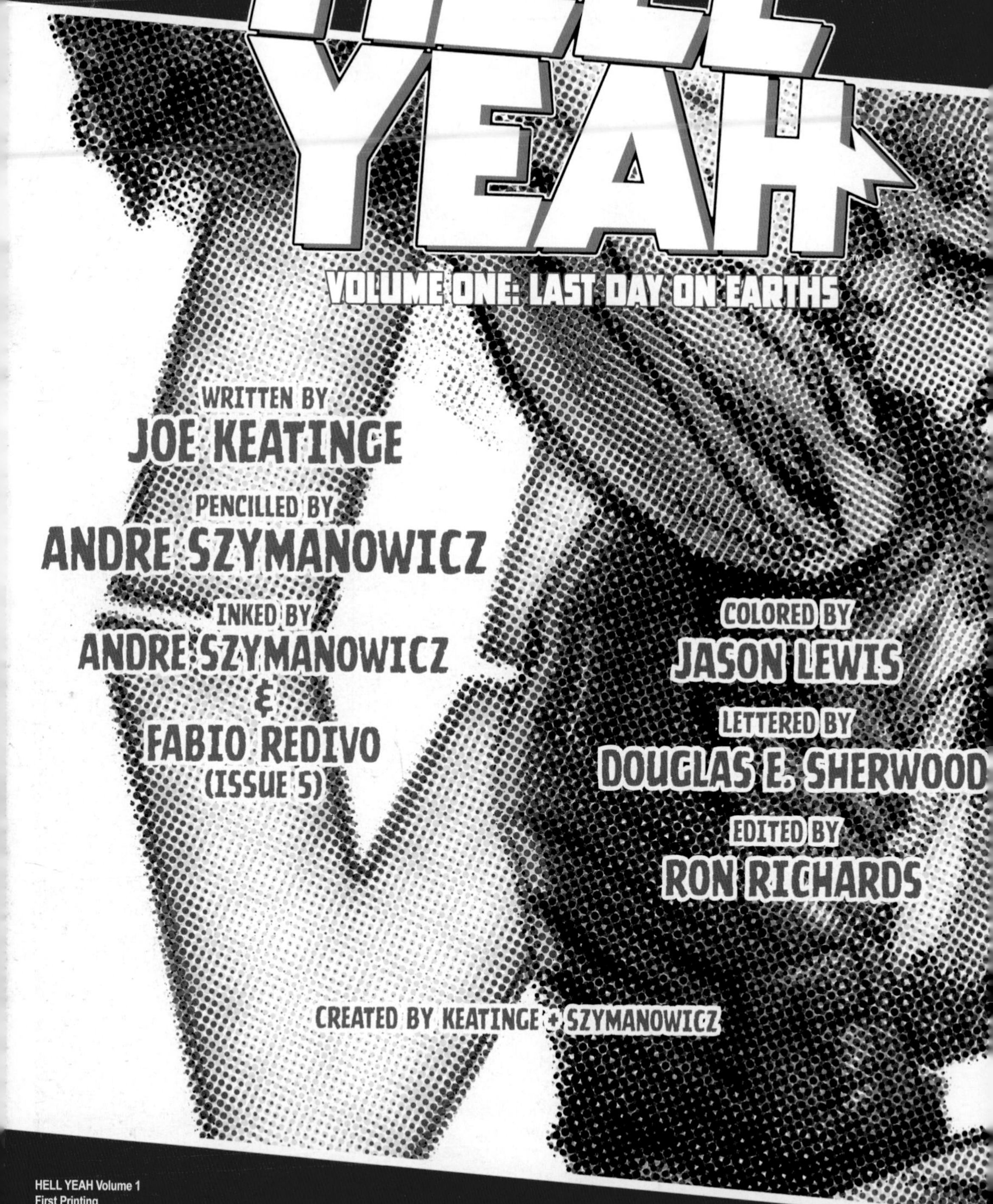

WRITTEN BY
JOE KEATINGE

PENCILLED BY
ANDRE SZYMANOWICZ

INKED BY
ANDRE SZYMANOWICZ
&
FABIO REDIVO
(ISSUE 5)

COLORED BY
JASON LEWIS

LETTERED BY
DOUGLAS E. SHERWOOD

EDITED BY
RON RICHARDS

CREATED BY KEATINGE + SZYMANOWICZ

HELL YEAH Volume 1
First Printing
ISBN: 978-1-60706-607-1

OE KEATINGE

o the original seven - Erik Larsen, Jim Lee, Rob Liefeld, Todd McFarlane, Whilce Portacio, arc Silvestri, Jim Valentino - for blazing the trail, to Andre for joining me on the journey nd to J.N. for making sure we never take the easy way.

NDRE SZYMANOWICZ

nis book is dedicated to Erin, without whose love, support and encouragement, I wouldn't e able to do what I love. Its for my parents and family, for never, ever questioning if I hould be drawing so many cartoons. Finally, its for my comic book brothers for being upportive and helpful every step of the way.

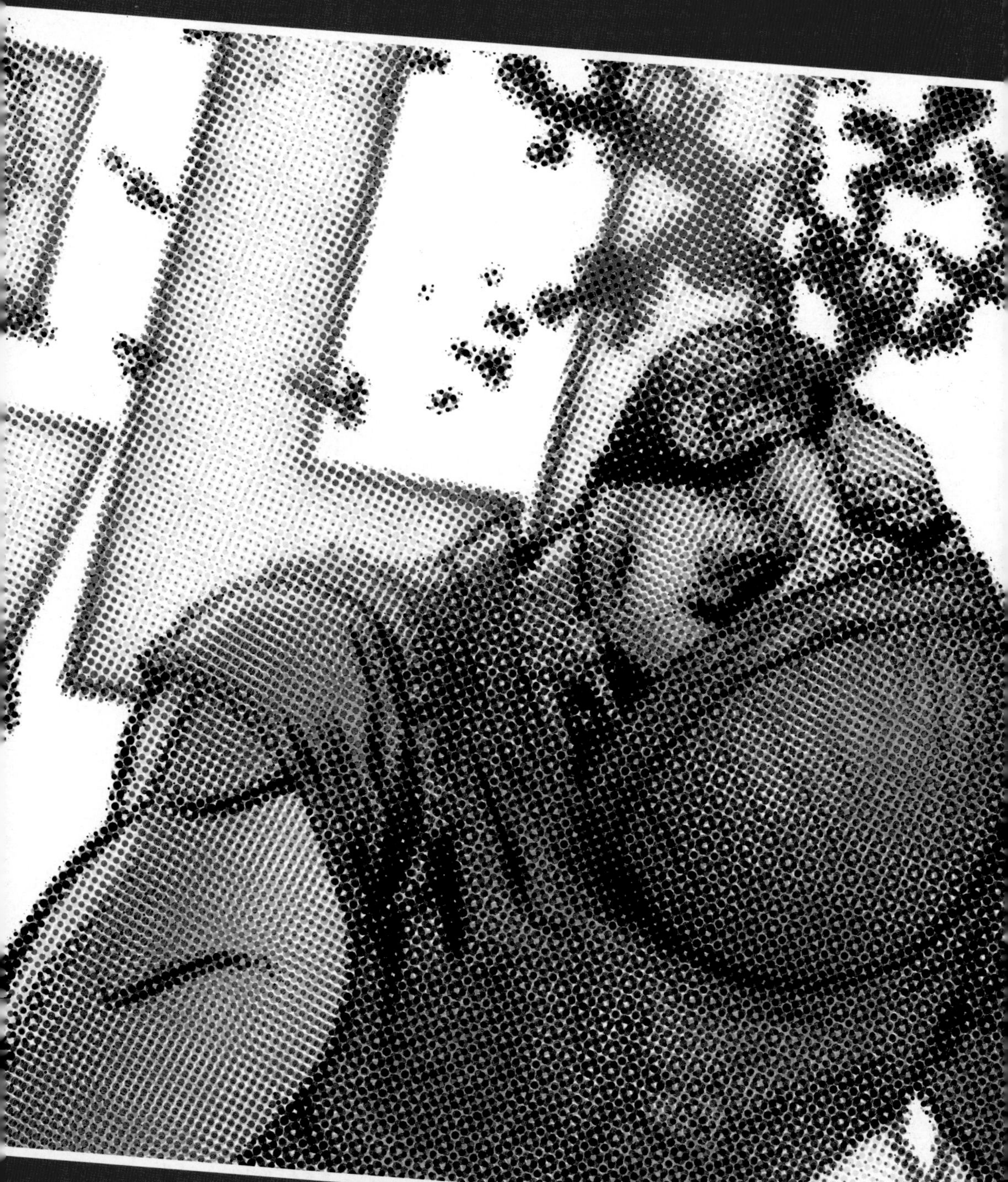

HECK YEAH!

An introduction by MICHAEL ALLRE

Ben Day! Hah! That's a pretty cool name giving an affectionate nod to this here comic book medium. In fact, that's HECK YEAH all over. Clearly the folks making this here comic book dig comics. And so do I. And it's all about me, right? I mean, that's why I was asked to do this intro, right? So I could go on and on about me?

Maybe later.

First I wanna talk just a little bit about the creators of this here comic book.

Let's start with Andre Szymanowicz. I love Andre! Known him for years. Enthusiastic upbeat talent! The more time you spend with Andre the more you want. And it's never enough. A while back he did an amazing Madman painting based on a classic Creem Magazine cover of David and Angie Bowie that blew me away! A kindred spirit! He's rock n roll! And it's a thrill to see him draw a comic book that gives him a chance to show off his rock n roll spirit. Cool references to Led Zeppelin, The Doors, and Portland Pals, The Dandy Warhols. I love Andre's raw cool style. Love it!

Terrific work from colorist Jason Lewis and letterer Douglas Sherwood too!

Now I'd like to say a few things about Joe Keatinge.

Actually, First I want to bring it back to me. Sorta. You know in the indicia where it says " any resemblance to actual persons blah blah blah is coincidental"? Well it's all lies. Ben Day is based on my son, Bond Allred. Even down to the bar code tattoo on the back of his neck. And the alternate versions of him in multiple universes. You'll notice my band, The Gear, is on the marquee for Portland's The Crystal Ballroom in chapter one? And my friend Jonathan Ross makes an appearance? When Joe Keatinge moved to Portland a few years ago, it was left to me to show him around (though I'm pretty sure he found the Mary's Club All Nude Revue without my help), and one of the coolest decisions in the creation of HELL YEAH is setting it in Portland. Well, clearly this book couldn't exist without me.

Now, I know you're all eager to hear more about me, so I'll oblige.

Several years ago my wife Laura and I bought a vacation lake house on the Oregon coast. We eventually moved the family there full time and I was blissfully happy making comic books in paradise and became a master carpenter as I more than doubled the size of the house. I started turning down invitations to make appearances at conventions and store signings. I never wanted to leave my little citadel where we got our mail by boat.

I became a full on recluse. But then I started a new Madman series with Image comics and was told their new Marketing Director, Joe Keatinge, was a big fan of my work. All of my work. Every book, movie, song, I ever did. So, of course I immediately liked him. Such a wise man with impeccable taste! Somehow he talked me into doing a weird Stardust story with him, then the cover to his award-winning Popgun anthology. And of course we bonded with similar tastes in music, comics, movies and a mad obsession with Moebius.

Then somehow Joe talked me into getting out in the world again, arranging a massive event in San Francisco at Neon Monster. My pal Courtney Taylor of The Dandy Warhols dropped by and Joe and I talked him into turning a screenplay he wrote into the fantastic graphic novel ONE MODEL NATION. We took turns driving a Tesla electric sports car on the hills of San Francisco and hung out with The Dandy Warhols after their show (why Courtney was in town). But, best of all I was reminded what a blast it is to get out in the world and visit with folks who dig comic books.

Thanks to Joe we broke from the reclusiveness that had snuck up on me. It may not be an exaggeration to say he restored my life. You can read me write more about me in the special extended edition of this book which doesn't exist. Yet.

And now Joe, along with Andre and co. is living the dream! Creating super cool comic books! All thanks to ME! Seriously, I owe Joe more than I could ever say in this limited space. And its a huge thrill to see this crazy cool comic book get collected.

Love these guys and this wild weird comic book. There's a lot of heart and soul on these pages (and a lot of blood and guts). Now run to the top of the nearest roof and yell loudly and proudly, "HECK YEAH"!

I'm a fan.

Yer pal forever,
Doc

HELL YEAH
CHAPTER ONE
ENLIST NOW
ALL NEW
ANDRÉ 2011
KEATINGE + SZYMANOWICZ

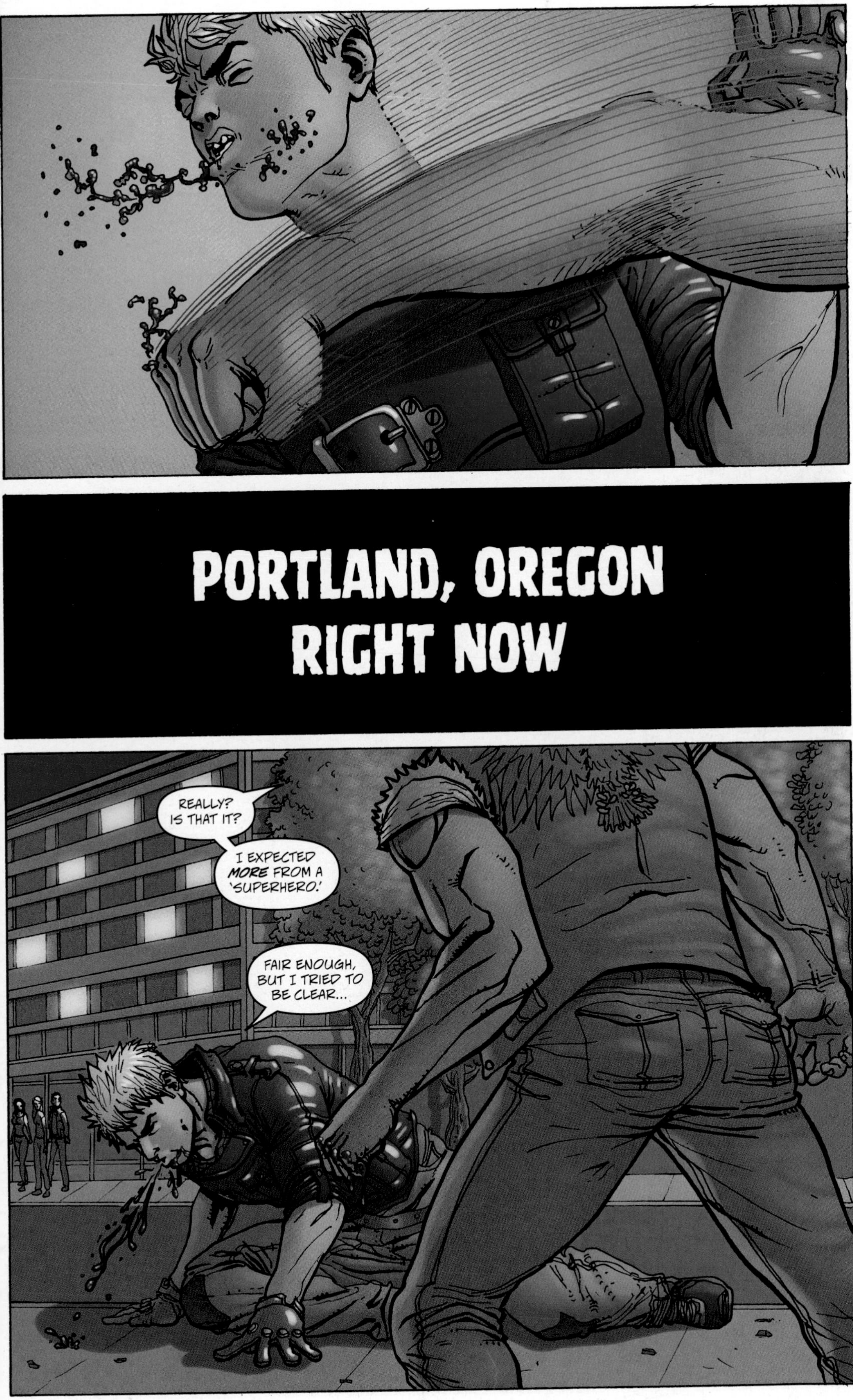
PORTLAND, OREGON
RIGHT NOW
REALLY? IS THAT IT?
I EXPECTED MORE FROM A 'SUPERHERO.'
FAIR ENOUGH, BUT I TRIED TO BE CLEAR...

IMAGE COMICS PRESENTS

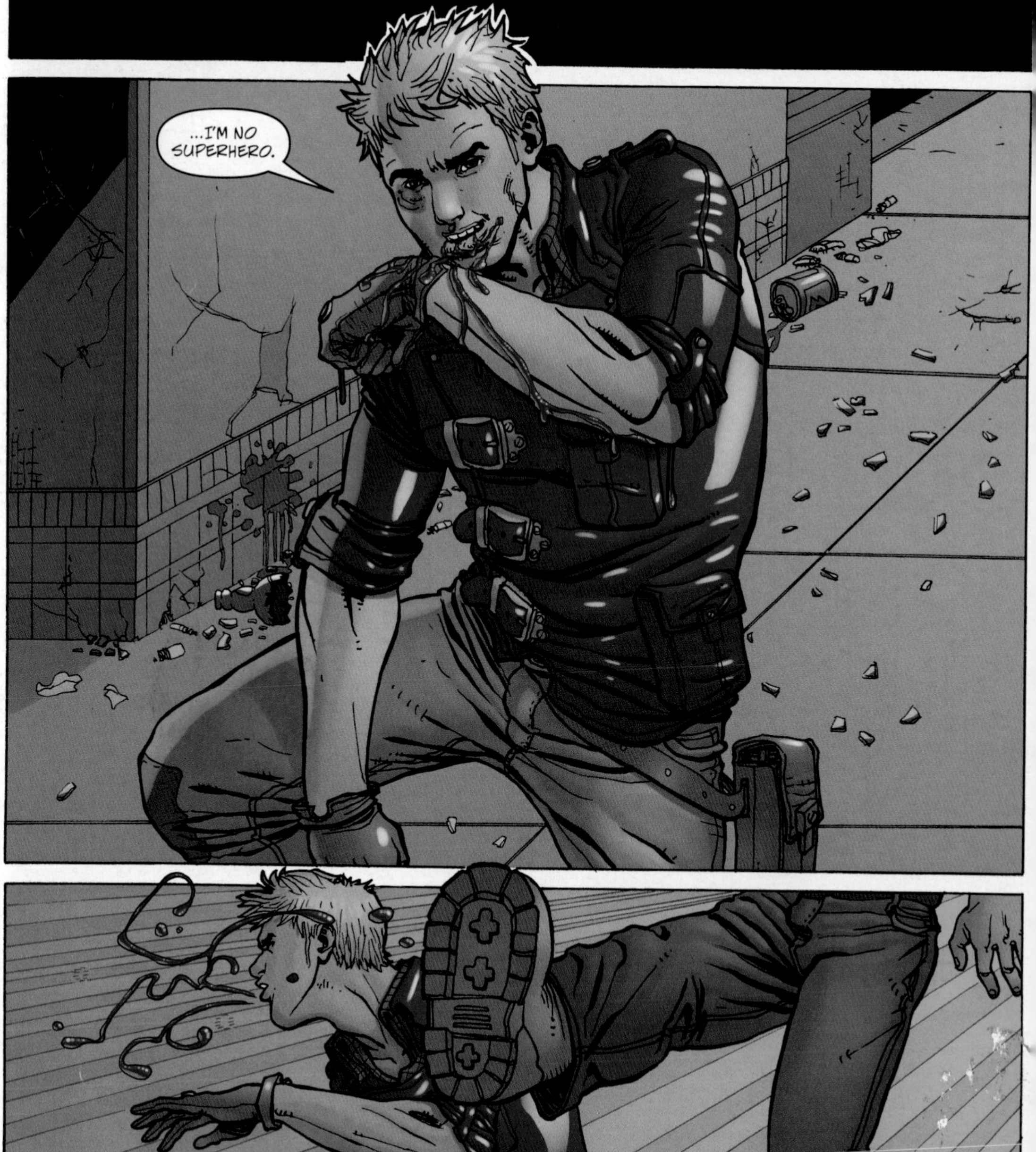

...I'M NO SUPERHERO.

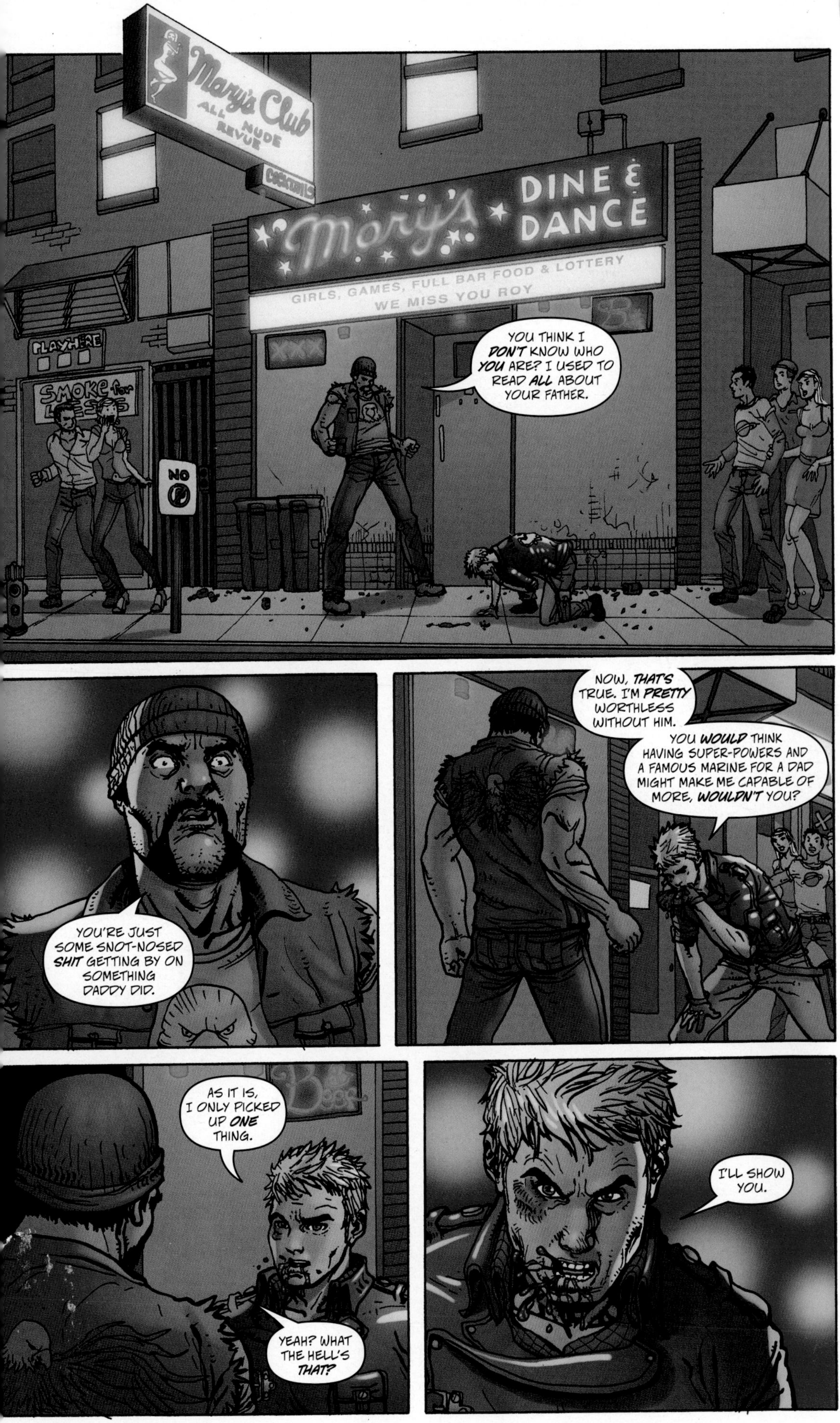
Mary's Club
ALL NUDE REVUE
COCKTAILS
Mary's
DINE & DANCE
GIRLS, GAMES, FULL BAR FOOD & LOTTERY
WE MISS YOU ROY
XXX
PLAYHERE
SMOKE for LESS
NO
YOU THINK I DON'T KNOW WHO YOU ARE? I USED TO READ ALL ABOUT YOUR FATHER.
YOU'RE JUST SOME SNOT-NOSED SHIT GETTING BY ON SOMETHING DADDY DID.
NOW, THAT'S TRUE. I'M PRETTY WORTHLESS WITHOUT HIM.
YOU WOULD THINK HAVING SUPER-POWERS AND A FAMOUS MARINE FOR A DAD MIGHT MAKE ME CAPABLE OF MORE, WOULDN'T YOU?
AS IT IS, I ONLY PICKED UP ONE THING.
YEAH? WHAT THE HELL'S THAT?
I'LL SHOW YOU.

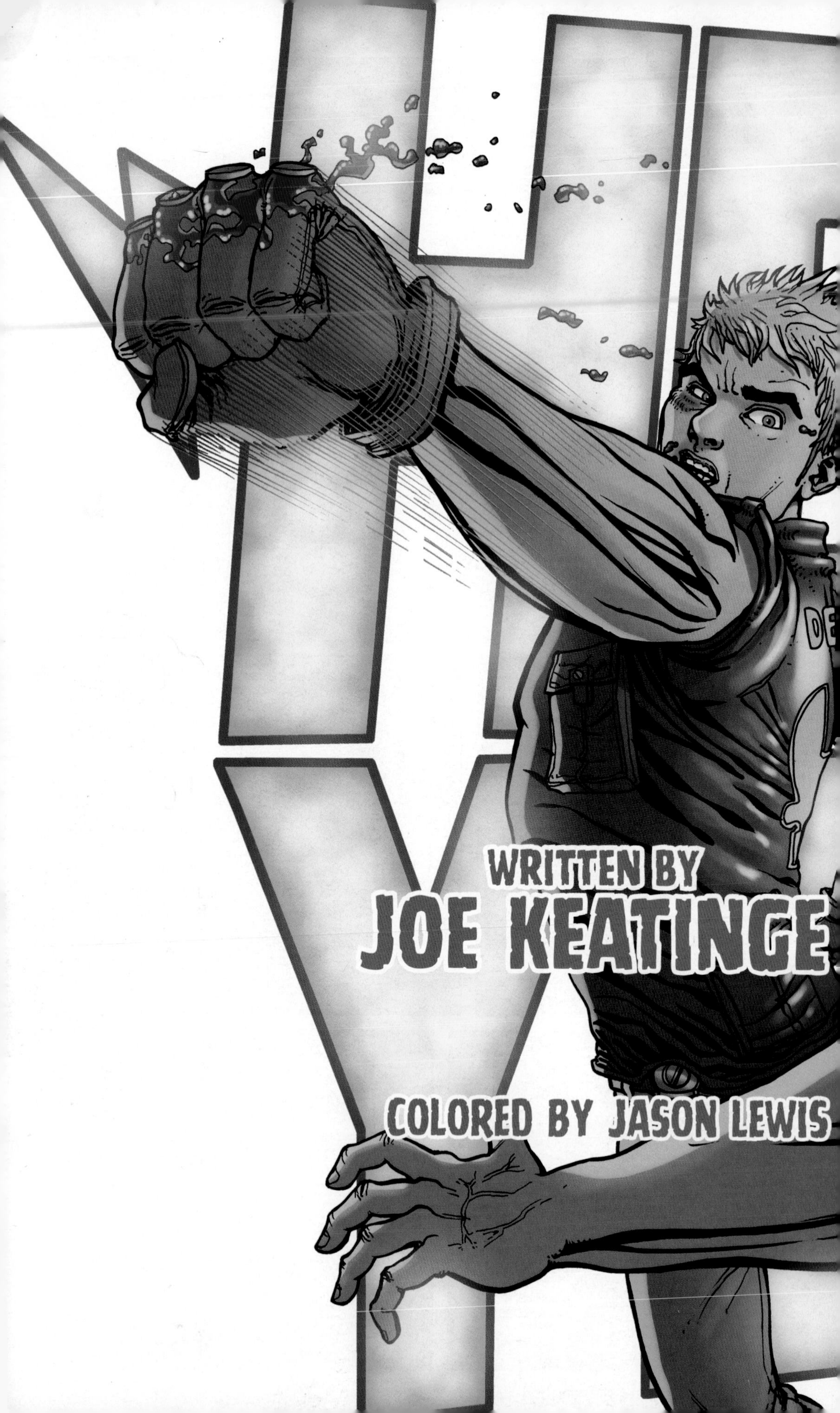
WRITTEN BY
JOE KEATINGE
COLORED BY JASON LEWIS

KA-POW, ASSHOLE!
ILLUSTRATED BY
ANDRE SZYMANOWICZ
LETTERED BY DOUGLAS E. SHERWOOD
CREATED BY KEATINGE + SZYMANOWICZ

BOOK ONE
LAST DAY ON EARTHS

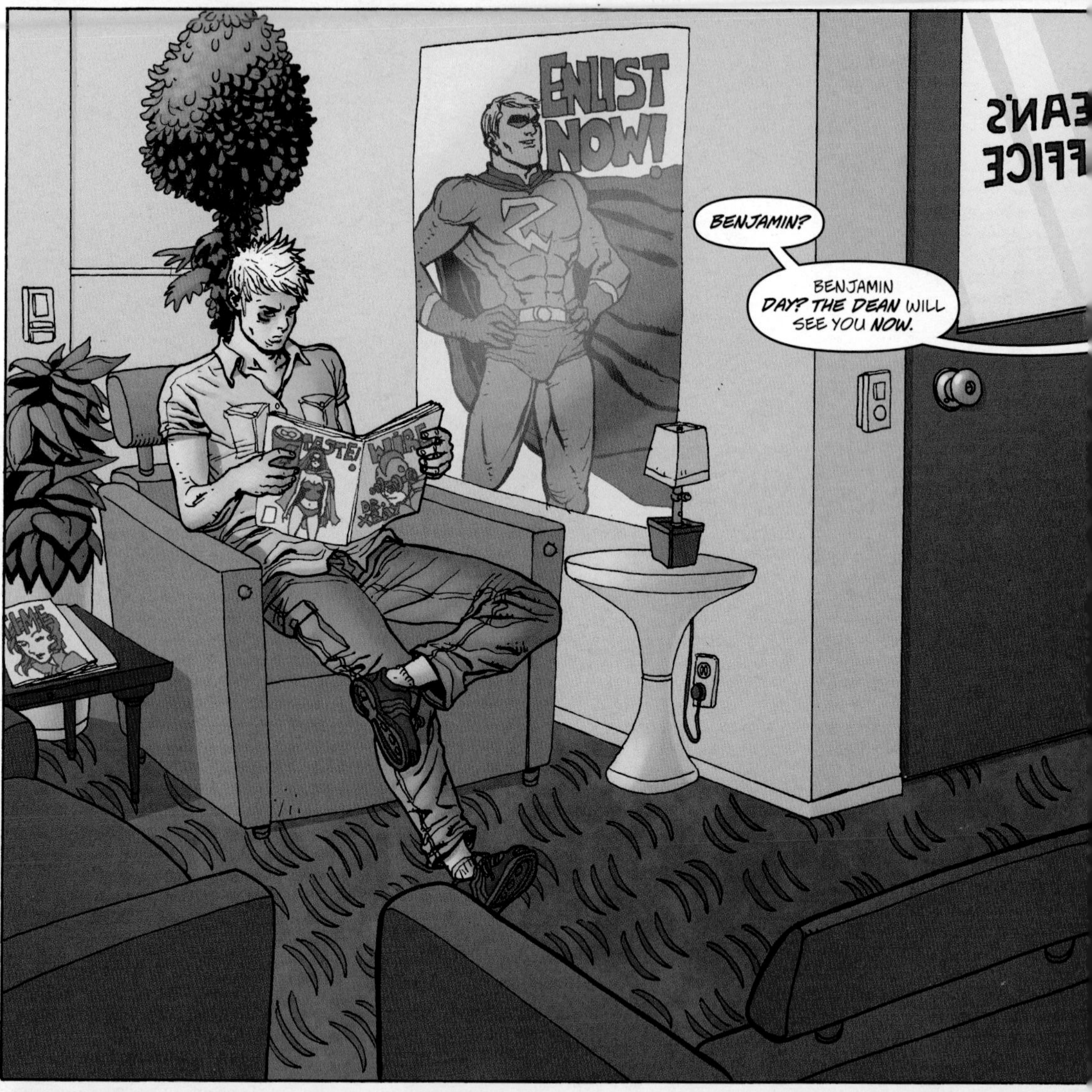
ENLIST NOW!
BENJAMIN?
BENJAMIN DAY? THE DEAN WILL SEE YOU NOW.

CHAPTER ONE
THE WORLD THEY MADE

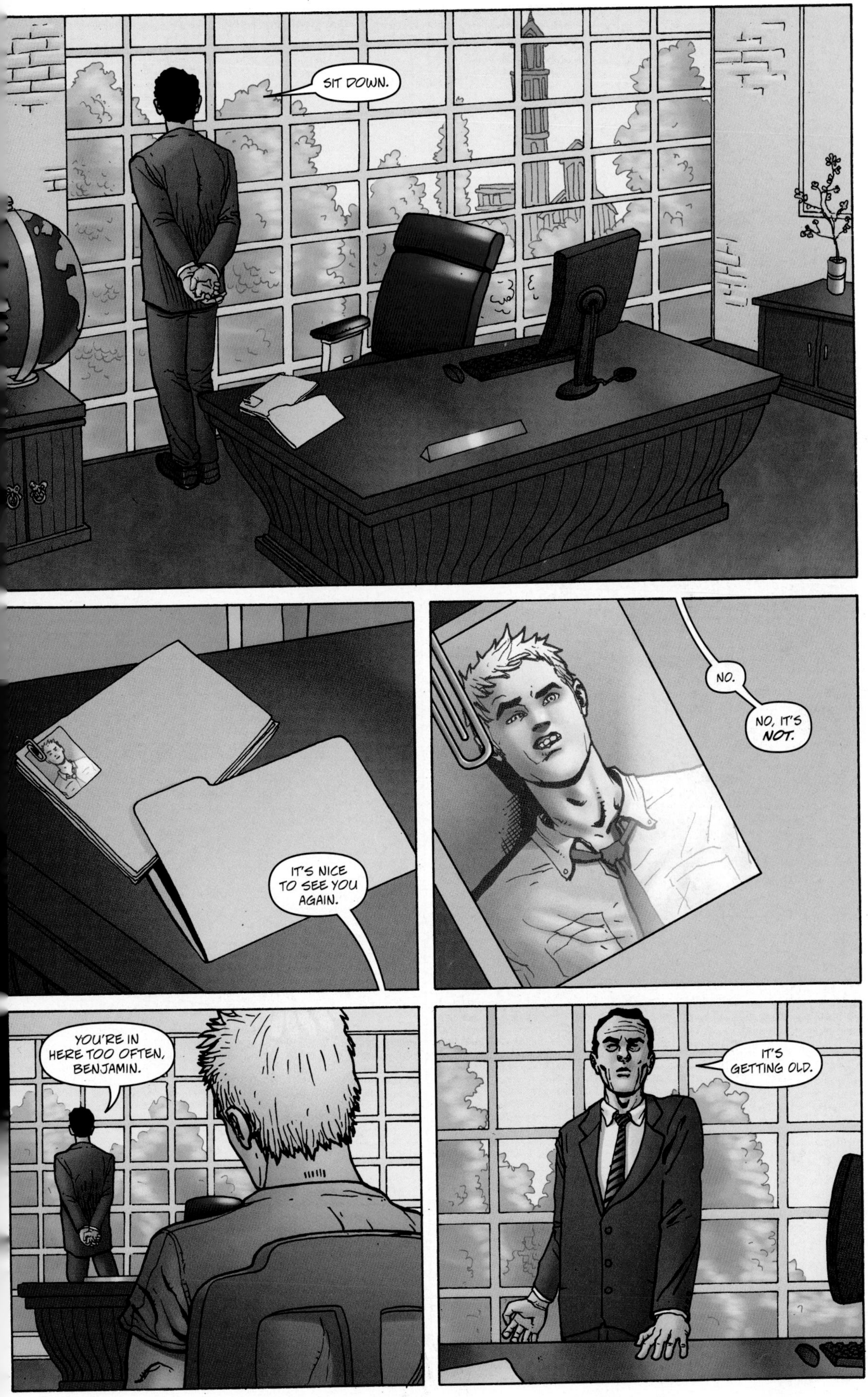
SIT DOWN.
IT'S NICE TO SEE YOU AGAIN.
NO.
NO, IT'S NOT.
YOU'RE IN HERE TOO OFTEN, BENJAMIN.
IT'S GETTING OLD.

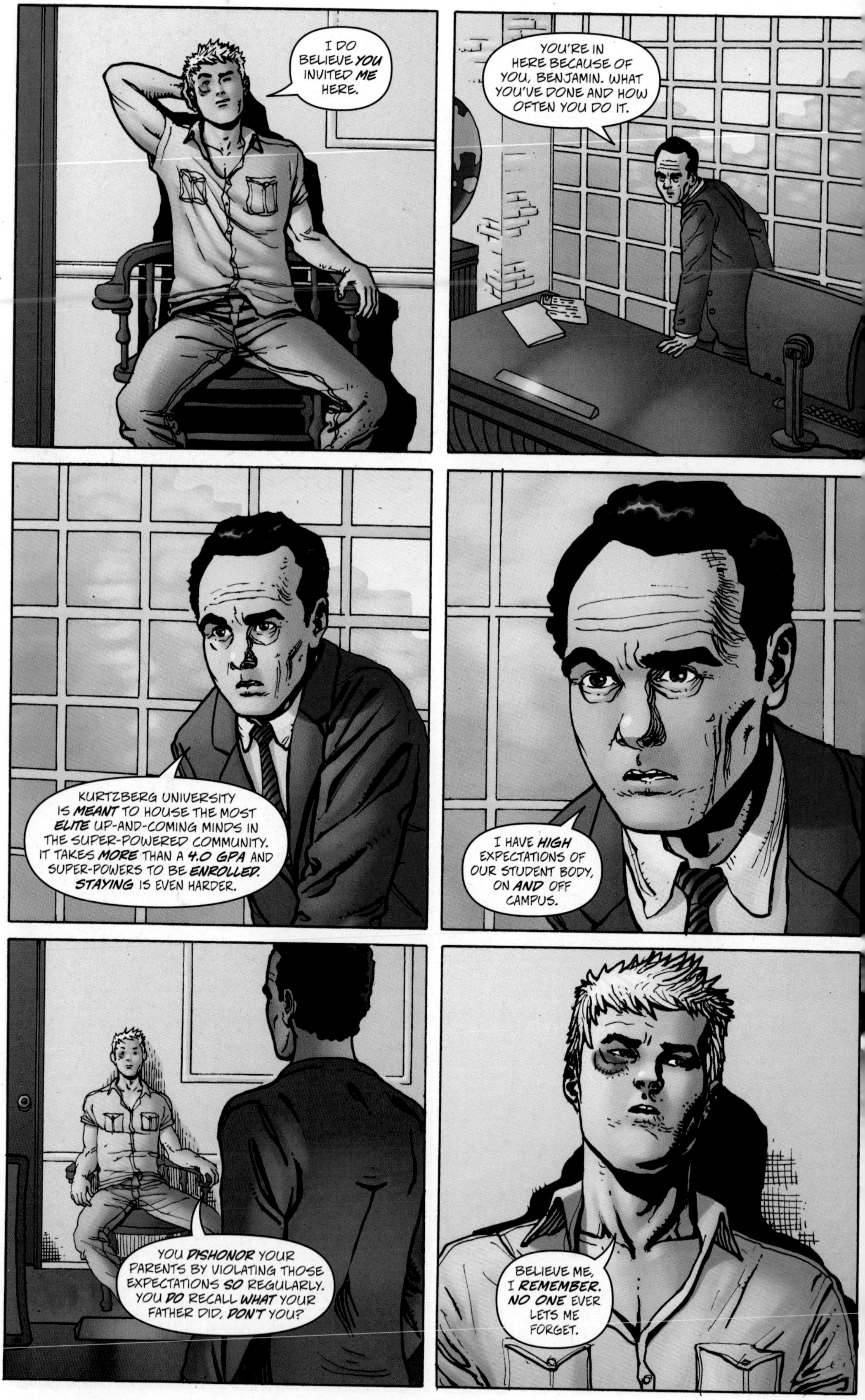
I DO BELIEVE YOU INVITED ME HERE.
YOU'RE IN HERE BECAUSE OF YOU, BENJAMIN. WHAT YOU'VE DONE AND HOW OFTEN YOU DO IT.
KURTZBERG UNIVERSITY IS MEANT TO HOUSE THE MOST ELITE UP-AND-COMING MINDS IN THE SUPER-POWERED COMMUNITY. IT TAKES MORE THAN A 4.0 GPA AND SUPER-POWERS TO BE ENROLLED. STAYING IS EVEN HARDER.
I HAVE HIGH EXPECTATIONS OF OUR STUDENT BODY, ON AND OFF CAMPUS.
YOU DISHONOR YOUR PARENTS BY VIOLATING THOSE EXPECTATIONS SO REGULARLY. YOU DO RECALL WHAT YOUR FATHER DID, DON'T YOU?
BELIEVE ME, I REMEMBER. NO ONE EVER LETS ME FORGET.

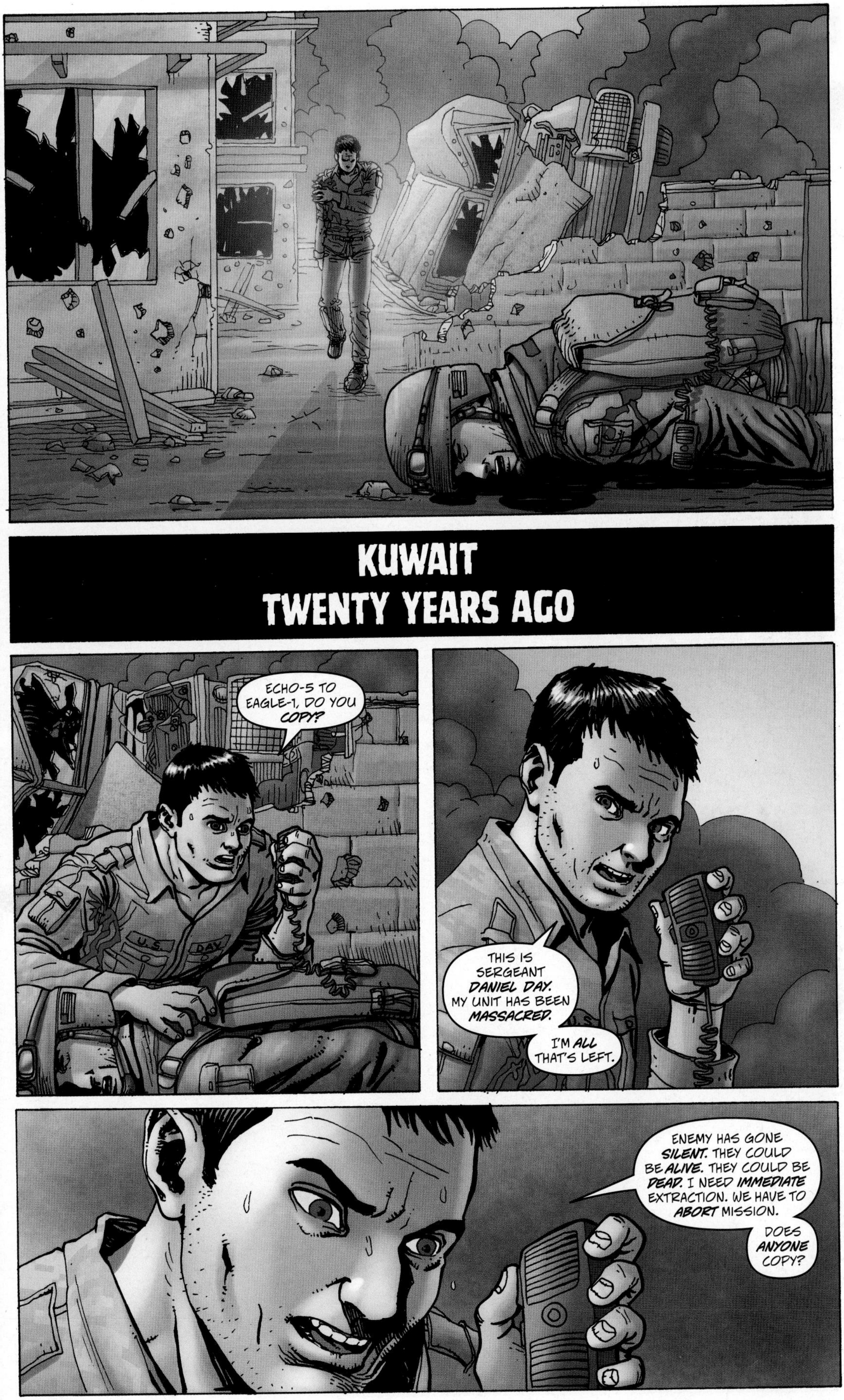
KUWAIT
TWENTY YEARS AGO
ECHO-5 TO EAGLE-1, DO YOU COPY?
THIS IS SERGEANT DANIEL DAY. MY UNIT HAS BEEN MASSACRED.
I'M ALL THAT'S LEFT.
ENEMY HAS GONE SILENT. THEY COULD BE ALIVE. THEY COULD BE DEAD. I NEED IMMEDIATE EXTRACTION. WE HAVE TO ABORT MISSION.
DOES ANYONE COPY?

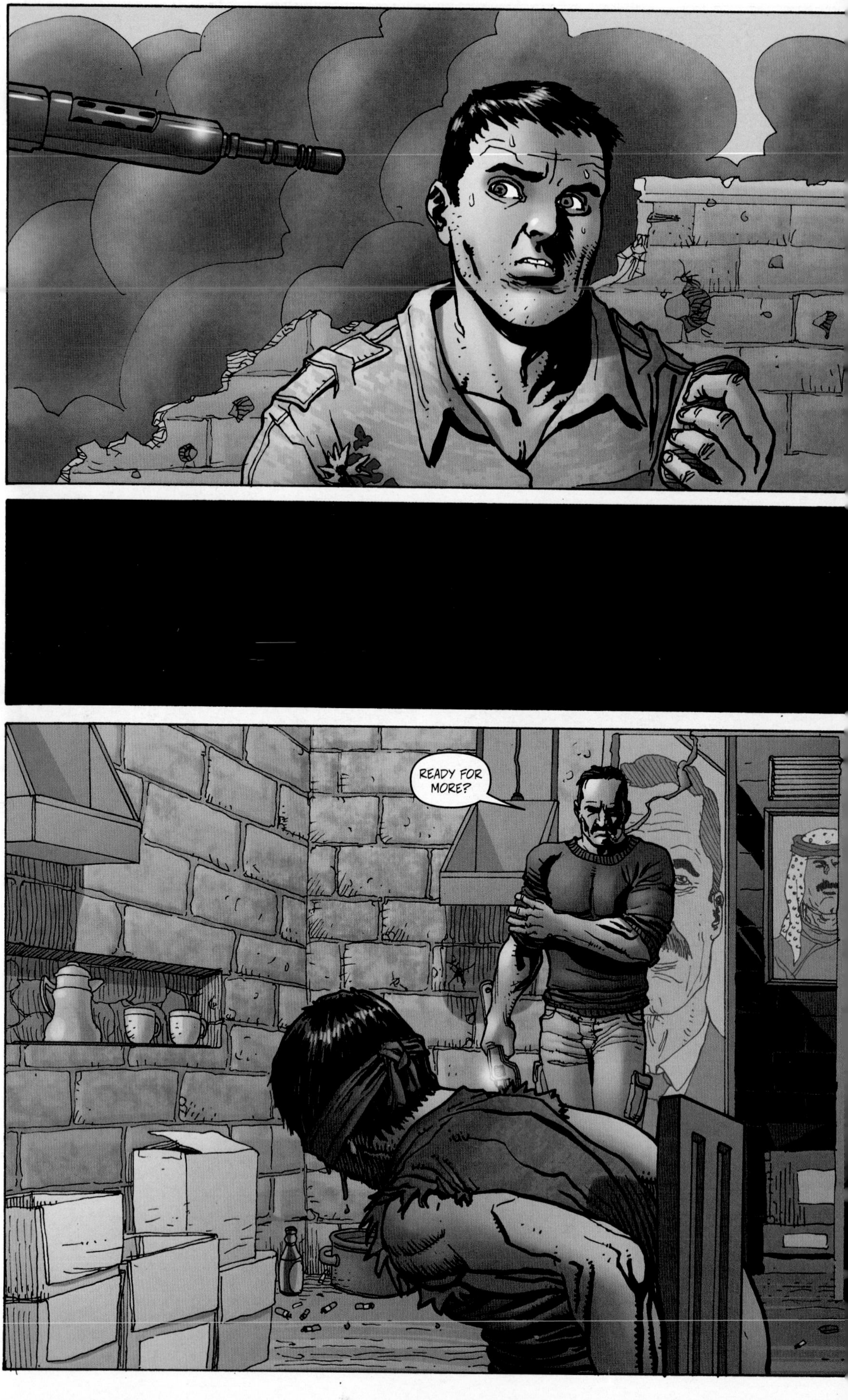
READY FOR MORE?

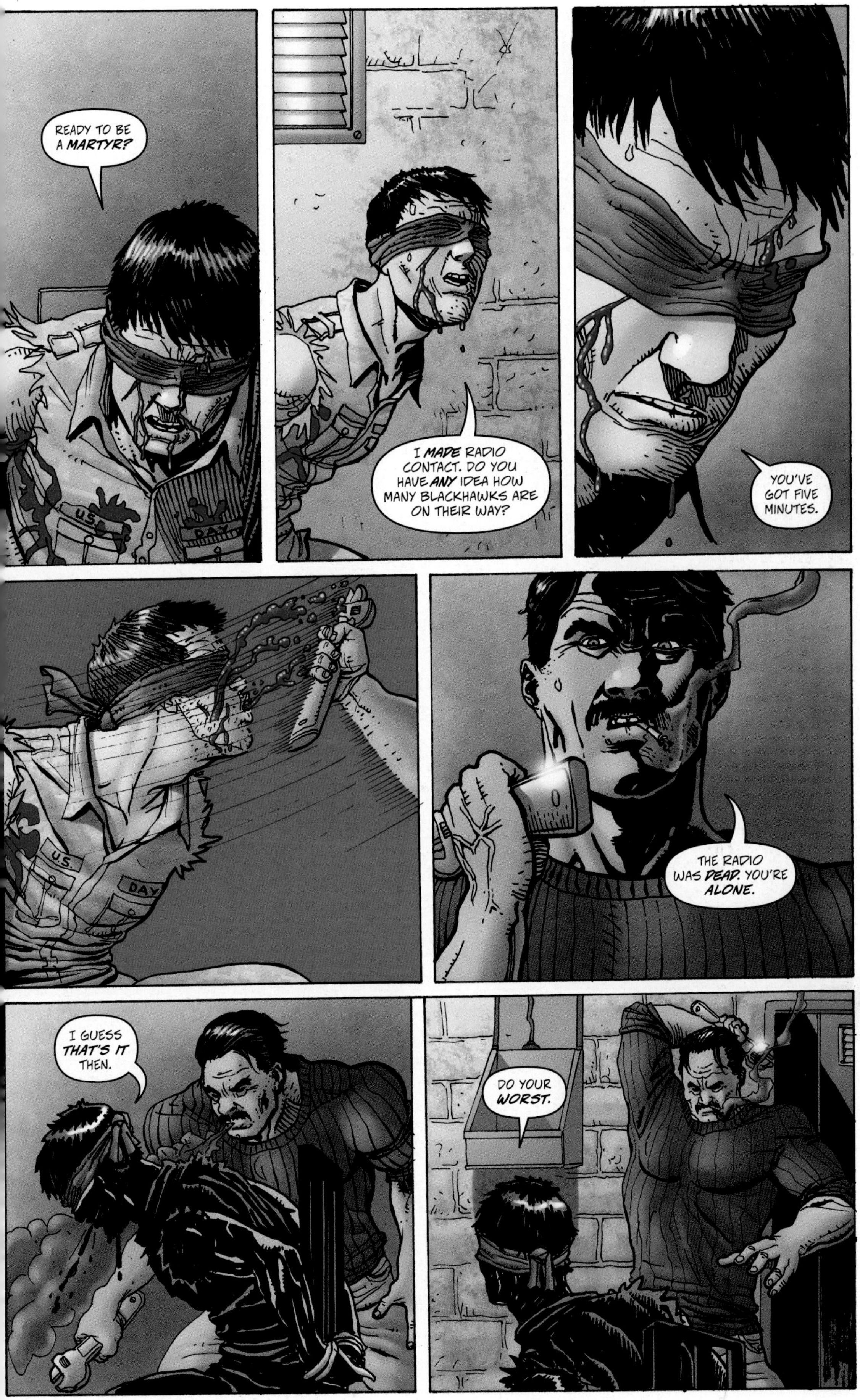
READY TO BE A MARTYR?
I MADE RADIO CONTACT. DO YOU HAVE ANY IDEA HOW MANY BLACKHAWKS ARE ON THEIR WAY?
YOU'VE GOT FIVE MINUTES.
THE RADIO WAS DEAD. YOU'RE ALONE.
I GUESS THAT'S IT THEN.
DO YOUR WORST.

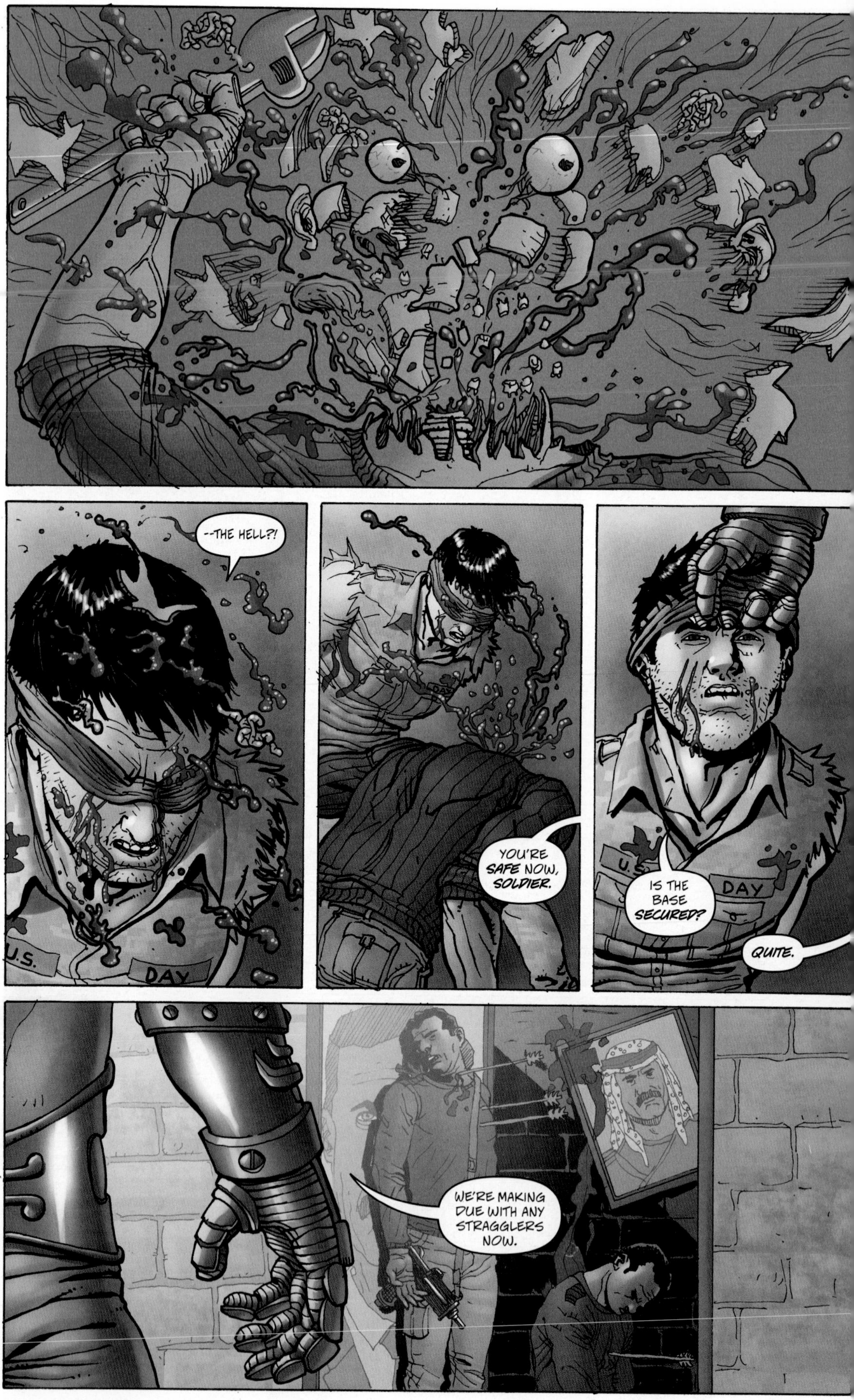
--THE HELL?!
YOU'RE SAFE NOW, SOLDIER.
U.S.
DAY
IS THE BASE SECURED?
QUITE.
WE'RE MAKING DUE WITH ANY STRAGGLERS NOW.

HOW DID YOU FIND ME?

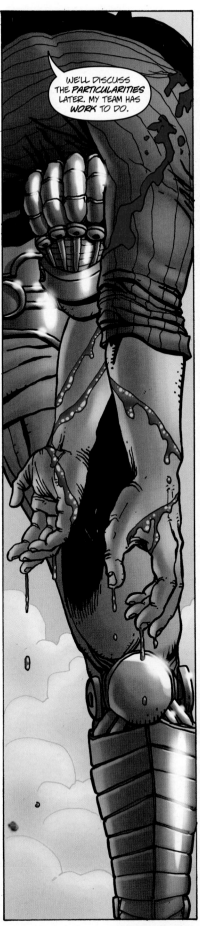

WE'LL DISCUSS THE *PARTICULARITIES* LATER. MY TEAM HAS *WORK* TO DO.

EXCUSE ME?

WHICH *UNIT* ARE YOU *WITH*?

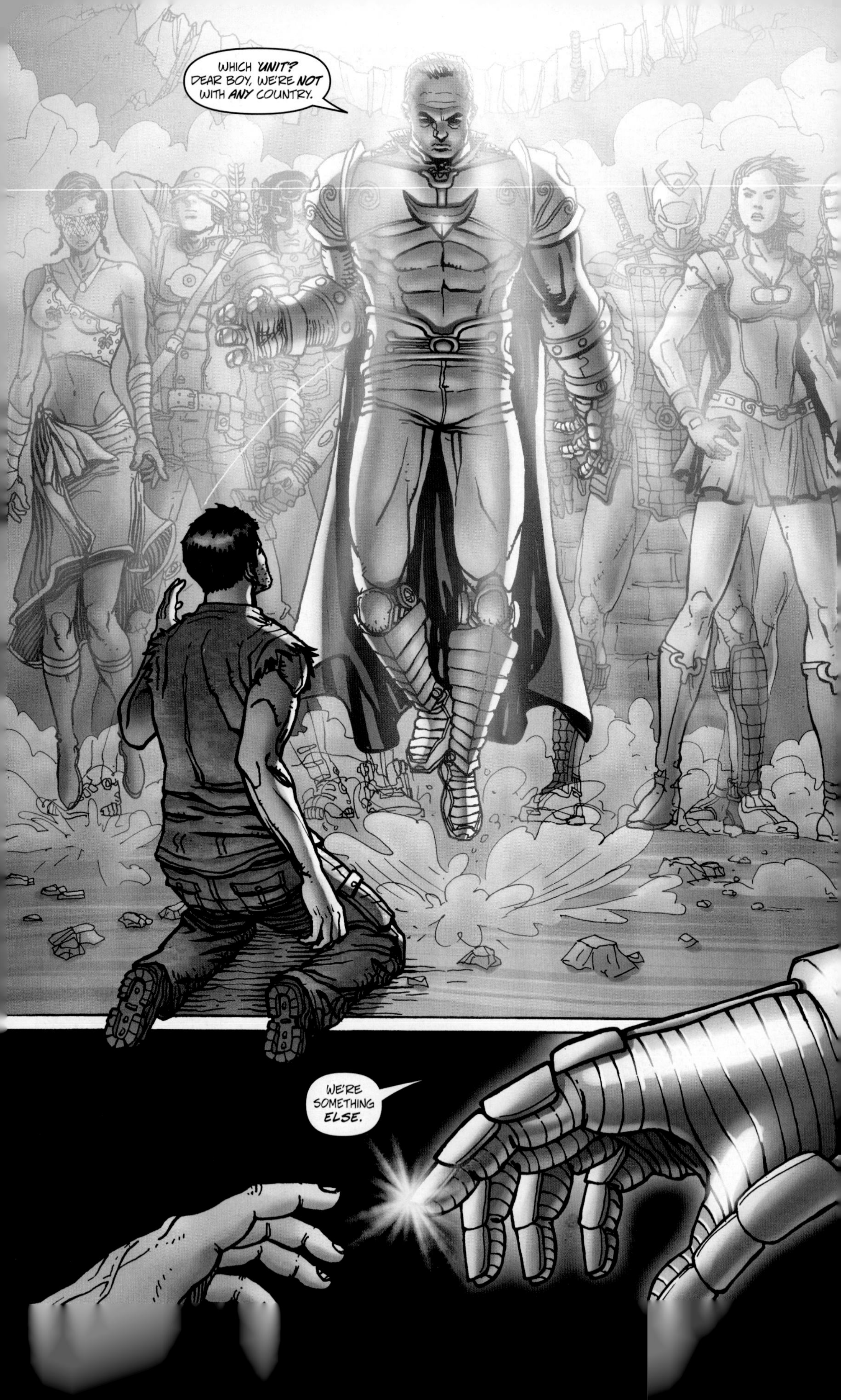
WHICH UNIT? DEAR BOY, WE'RE NOT WITH ANY COUNTRY.
WE'RE SOMETHING ELSE.

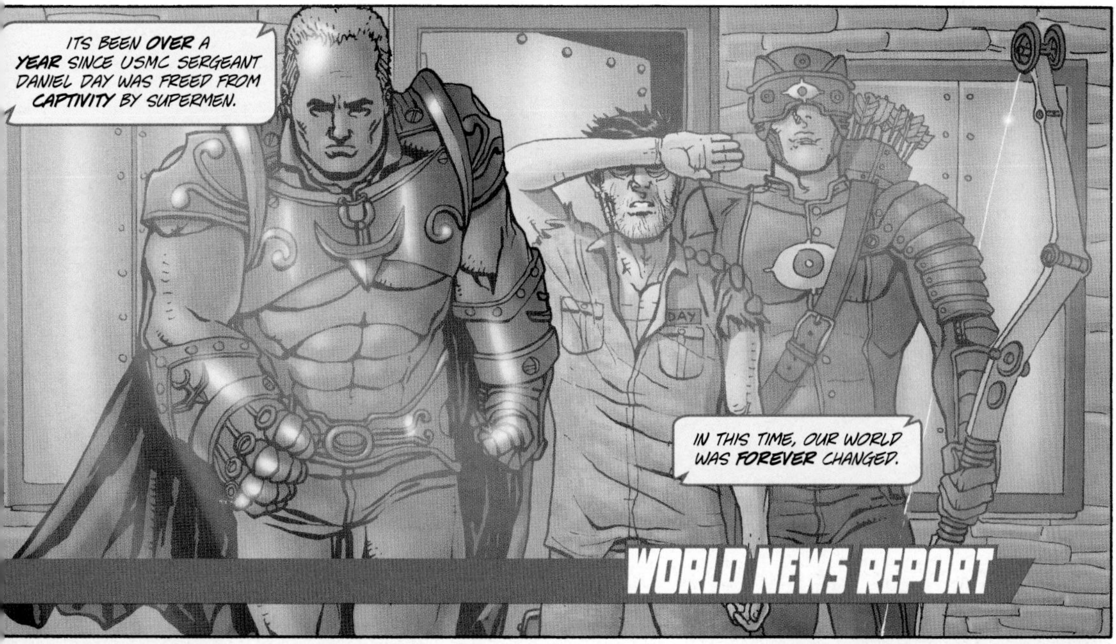
ITS BEEN OVER A YEAR SINCE USMC SERGEANT DANIEL DAY WAS FREED FROM CAPTIVITY BY SUPERMEN.
DAY
IN THIS TIME, OUR WORLD WAS FOREVER CHANGED.
WORLD NEWS REPORT

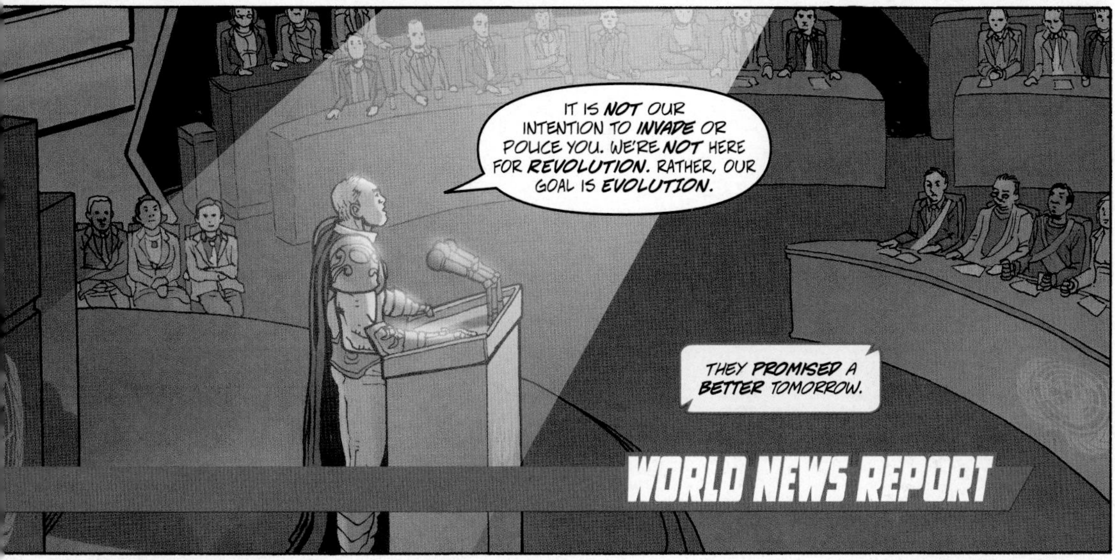
IT IS NOT OUR INTENTION TO INVADE OR POLICE YOU. WE'RE NOT HERE FOR REVOLUTION. RATHER, OUR GOAL IS EVOLUTION.
THEY PROMISED A BETTER TOMORROW.
WORLD NEWS REPORT

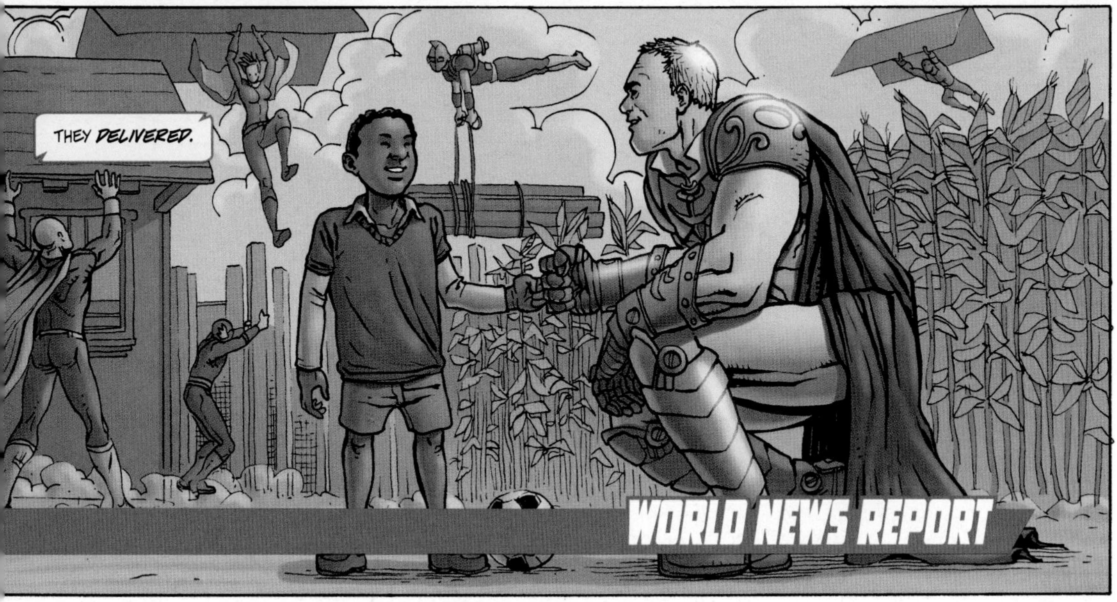
THEY DELIVERED.
WORLD NEWS REPORT

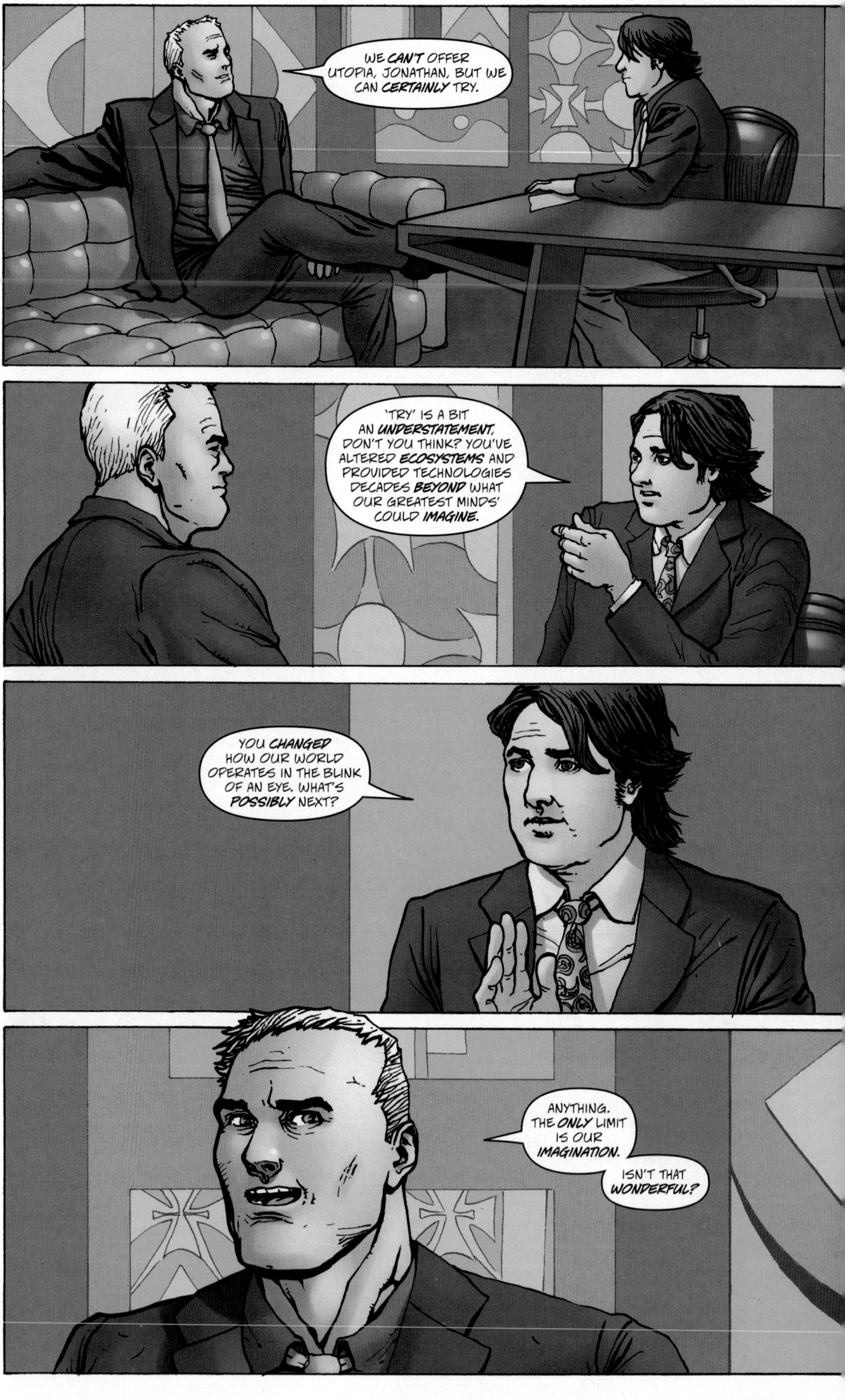
WE CAN'T OFFER UTOPIA, JONATHAN, BUT WE CAN CERTAINLY TRY.
'TRY' IS A BIT AN UNDERSTATEMENT, DON'T YOU THINK? YOU'VE ALTERED ECOSYSTEMS AND PROVIDED TECHNOLOGIES DECADES BEYOND WHAT OUR GREATEST MINDS' COULD IMAGINE.
YOU CHANGED HOW OUR WORLD OPERATES IN THE BLINK OF AN EYE. WHAT'S POSSIBLY NEXT?
ANYTHING. THE ONLY LIMIT IS OUR IMAGINATION.
ISN'T THAT WONDERFUL?

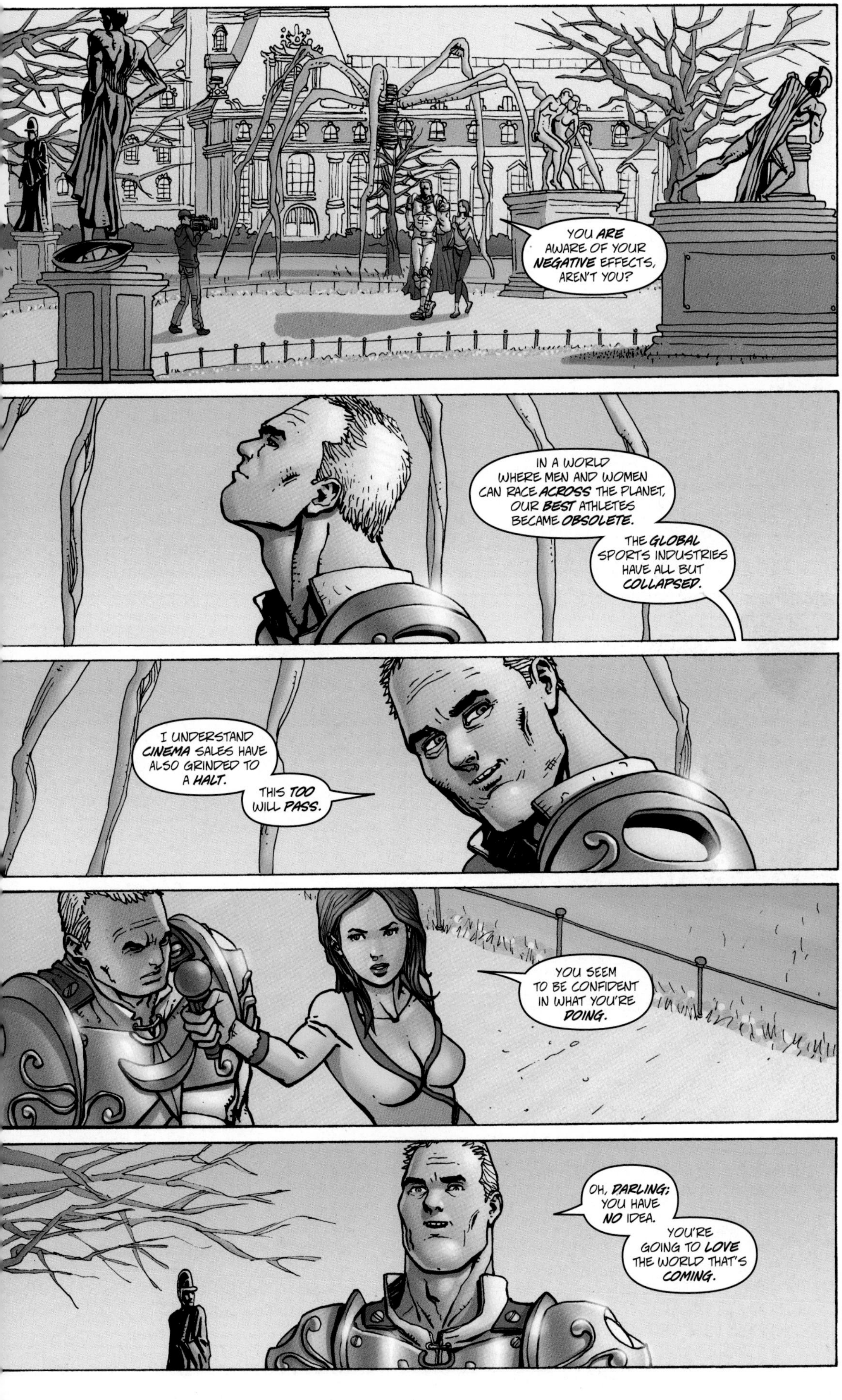

YOU ARE AWARE OF YOUR NEGATIVE EFFECTS, AREN'T YOU?
IN A WORLD WHERE MEN AND WOMEN CAN RACE ACROSS THE PLANET, OUR BEST ATHLETES BECAME OBSOLETE.
THE GLOBAL SPORTS INDUSTRIES HAVE ALL BUT COLLAPSED.
I UNDERSTAND CINEMA SALES HAVE ALSO GRINDED TO A HALT.
THIS TOO WILL PASS.
YOU SEEM TO BE CONFIDENT IN WHAT YOU'RE DOING.
OH, DARLING; YOU HAVE NO IDEA.
YOU'RE GOING TO LOVE THE WORLD THAT'S COMING.

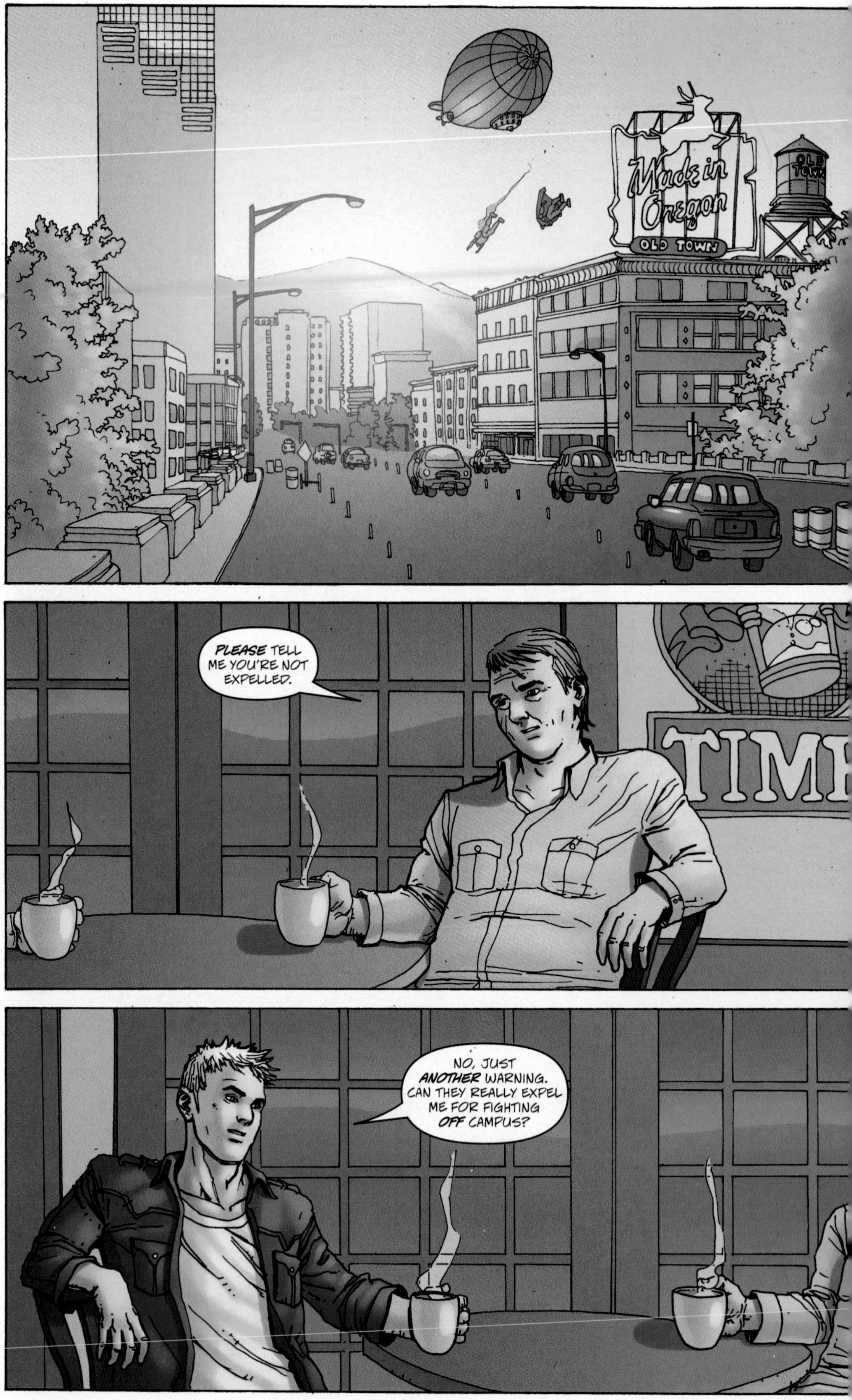
Made in Oregon
OLD TOWN
OLD TOWN
PLEASE TELL ME YOU'RE NOT EXPELLED.
TIM
NO, JUST ANOTHER WARNING. CAN THEY REALLY EXPEL ME FOR FIGHTING OFF CAMPUS?

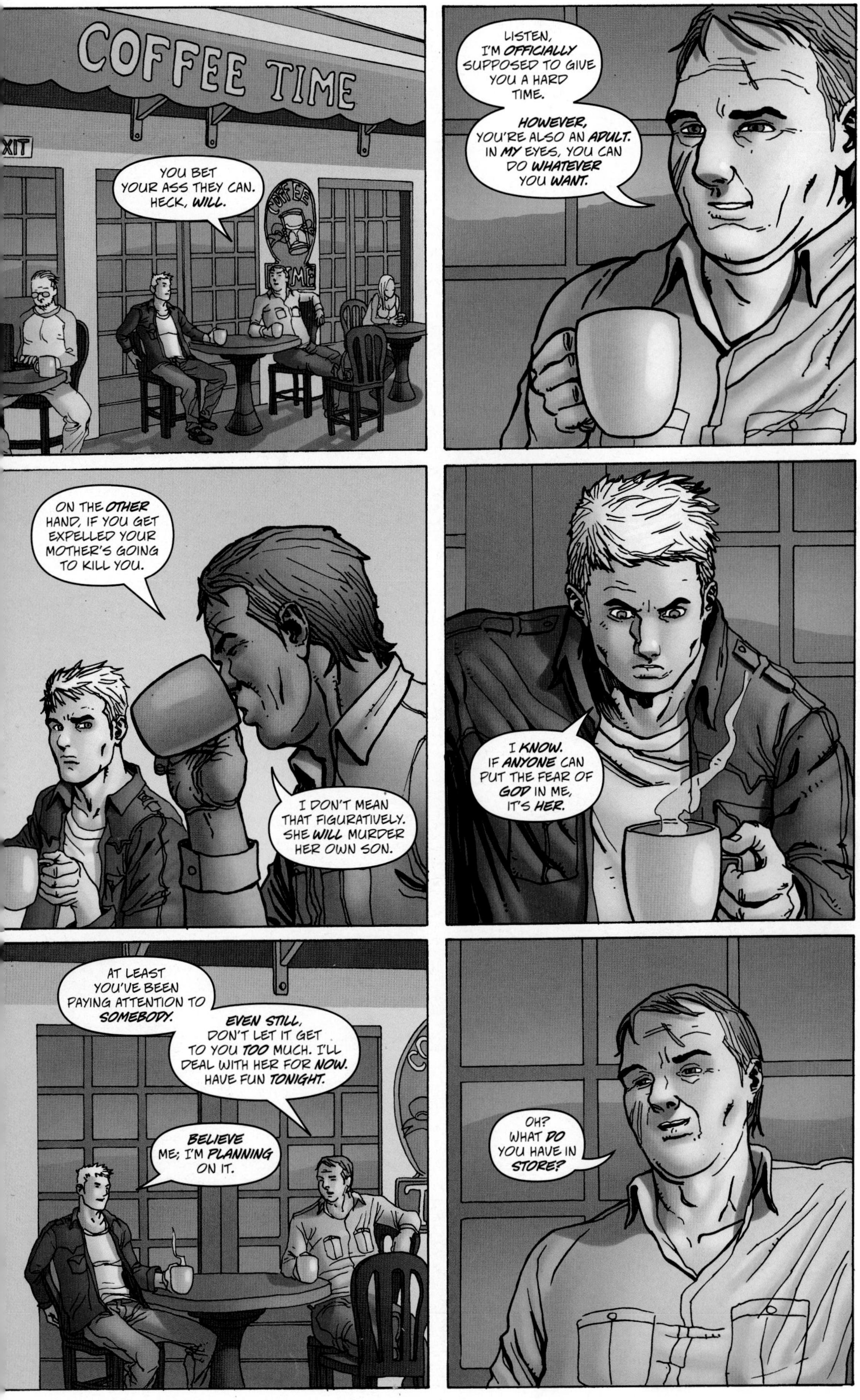
COFFEE TIME
YOU BET YOUR ASS THEY CAN. HECK, WILL.
LISTEN, I'M OFFICIALLY SUPPOSED TO GIVE YOU A HARD TIME.
HOWEVER, YOU'RE ALSO AN ADULT. IN MY EYES, YOU CAN DO WHATEVER YOU WANT.
ON THE OTHER HAND, IF YOU GET EXPELLED YOUR MOTHER'S GOING TO KILL YOU.
I DON'T MEAN THAT FIGURATIVELY. SHE WILL MURDER HER OWN SON.
I KNOW. IF ANYONE CAN PUT THE FEAR OF GOD IN ME, IT'S HER.
AT LEAST YOU'VE BEEN PAYING ATTENTION TO SOMEBODY.
EVEN STILL, DON'T LET IT GET TO YOU TOO MUCH. I'LL DEAL WITH HER FOR NOW. HAVE FUN TONIGHT.
BELIEVE ME; I'M PLANNING ON IT.
OH? WHAT DO YOU HAVE IN STORE?

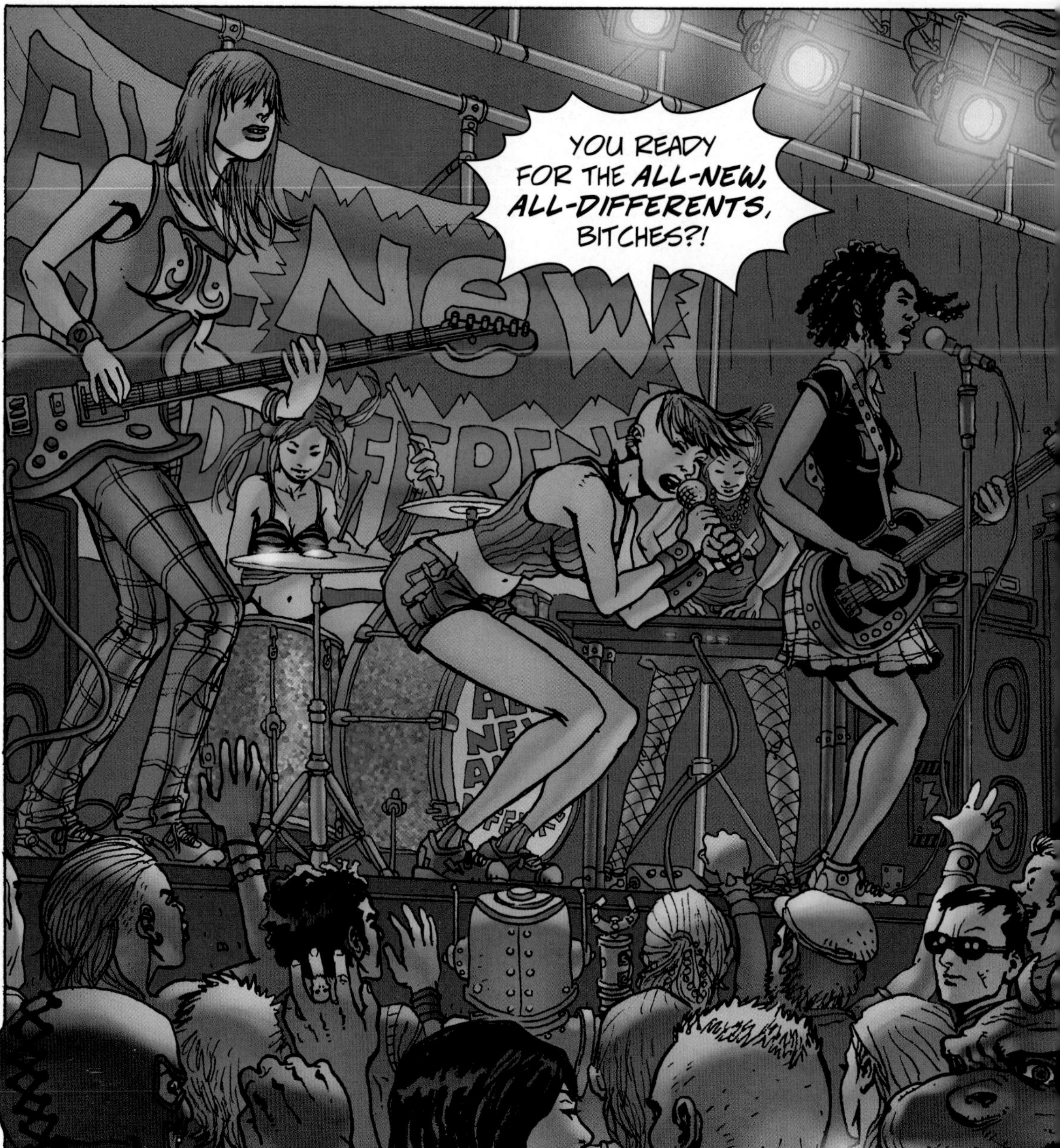
YOU READY FOR THE ALL-NEW, ALL-DIFFERENTS, BITCHES?!

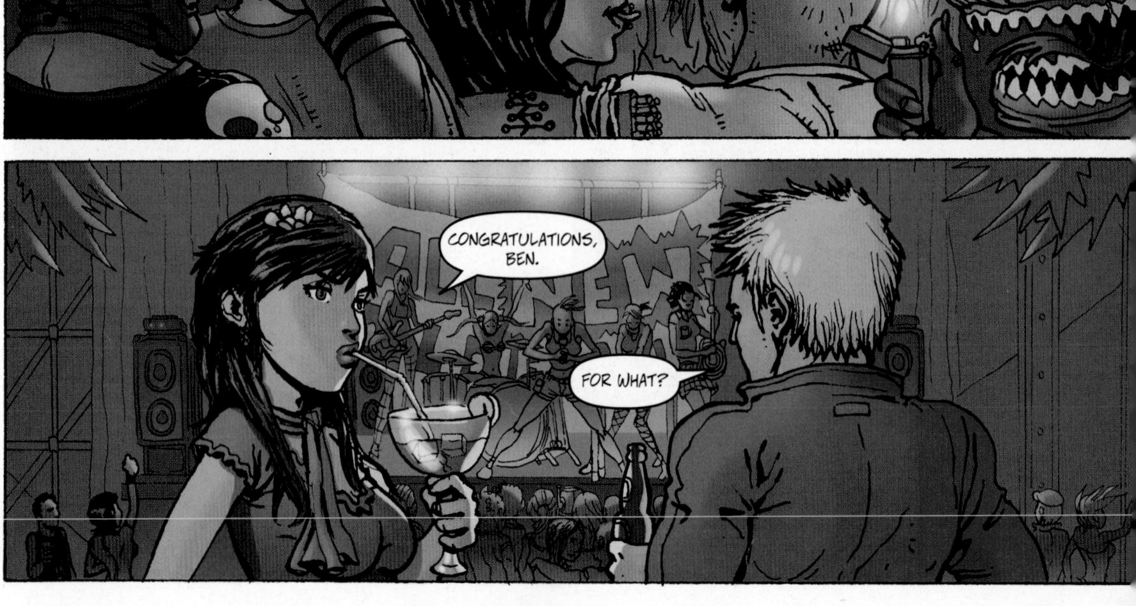
CONGRATULATIONS, BEN.
FOR WHAT?

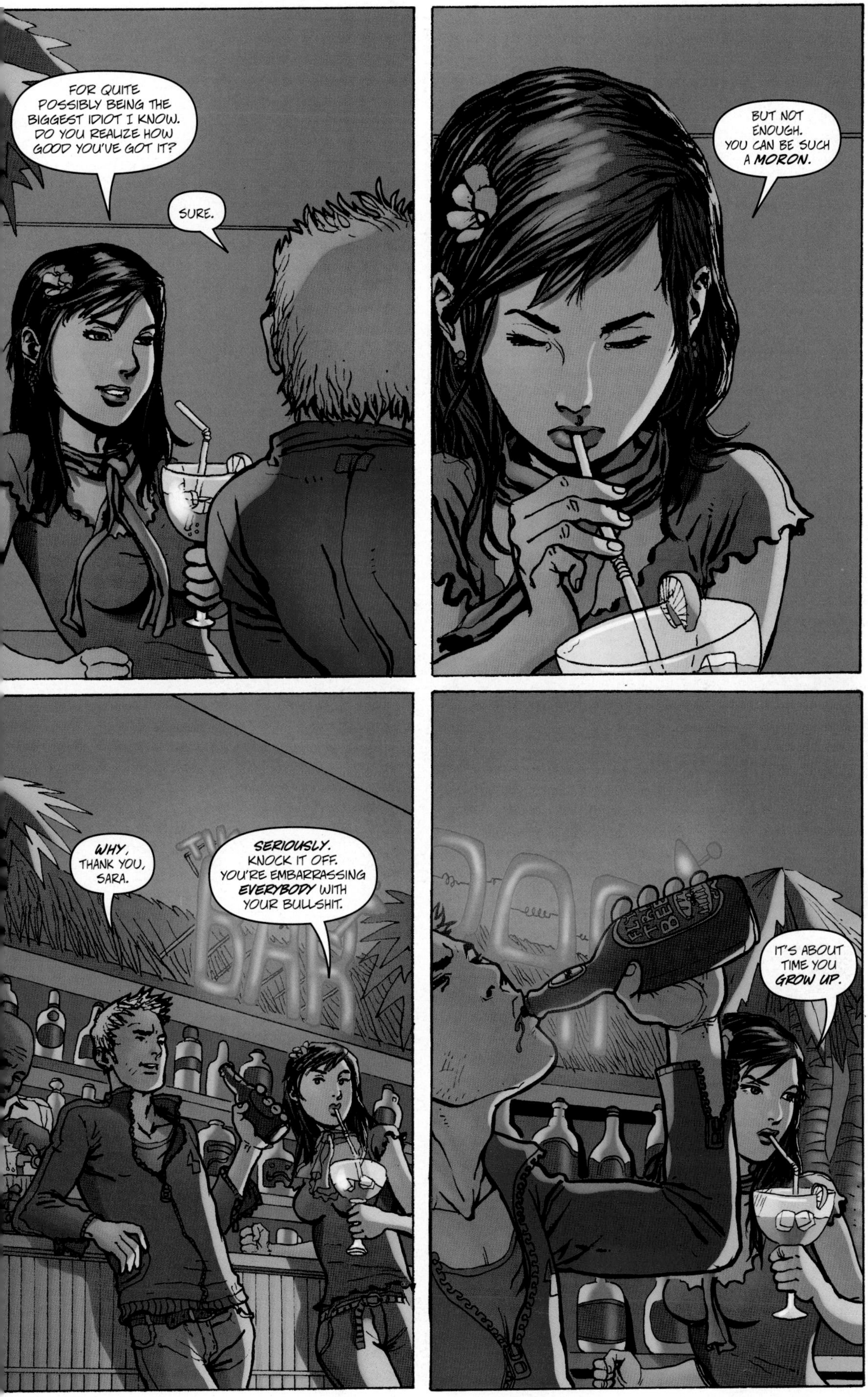
FOR QUITE POSSIBLY BEING THE BIGGEST IDIOT I KNOW. DO YOU REALIZE HOW GOOD YOU'VE GOT IT?
SURE.
BUT NOT ENOUGH. YOU CAN BE SUCH A MORON.
WHY, THANK YOU, SARA.
SERIOUSLY. KNOCK IT OFF. YOU'RE EMBARRASSING EVERYBODY WITH YOUR BULLSHIT.
IT'S ABOUT TIME YOU GROW UP.

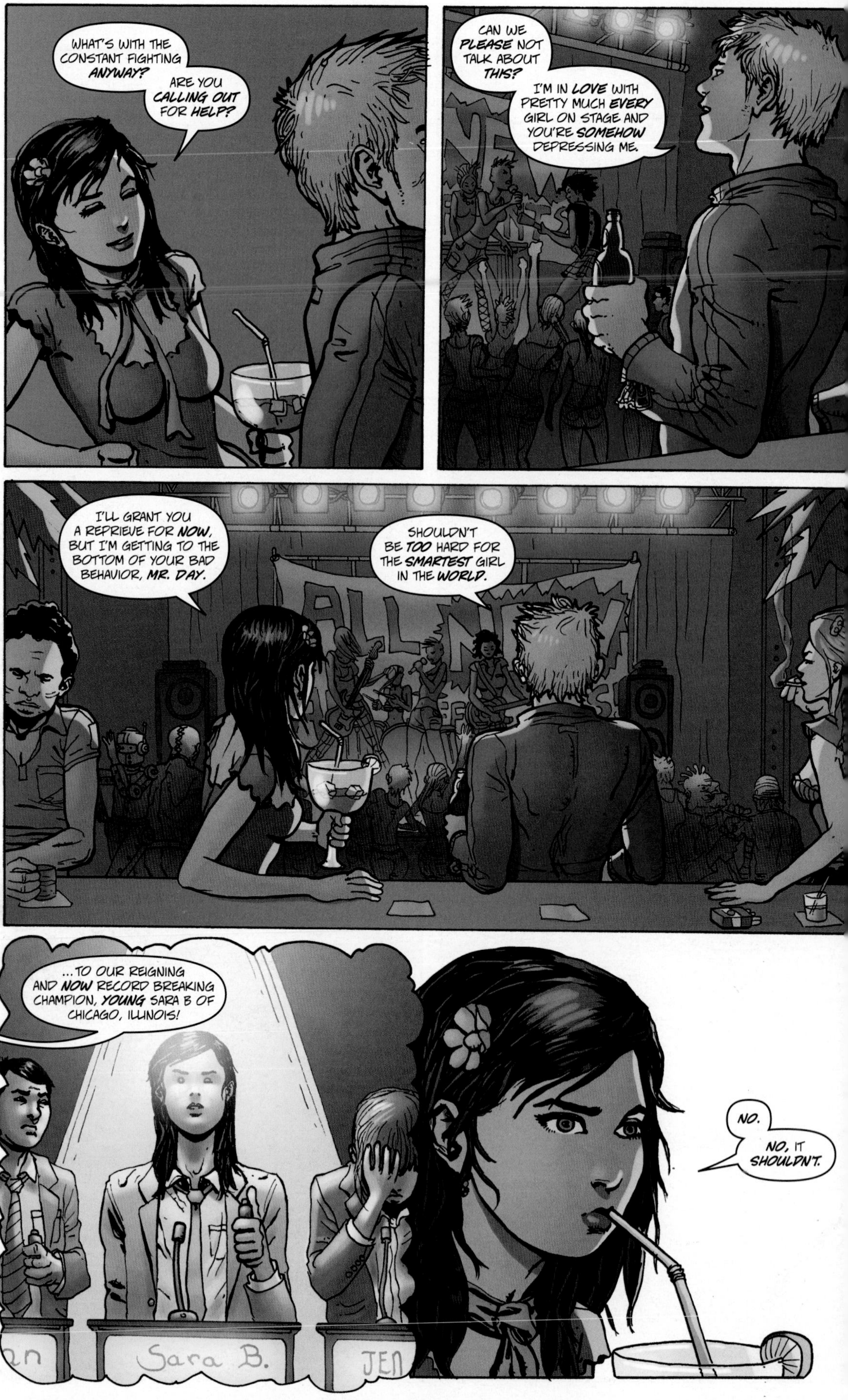
WHAT'S WITH THE CONSTANT FIGHTING ANYWAY?
ARE YOU CALLING OUT FOR HELP?
CAN WE PLEASE NOT TALK ABOUT THIS?
I'M IN LOVE WITH PRETTY MUCH EVERY GIRL ON STAGE AND YOU'RE SOMEHOW DEPRESSING ME.
I'LL GRANT YOU A REPRIEVE FOR NOW, BUT I'M GETTING TO THE BOTTOM OF YOUR BAD BEHAVIOR, MR. DAY.
SHOULDN'T BE TOO HARD FOR THE SMARTEST GIRL IN THE WORLD.
...TO OUR REIGNING AND NOW RECORD BREAKING CHAMPION, YOUNG SARA B OF CHICAGO, ILLINOIS!
Sara B.
JEN
NO.
NO, IT SHOULDN'T.

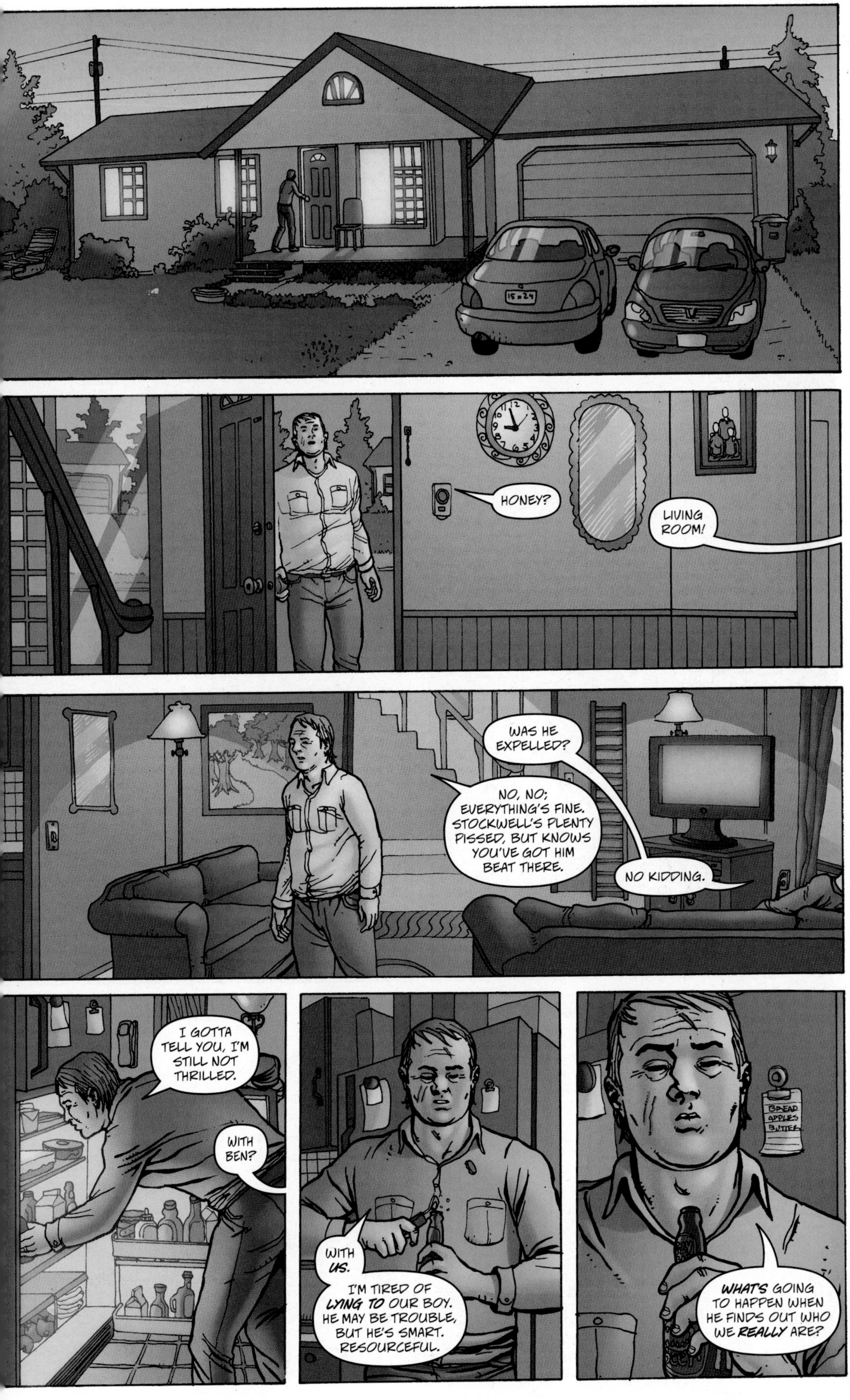
15 24
HONEY?
LIVING ROOM!
WAS HE EXPELLED?
NO, NO; EVERYTHING'S FINE. STOCKWELL'S PLENTY PISSED, BUT KNOWS YOU'VE GOT HIM BEAT THERE.
NO KIDDING.
I GOTTA TELL YOU, I'M STILL NOT THRILLED.
WITH BEN?
WITH *US.*
I'M TIRED OF *LYING TO* OUR BOY. HE MAY BE TROUBLE, BUT HE'S SMART. RESOURCEFUL.
BREAD
APPLES
BUTTER
WHAT'S GOING TO HAPPEN WHEN HE FINDS OUT WHO WE *REALLY* ARE?

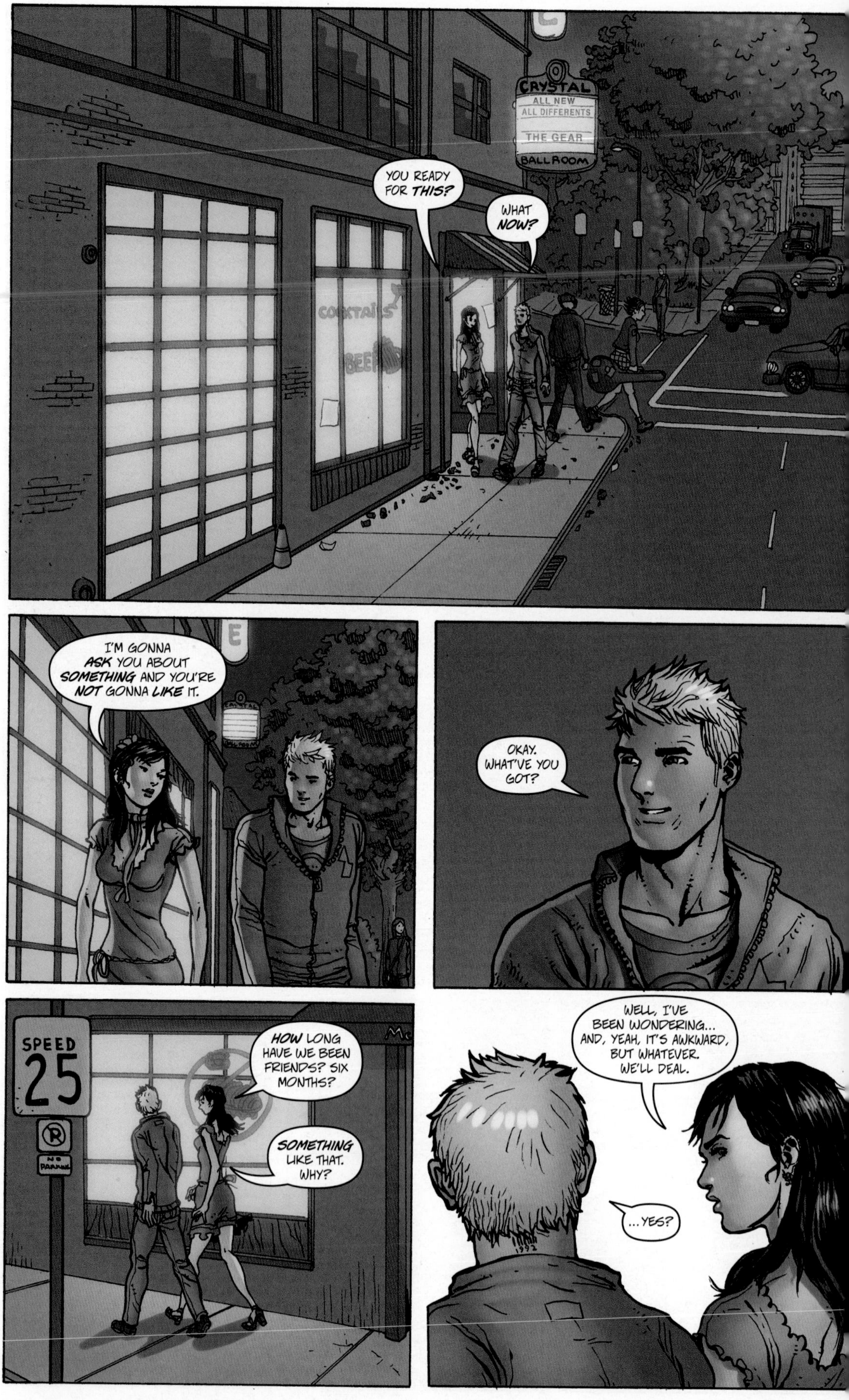
CRYSTAL
ALL NEW
ALL DIFFERENTS
THE GEAR
BALLROOM
YOU READY FOR THIS?
WHAT NOW?
COCKTAILS
I'M GONNA ASK YOU ABOUT SOMETHING AND YOU'RE NOT GONNA LIKE IT.
OKAY. WHAT'VE YOU GOT?
SPEED 25
HOW LONG HAVE WE BEEN FRIENDS? SIX MONTHS?
SOMETHING LIKE THAT. WHY?
WELL, I'VE BEEN WONDERING... AND, YEAH, IT'S AWKWARD, BUT WHATEVER. WE'LL DEAL.
...YES?

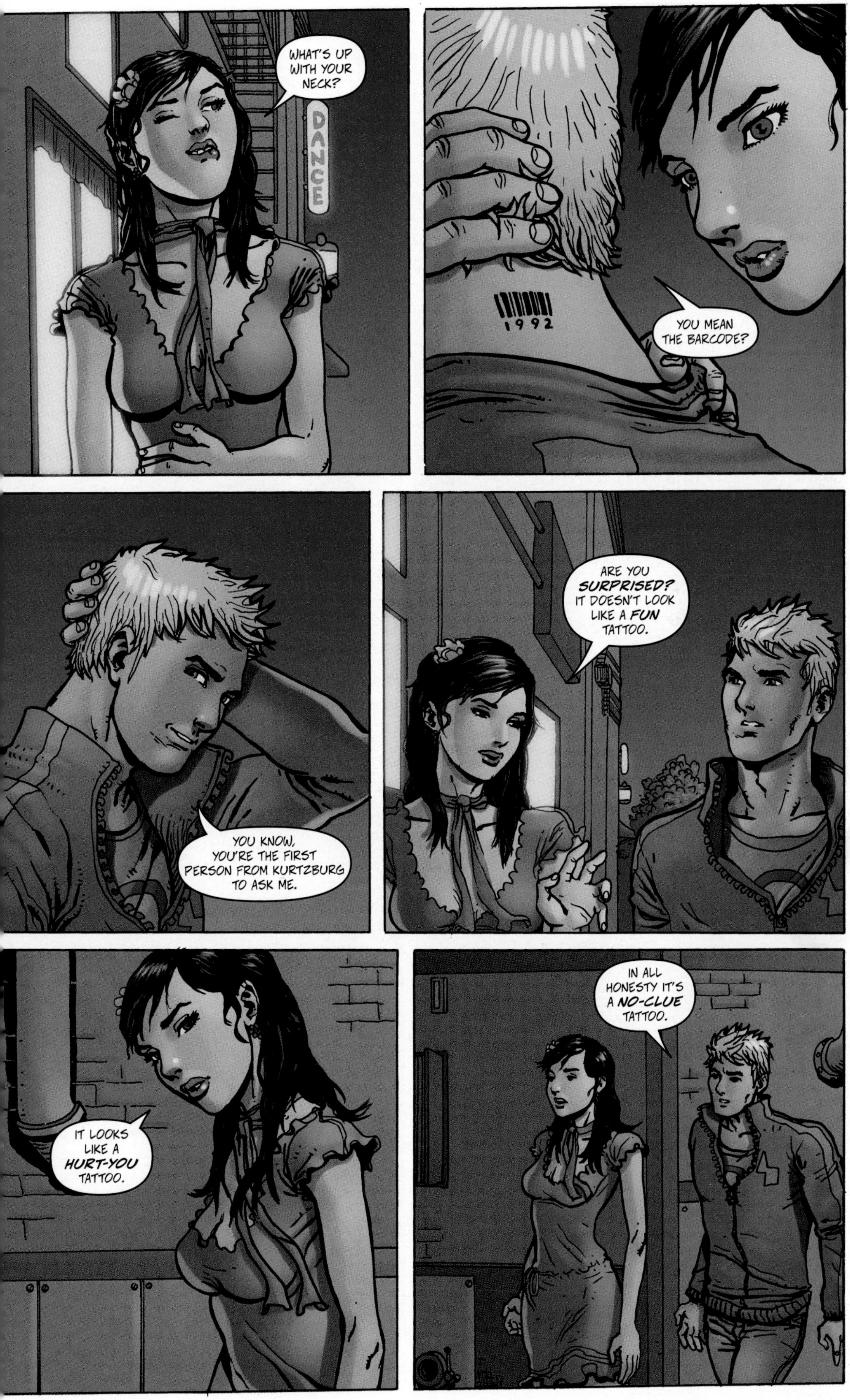
WHAT'S UP WITH YOUR NECK?
DANCE
1992
YOU MEAN THE BARCODE?
YOU KNOW, YOU'RE THE FIRST PERSON FROM KURTZBURG TO ASK ME.
ARE YOU SURPRISED? IT DOESN'T LOOK LIKE A FUN TATTOO.
IT LOOKS LIKE A HURT-YOU TATTOO.
IN ALL HONESTY IT'S A NO-CLUE TATTOO.

WERE YOU BORN WITH IT?

NO, WASN'T *BORN* WITH IT. THINK *WEIRDER*; EVEN FOR A WORLD LIKE OURS.

WHAT DO YOU MEAN?

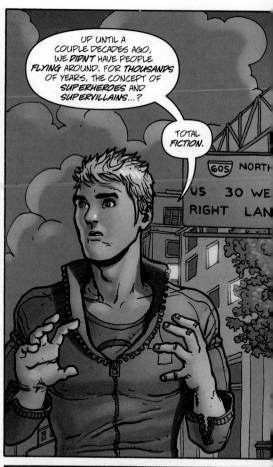

UP UNTIL A COUPLE DECADES AGO, WE *DIDN'T* HAVE PEOPLE *FLYING* AROUND. FOR *THOUSANDS* OF YEARS, THE CONCEPT OF *SUPERHEROES* AND *SUPERVILLAINS*...?

TOTAL *FICTION*.

THEN *ONE* DAY MY DAD'S *SAVED* BY A *BUNCH* OF THEM, ENDING THE GULF WAR. *SUDDENLY* THE WORLD'S *FULL* OF SUPER-PEOPLE AND *SOME* OF US ARE EVEN *BORN* WITH *POWERS*.

...AND *THIS* RELATES TO YOUR *TATTOO*?

COMPLETELY.

BECAUSE AS *WEIRD* AS A WORLD AS WE *LIVE* IN, HOW I HAVE *THIS* IS EVEN *WEIRDER*.

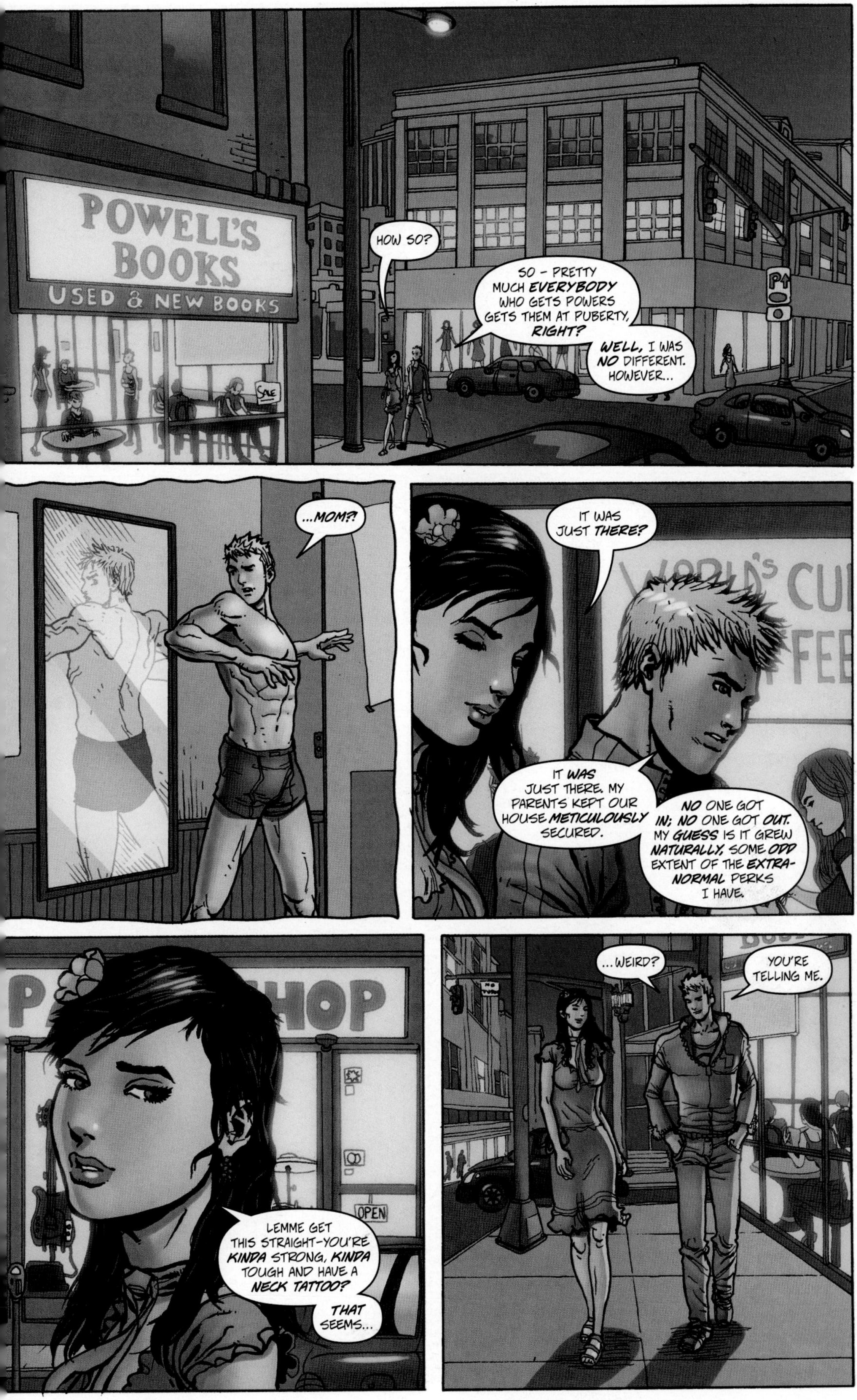
POWELL'S BOOKS
USED & NEW BOOKS
SALE
HOW SO?
SO - PRETTY MUCH EVERYBODY WHO GETS POWERS GETS THEM AT PUBERTY, RIGHT?
WELL, I WAS NO DIFFERENT. HOWEVER...
...MOM?!
IT WAS JUST THERE?
IT WAS JUST THERE. MY PARENTS KEPT OUR HOUSE METICULOUSLY SECURED.
NO ONE GOT IN; NO ONE GOT OUT. MY GUESS IS IT GREW NATURALLY, SOME ODD EXTENT OF THE EXTRA-NORMAL PERKS I HAVE.
OPEN
LEMME GET THIS STRAIGHT-YOU'RE KINDA STRONG, KINDA TOUGH AND HAVE A NECK TATTOO?
THAT SEEMS...
...WEIRD?
YOU'RE TELLING ME.

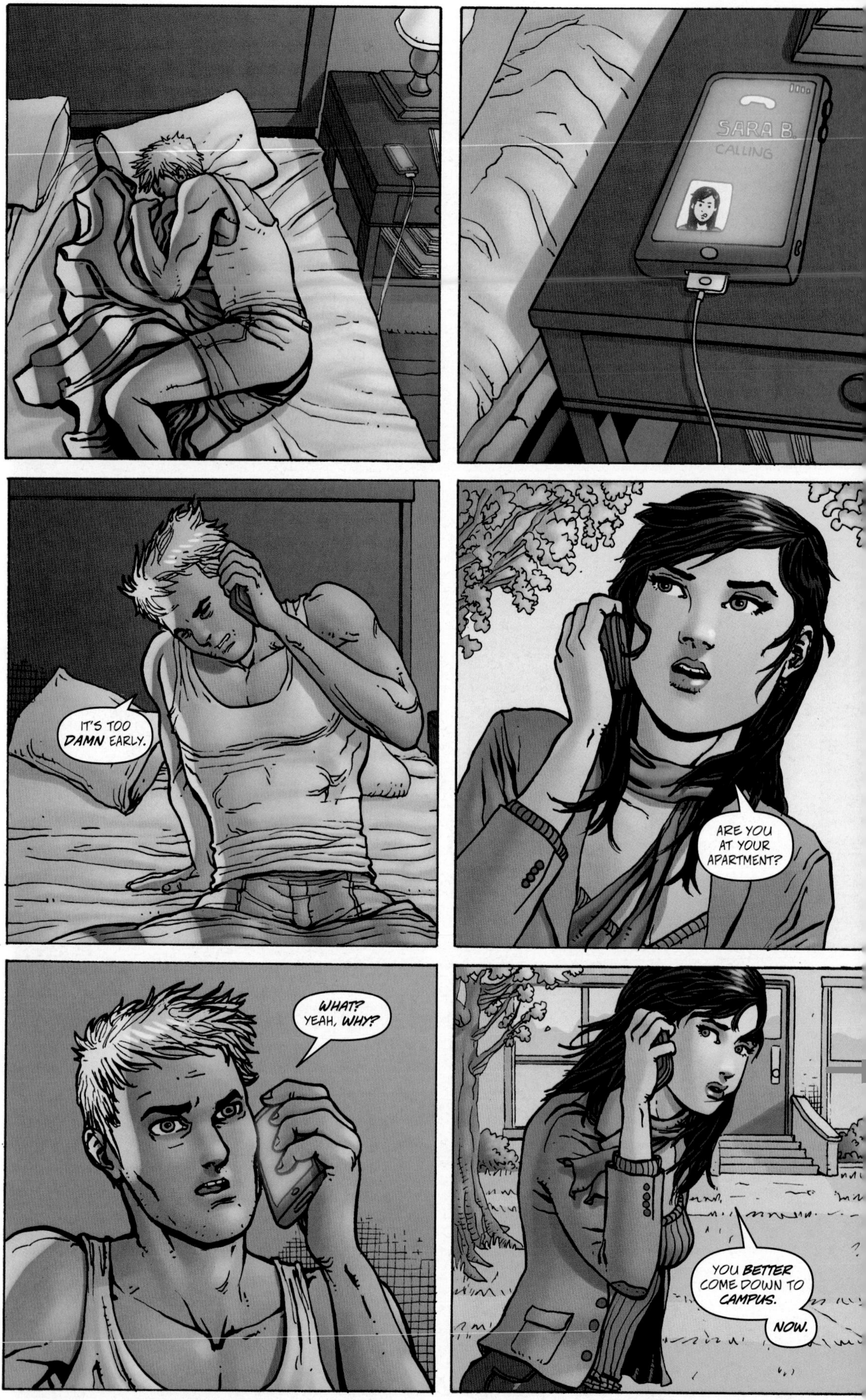
SARA B.
CALLING
IT'S TOO DAMN EARLY.
ARE YOU AT YOUR APARTMENT?
WHAT? YEAH, WHY?
YOU BETTER COME DOWN TO CAMPUS.
NOW.

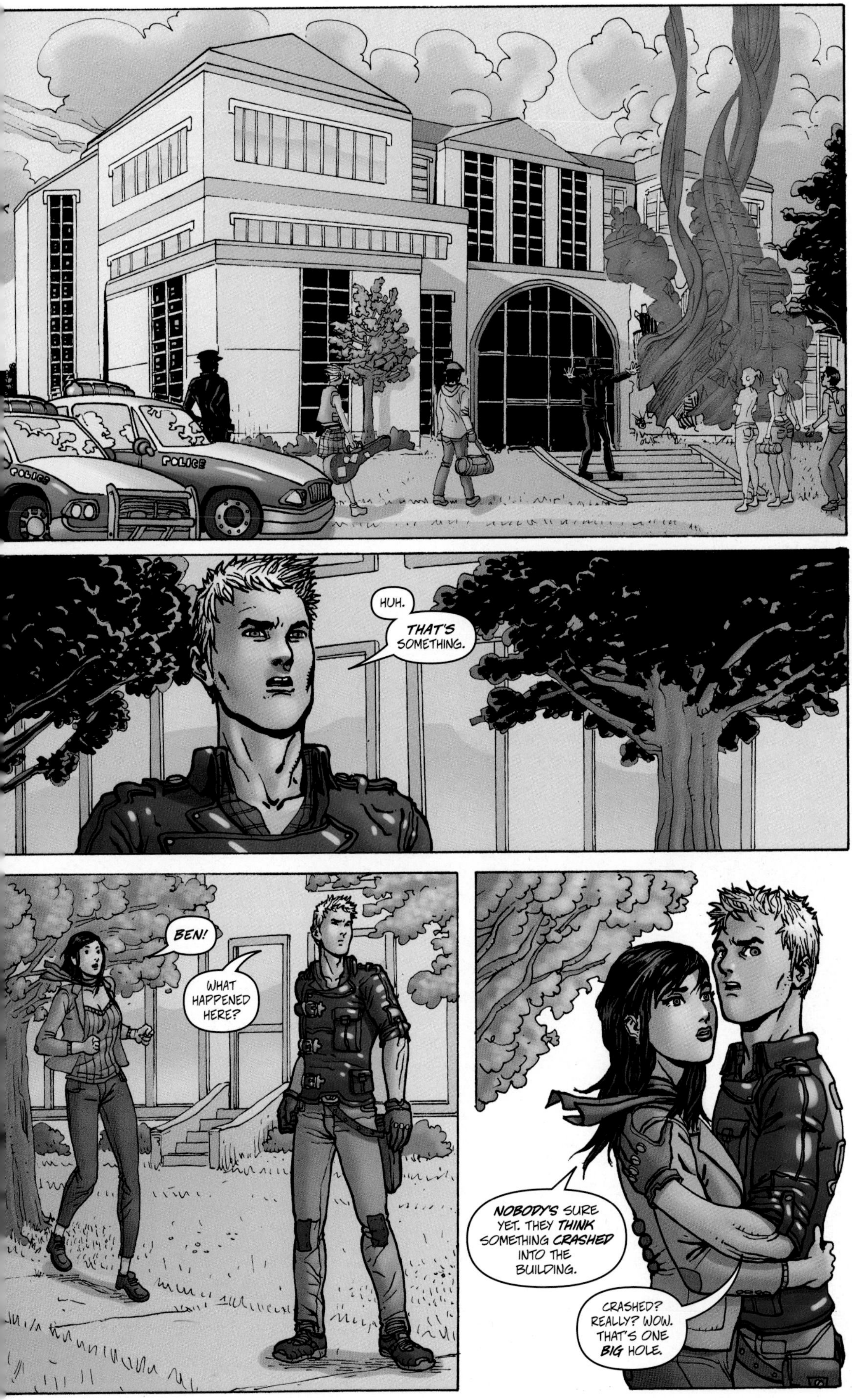
POLICE
POLICE
HUH.
THAT'S SOMETHING.
BEN!
WHAT HAPPENED HERE?
NOBODY'S SURE YET. THEY THINK SOMETHING CRASHED INTO THE BUILDING.
CRASHED? REALLY? WOW. THAT'S ONE BIG HOLE.

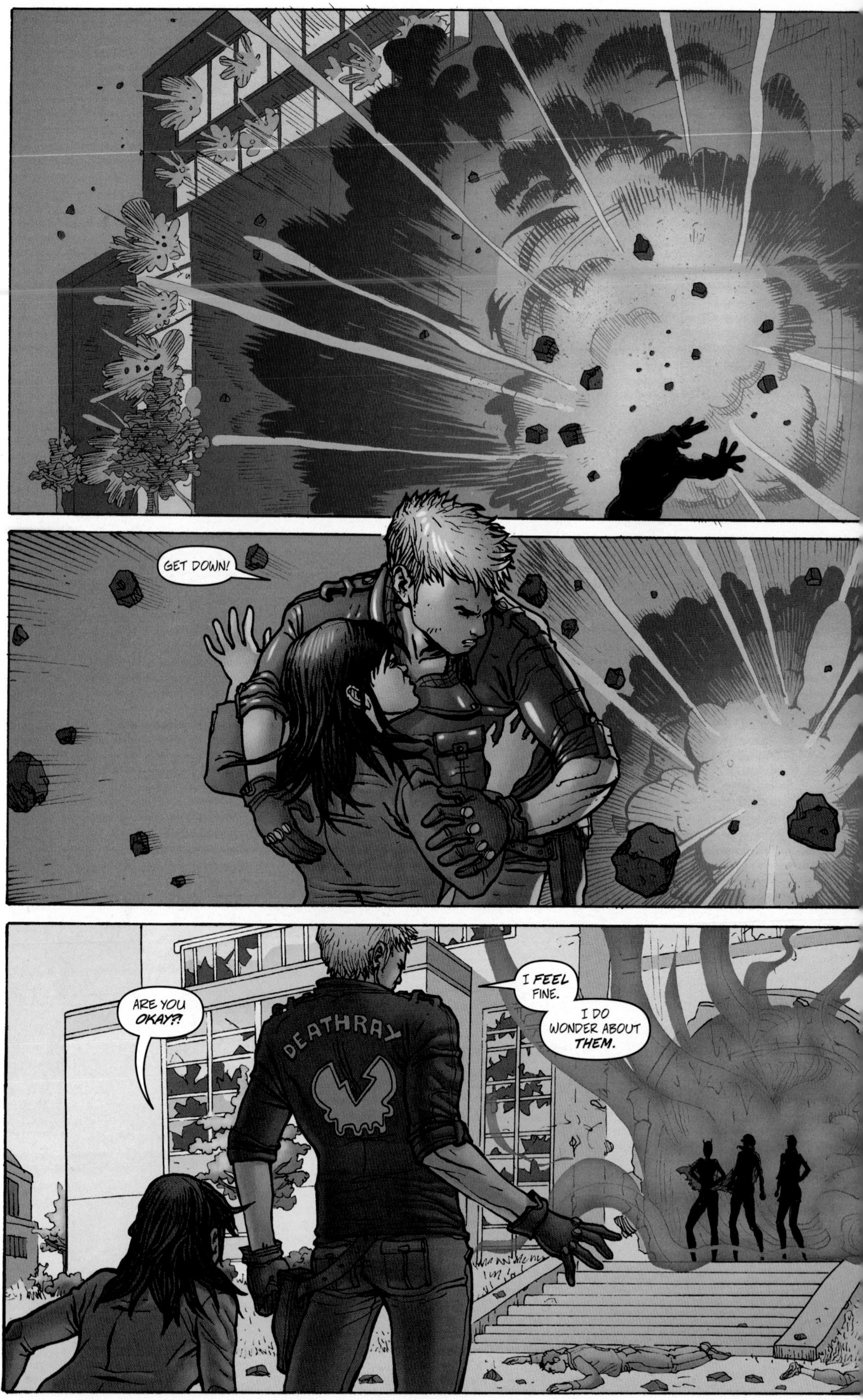
GET DOWN!
ARE YOU OKAY?!
I FEEL FINE.
I DO WONDER ABOUT THEM.
DEATHRAY

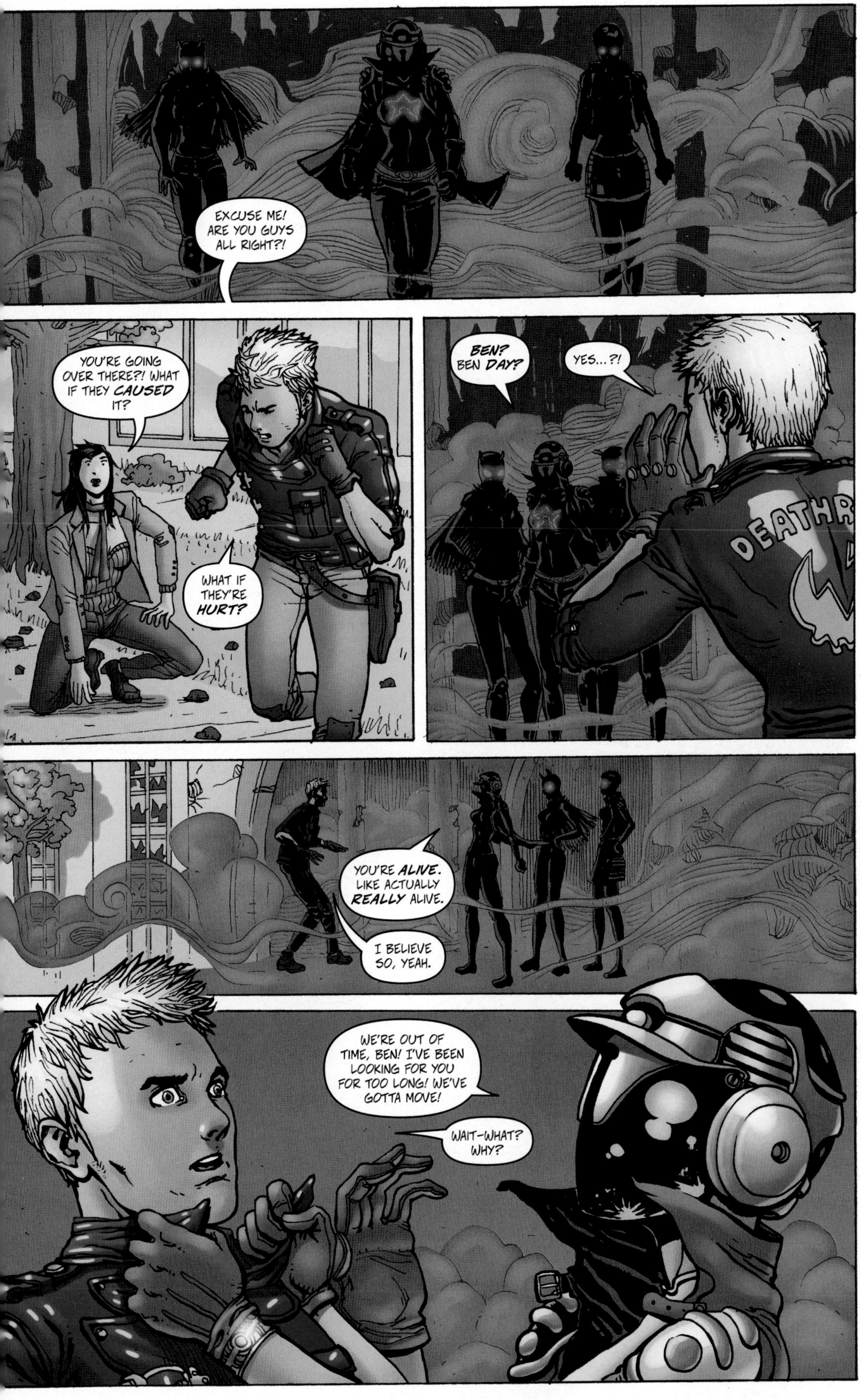
EXCUSE ME! ARE YOU GUYS ALL RIGHT?!
YOU'RE GOING OVER THERE?! WHAT IF THEY CAUSED IT?
WHAT IF THEY'RE HURT?
BEN? BEN DAY?
YES...?!
DEATHR
YOU'RE ALIVE. LIKE ACTUALLY REALLY ALIVE.
I BELIEVE SO, YEAH.
WE'RE OUT OF TIME, BEN! I'VE BEEN LOOKING FOR YOU FOR TOO LONG! WE'VE GOTTA MOVE!
WAIT-WHAT? WHY?

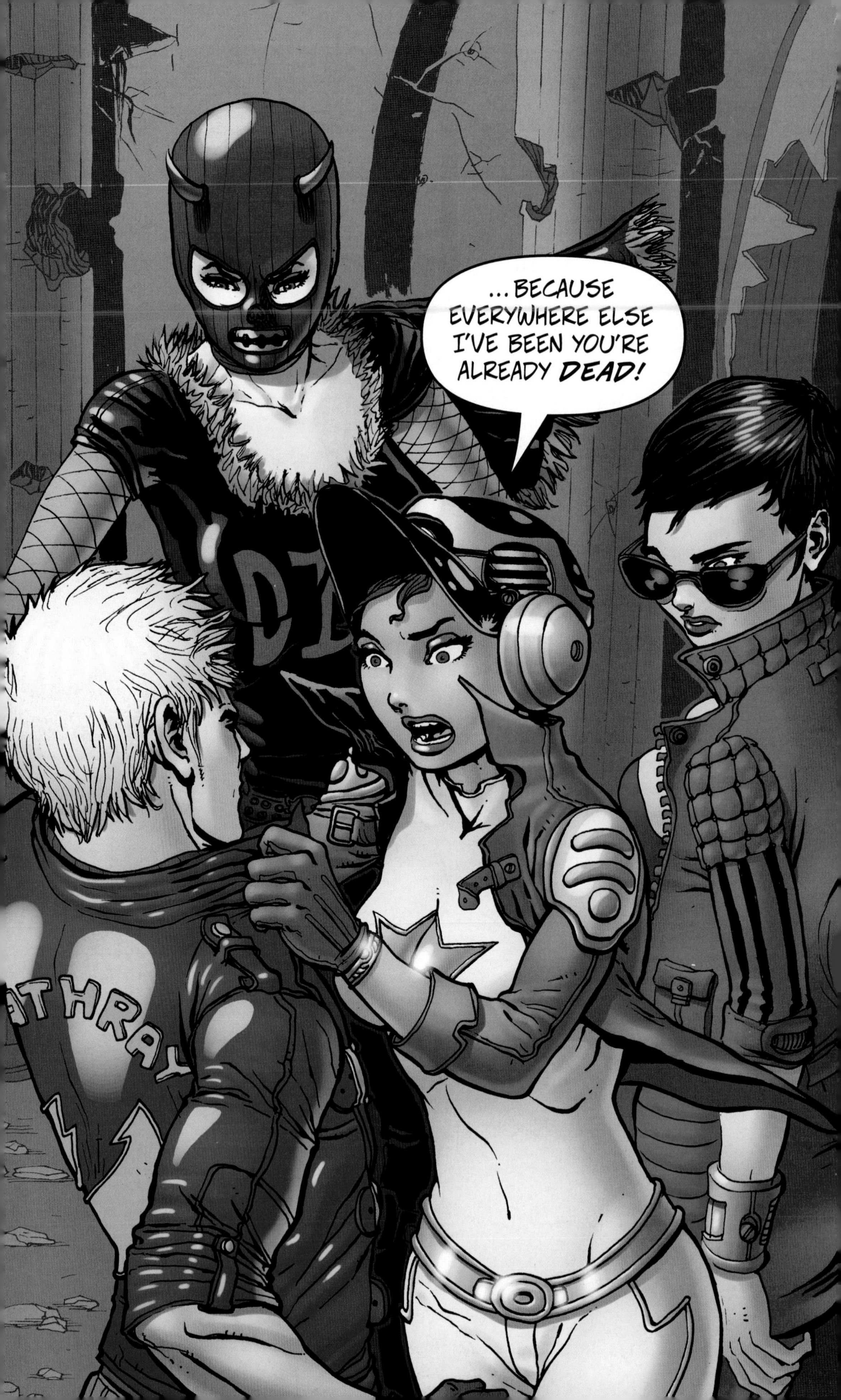
...BECAUSE EVERYWHERE ELSE I'VE BEEN YOU'RE ALREADY ***DEAD!***

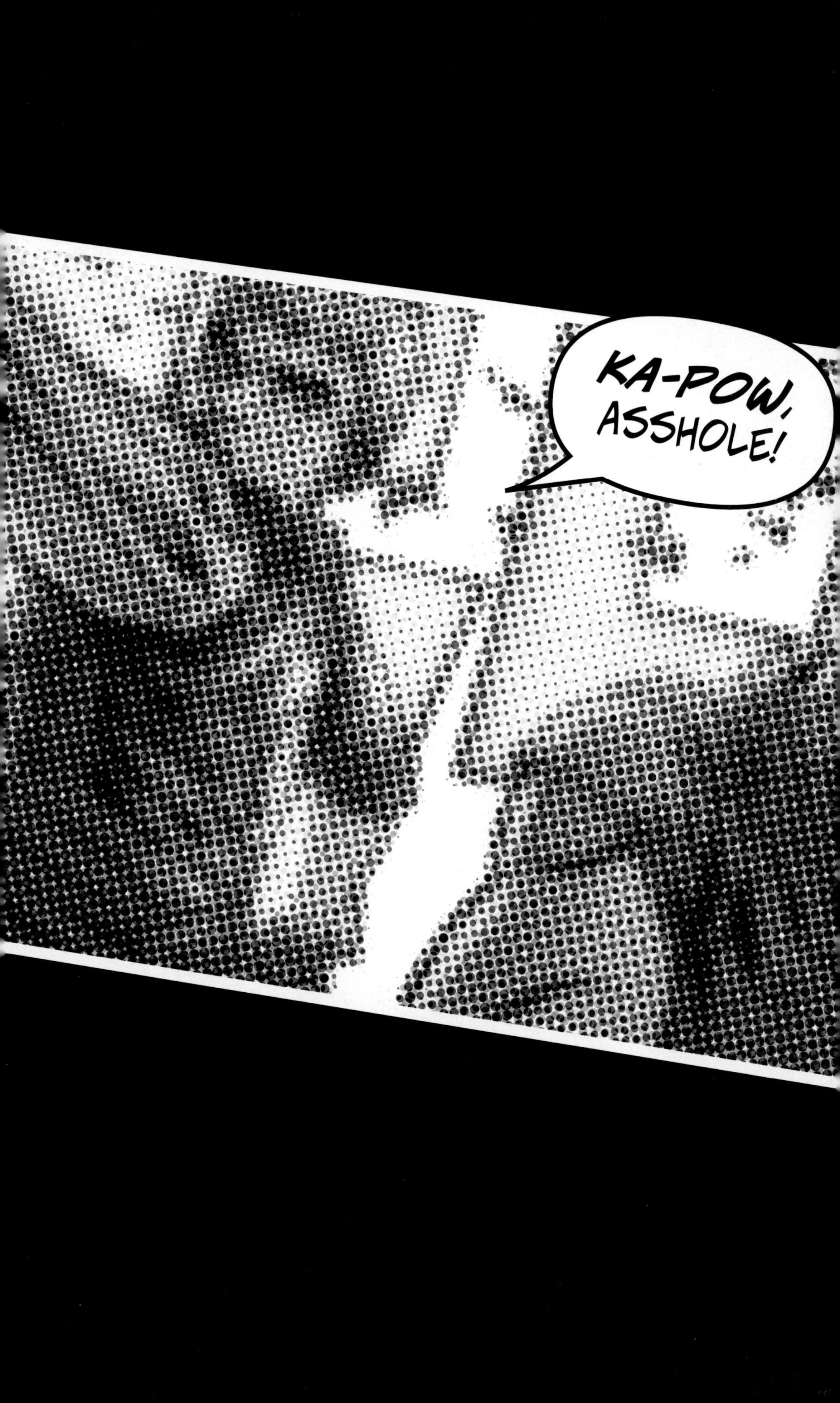
KA-POW, ASSHOLE!

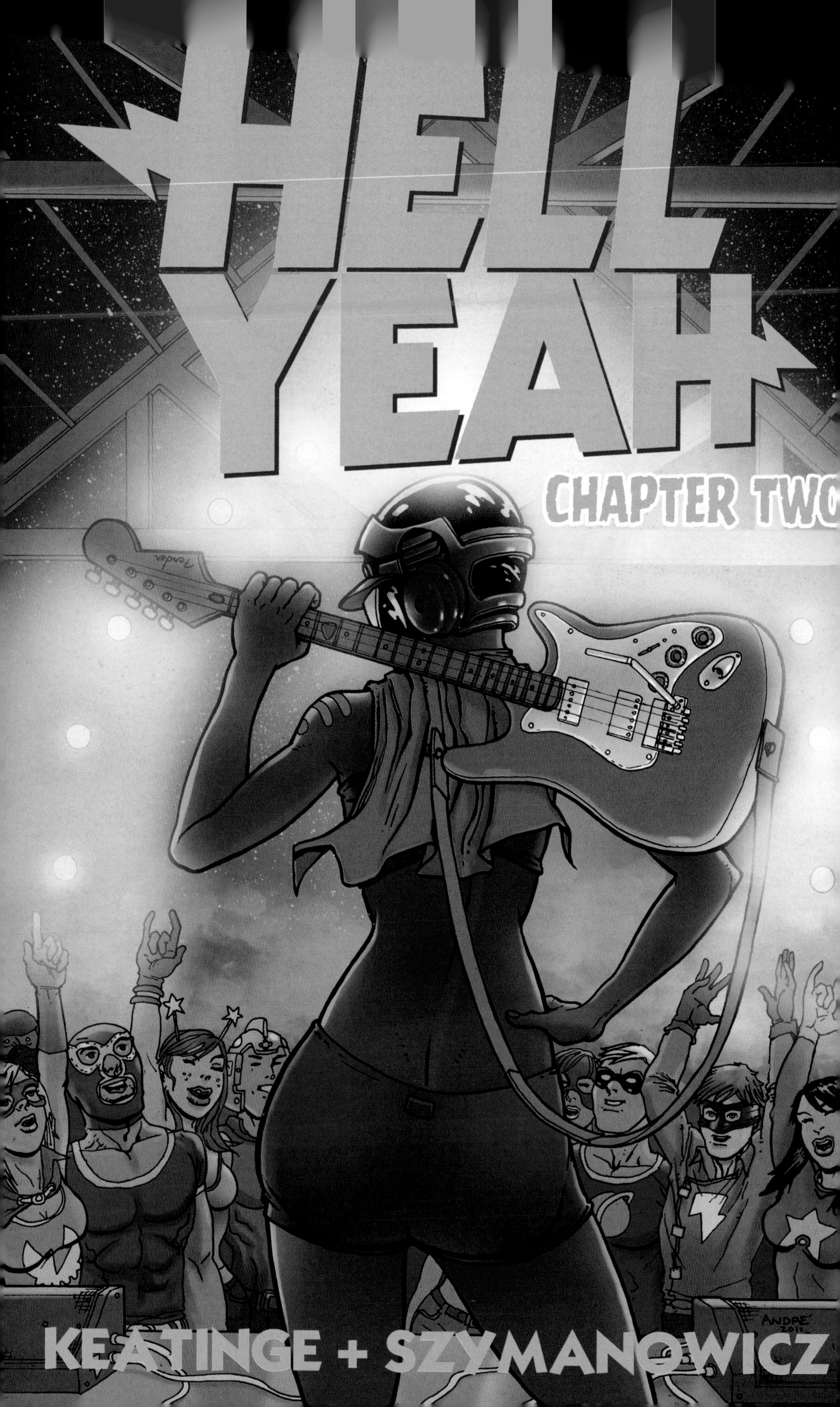
HELL YEAH
CHAPTER TWO
KEATINGE + SZYMANOWICZ

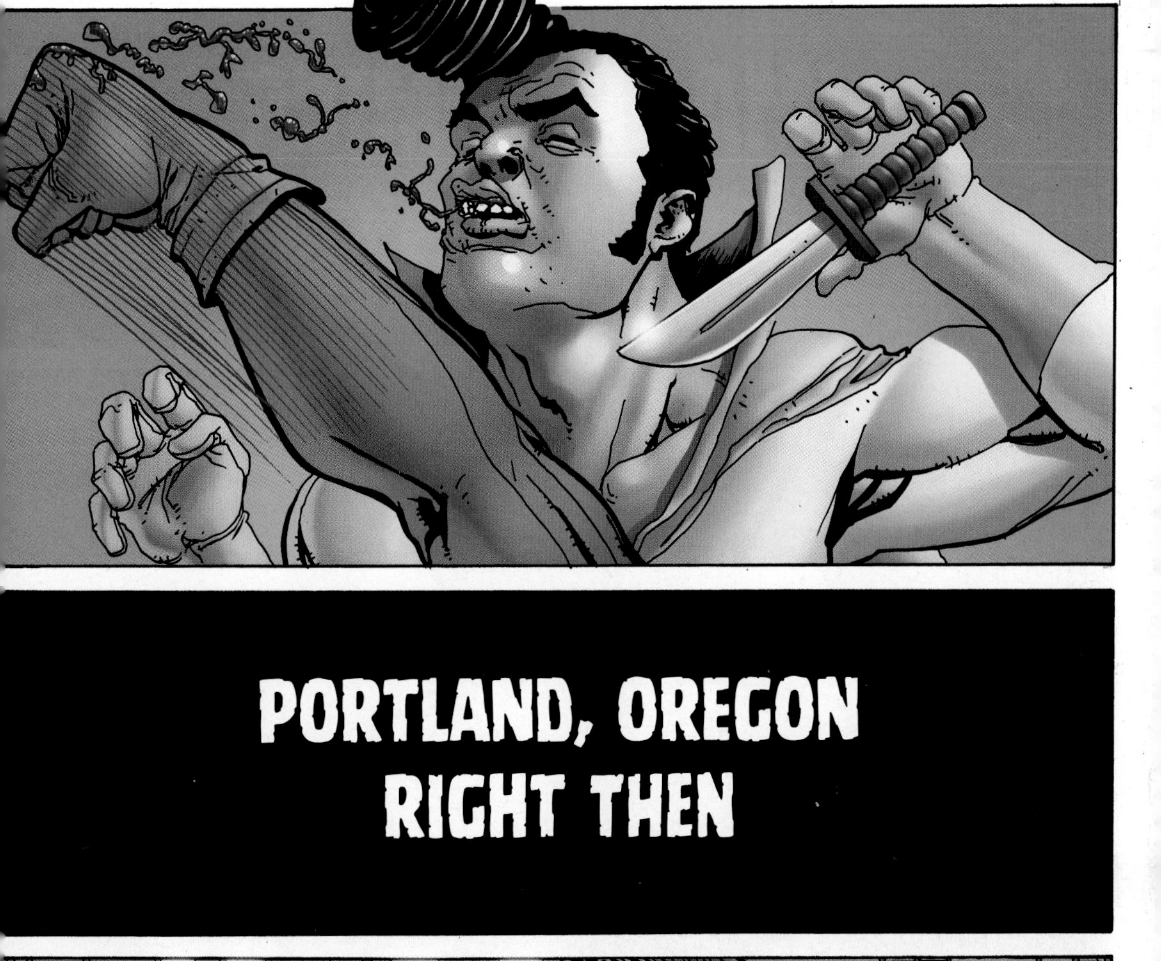

PORTLAND, OREGON
RIGHT THEN

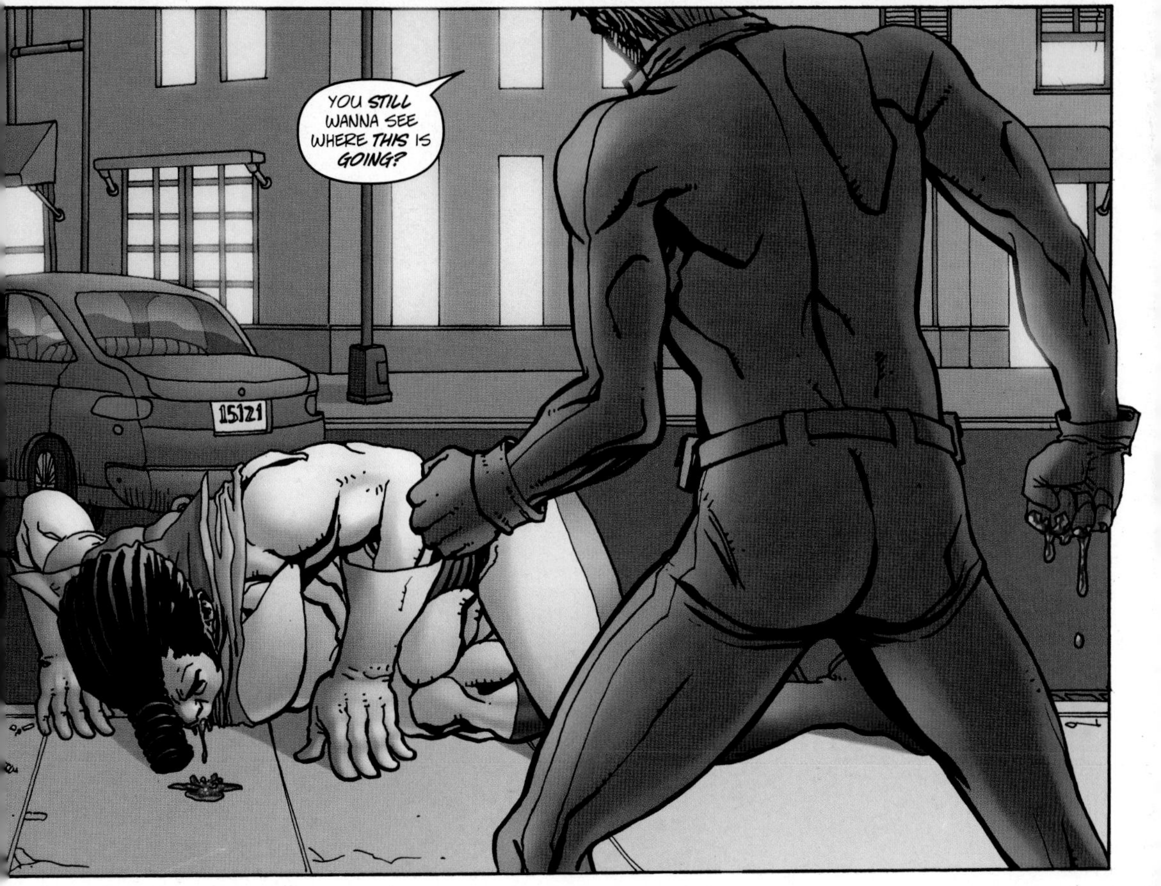
YOU STILL WANNA SEE WHERE THIS IS GOING?
15121

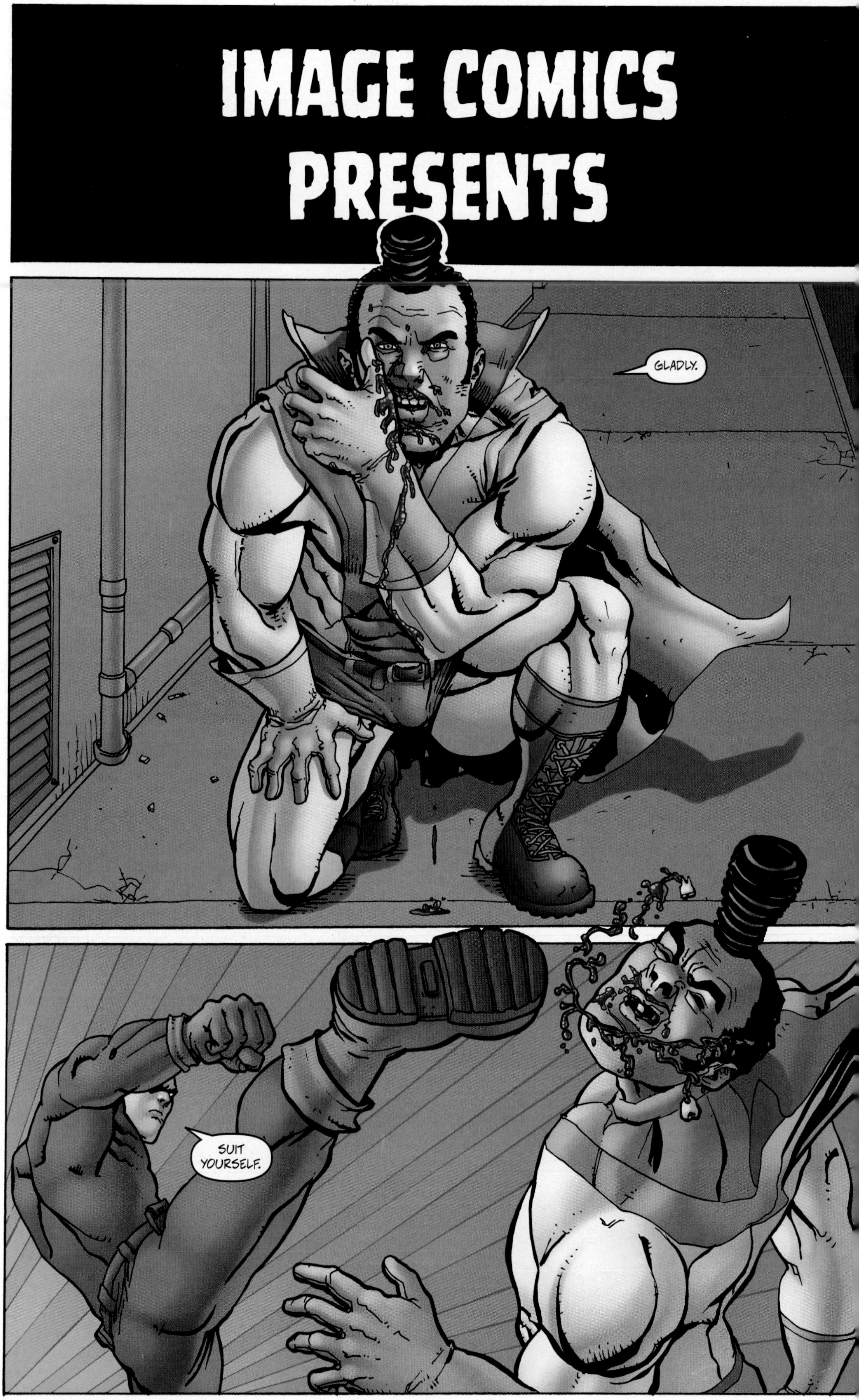
IMAGE COMICS PRESENTS
GLADLY.
SUIT YOURSELF.

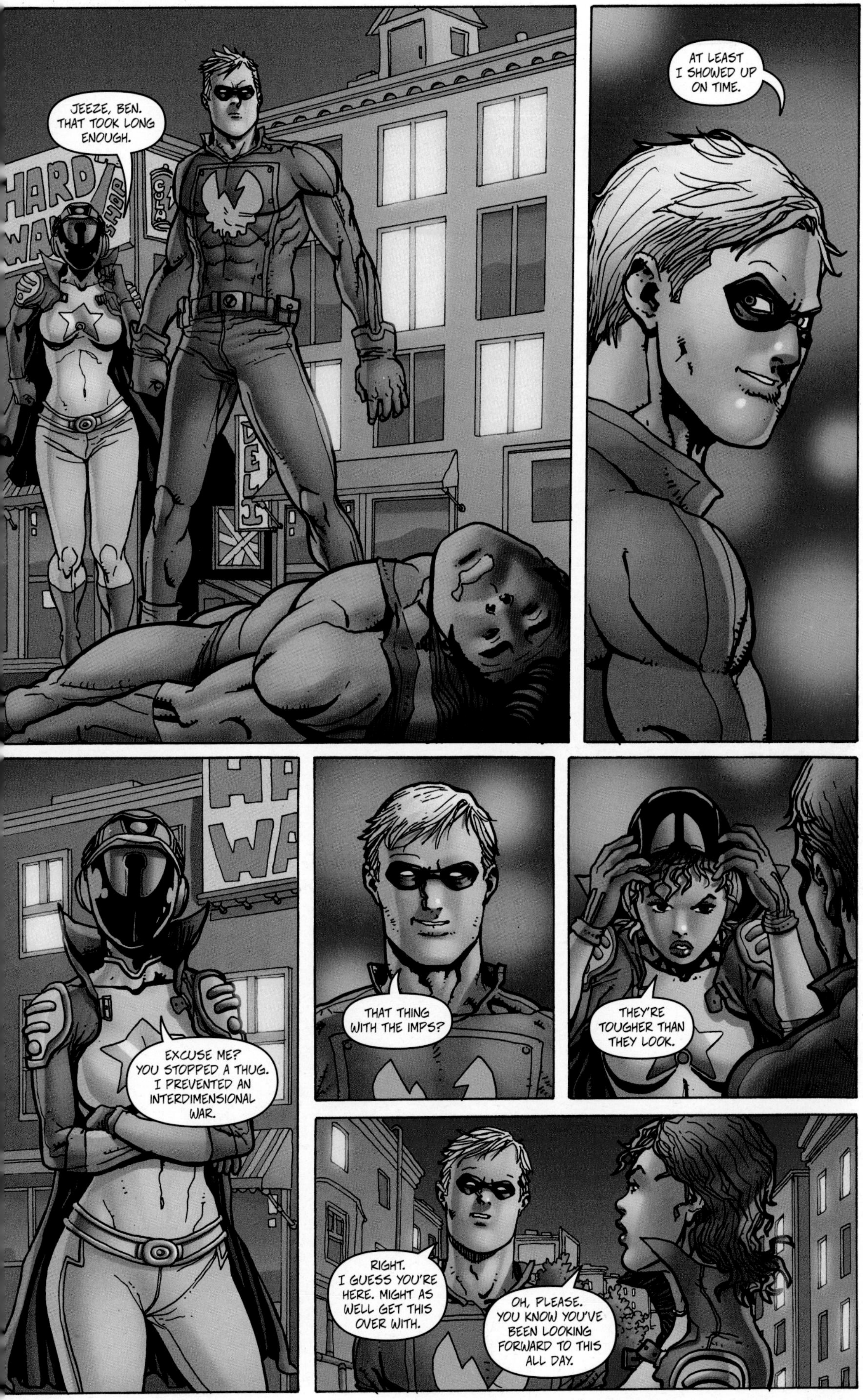

JEEZE, BEN. THAT TOOK LONG ENOUGH.
HARDWARE
DELI
AT LEAST I SHOWED UP ON TIME.
EXCUSE ME? YOU STOPPED A THUG. I PREVENTED AN INTERDIMENSIONAL WAR.
THAT THING WITH THE IMPS?
THEY'RE TOUGHER THAN THEY LOOK.
RIGHT. I GUESS YOU'RE HERE. MIGHT AS WELL GET THIS OVER WITH.
OH, PLEASE. YOU KNOW YOU'VE BEEN LOOKING FORWARD TO THIS ALL DAY.

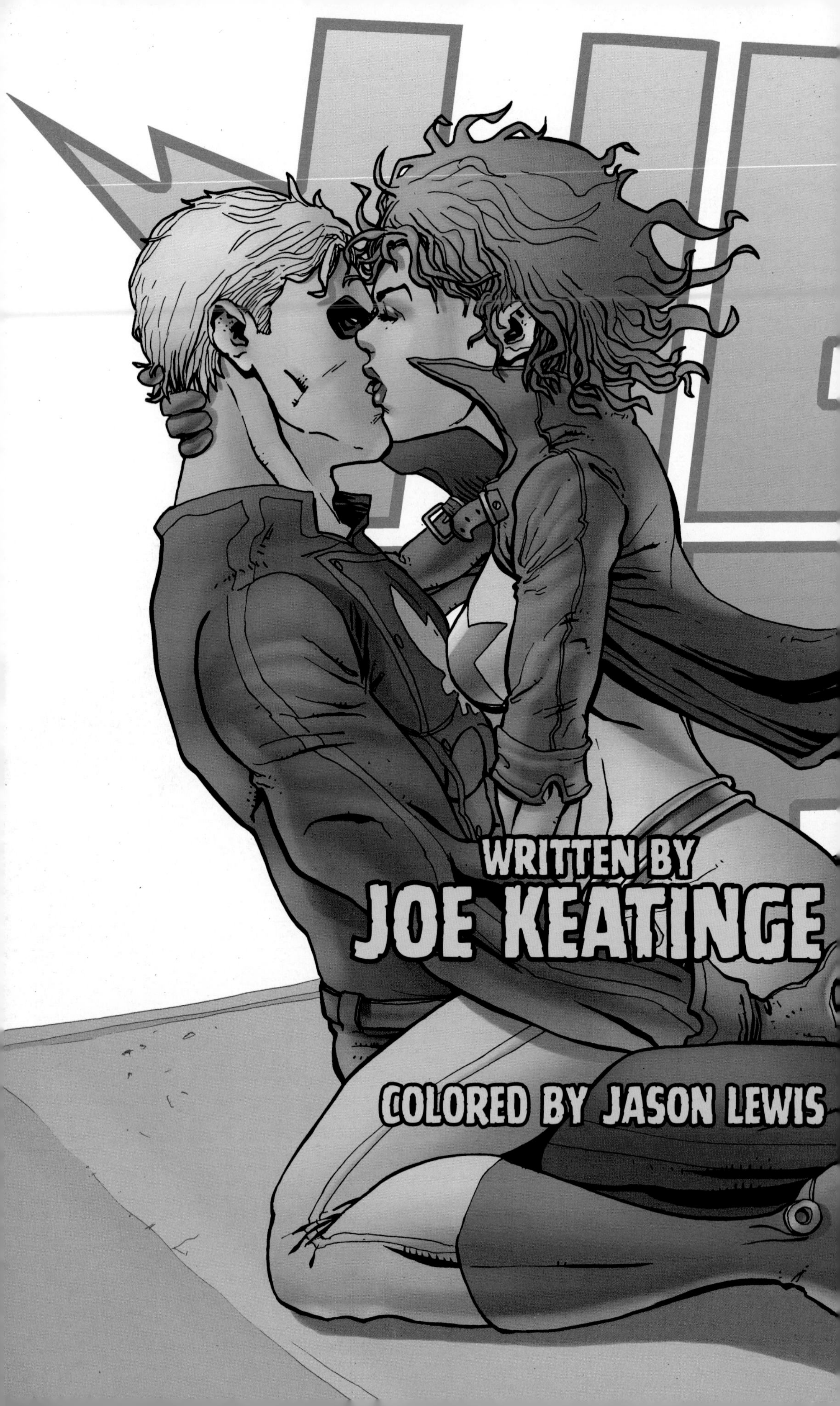
WRITTEN BY
JOE KEATINGE
COLORED BY JASON LEWIS

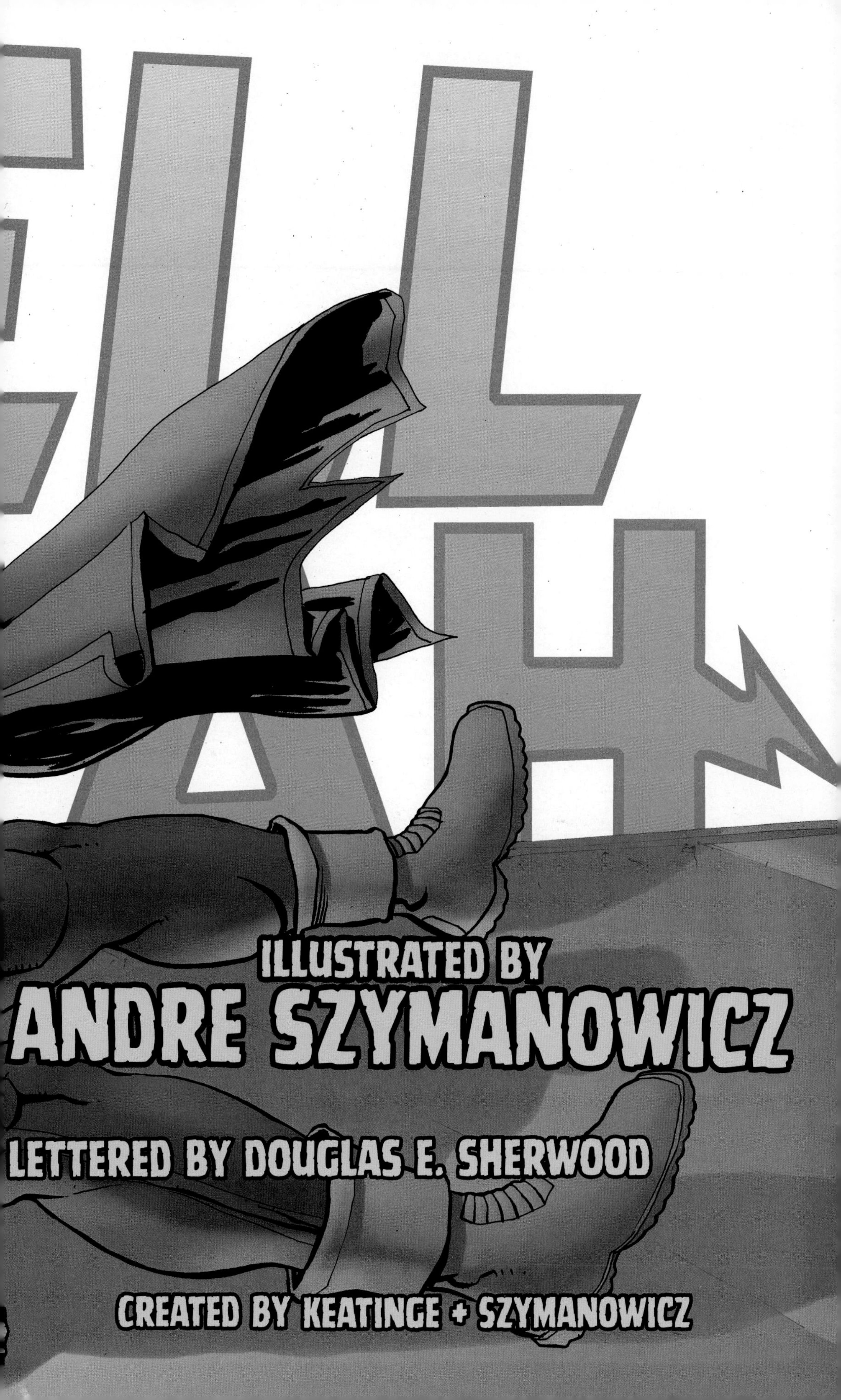
ILLUSTRATED BY
ANDRE SZYMANOWICZ
LETTERED BY DOUGLAS E. SHERWOOD
CREATED BY KEATINGE + SZYMANOWICZ

BOOK ONE
LAST DAY ON EARTHS

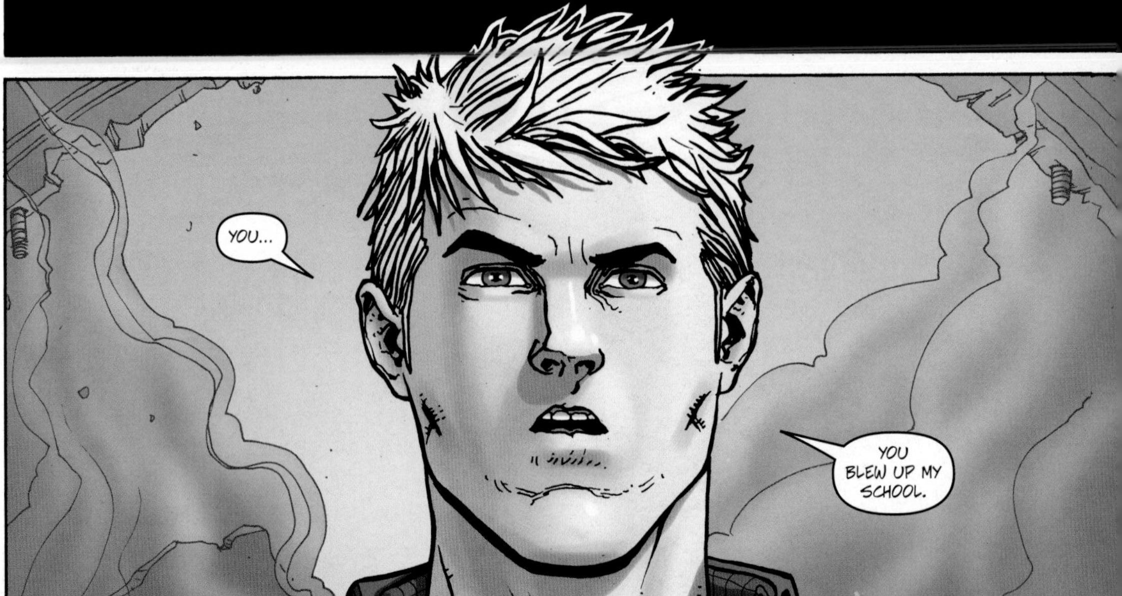

YOU...
YOU BLEW UP MY SCHOOL.

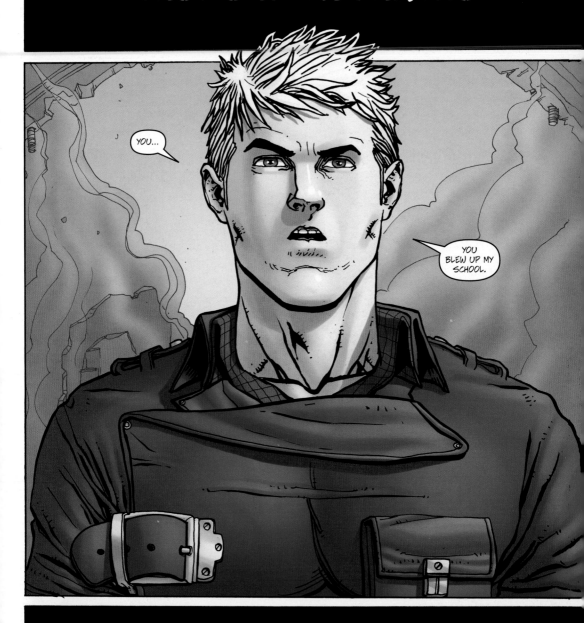

CHAPTER TWO
ALWAYS YOU

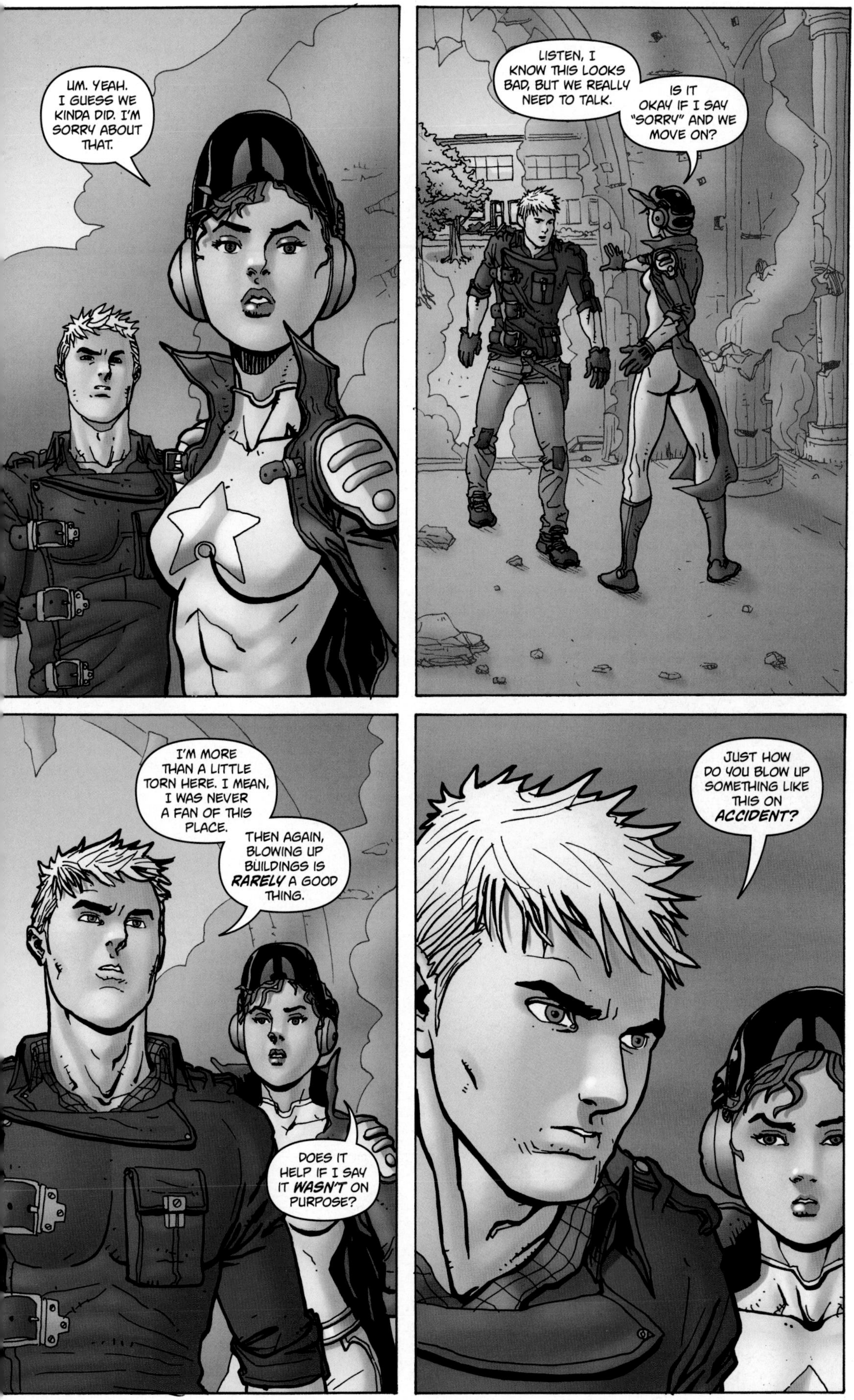
UM. YEAH. I GUESS WE KINDA DID. I'M SORRY ABOUT THAT.
LISTEN, I KNOW THIS LOOKS BAD, BUT WE REALLY NEED TO TALK.
IS IT OKAY IF I SAY "SORRY" AND WE MOVE ON?
I'M MORE THAN A LITTLE TORN HERE. I MEAN, I WAS NEVER A FAN OF THIS PLACE.
THEN AGAIN, BLOWING UP BUILDINGS IS RARELY A GOOD THING.
DOES IT HELP IF I SAY IT WASN'T ON PURPOSE?
JUST HOW DO YOU BLOW UP SOMETHING LIKE THIS ON ACCIDENT?

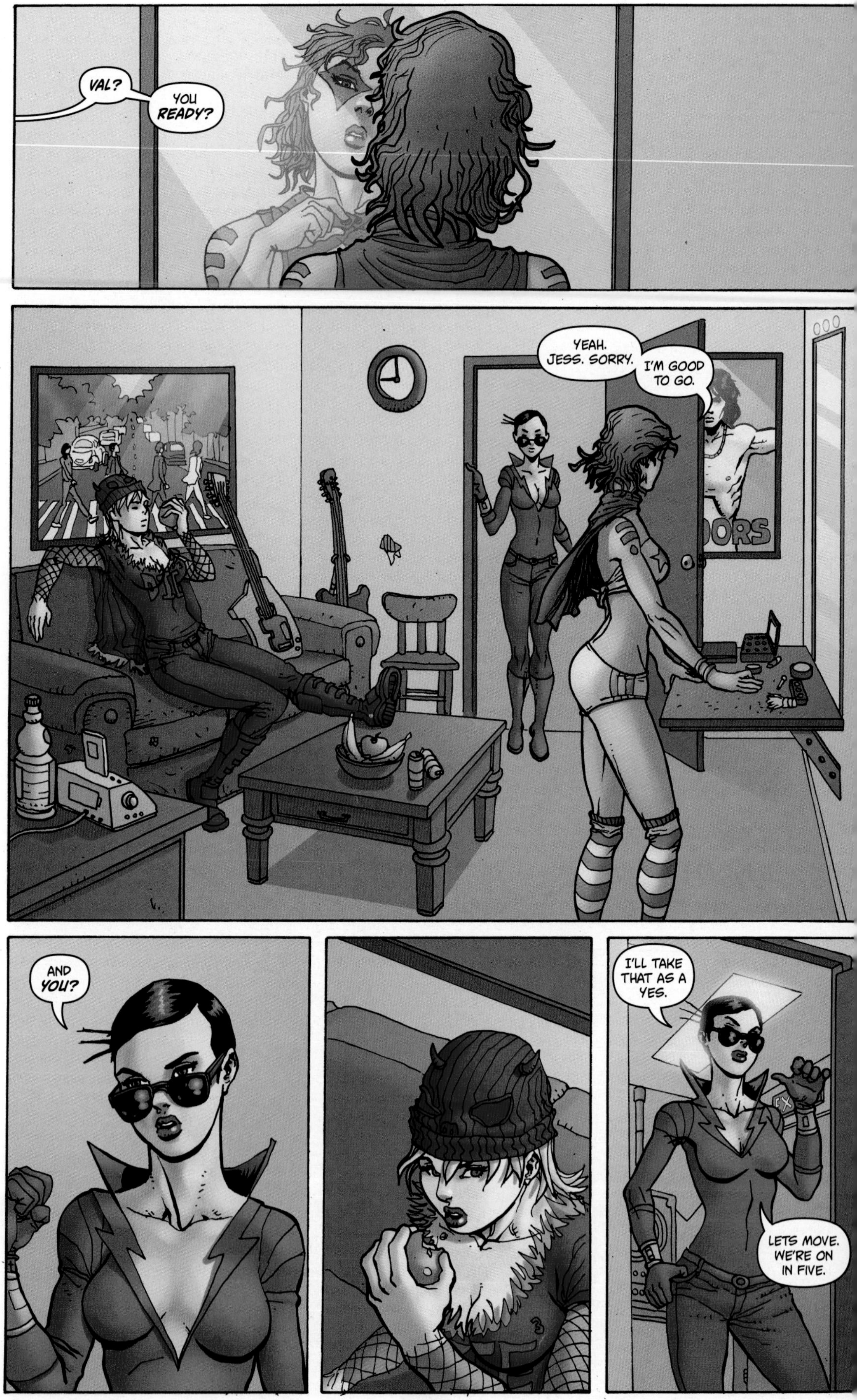
VAL?
YOU READY?
YEAH. JESS. SORRY.
I'M GOOD TO GO.
DOORS
AND YOU?
I'LL TAKE THAT AS A YES.
LETS MOVE. WE'RE ON IN FIVE.

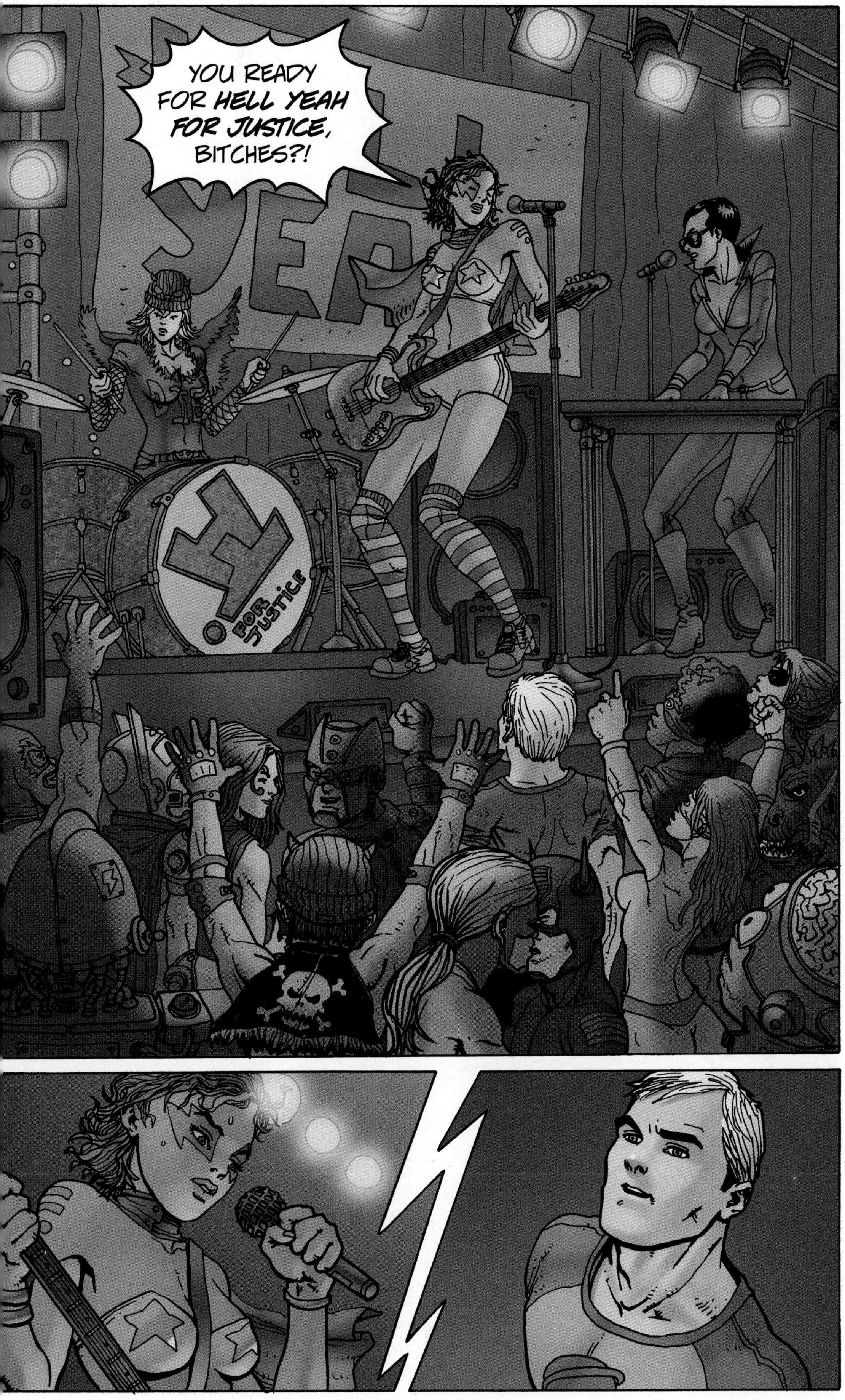
YOU READY FOR HELL YEAH FOR JUSTICE, BITCHES?!
FOR JUSTICE

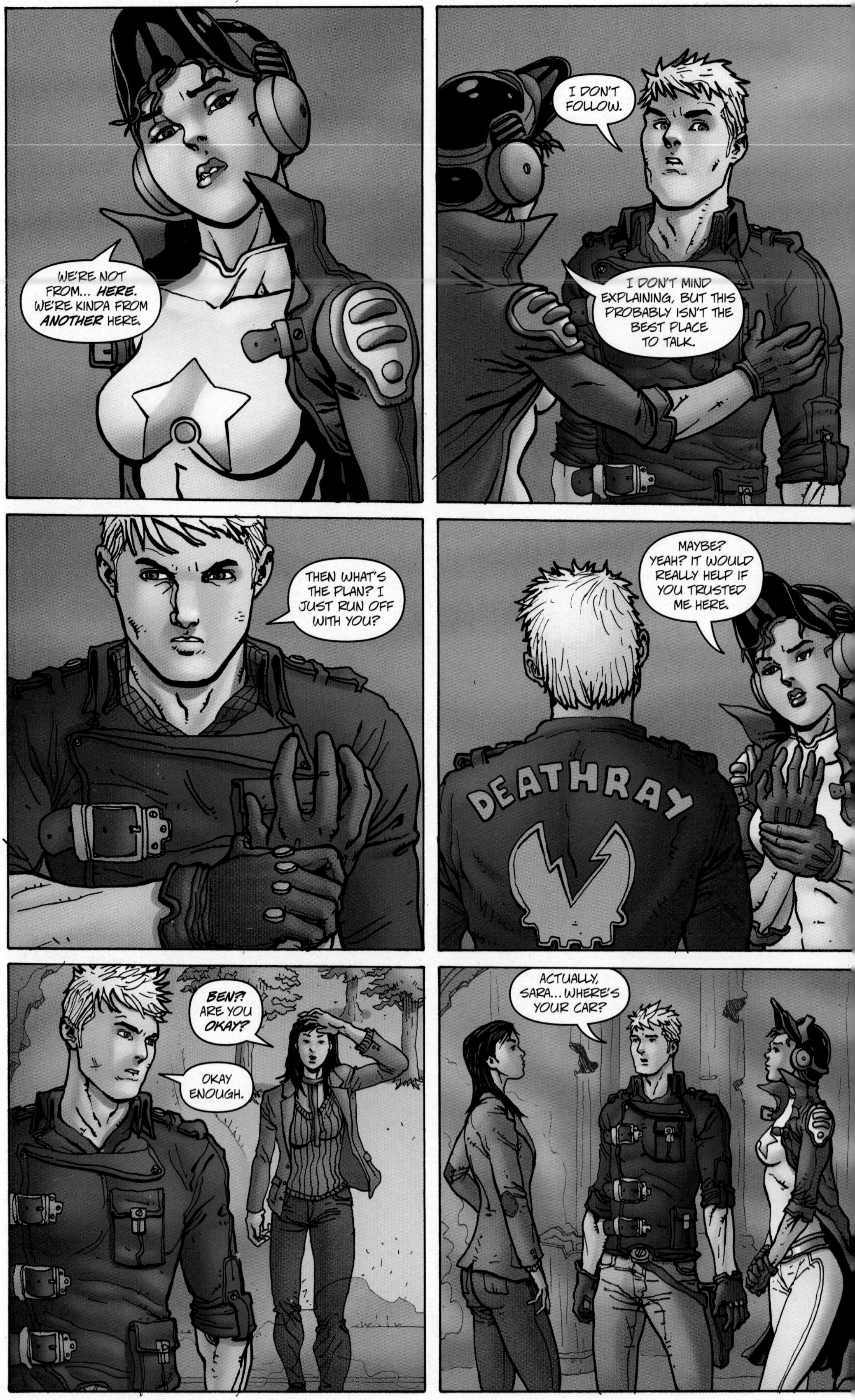
WE'RE NOT FROM... HERE. WE'RE KINDA FROM ANOTHER HERE.
I DON'T FOLLOW.
I DON'T MIND EXPLAINING, BUT THIS PROBABLY ISN'T THE BEST PLACE TO TALK.
THEN WHAT'S THE PLAN? I JUST RUN OFF WITH YOU?
MAYBE? YEAH? IT WOULD REALLY HELP IF YOU TRUSTED ME HERE.
DEATHRAY
BEN?! ARE YOU OKAY?
OKAY ENOUGH.
ACTUALLY, SARA... WHERE'S YOUR CAR?

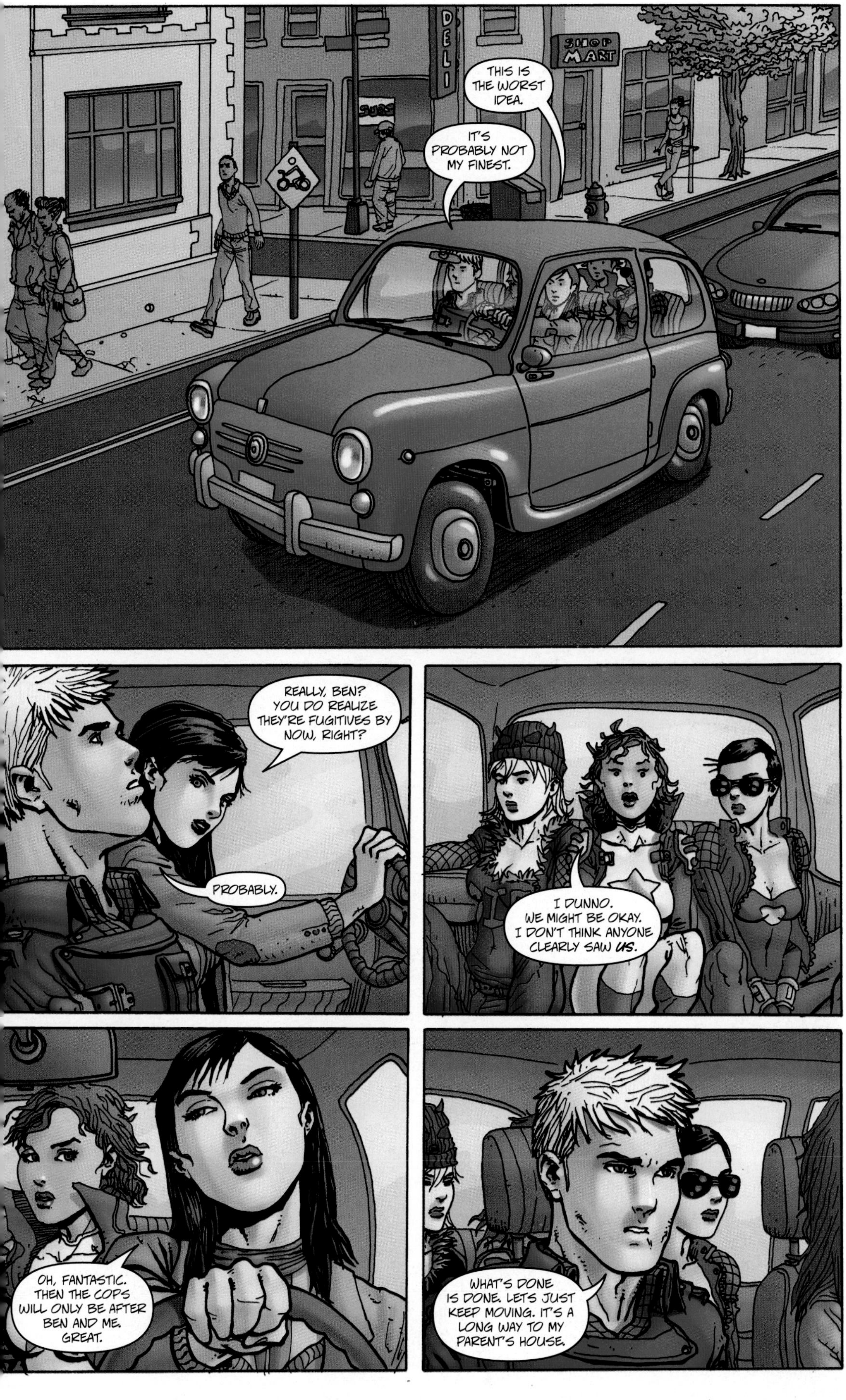

THIS IS THE WORST IDEA.
IT'S PROBABLY NOT MY FINEST.
DELI
SHOP MART
SUBS
REALLY, BEN? YOU DO REALIZE THEY'RE FUGITIVES BY NOW, RIGHT?
PROBABLY.
I DUNNO. WE MIGHT BE OKAY. I DON'T THINK ANYONE CLEARLY SAW US.
OH, FANTASTIC. THEN THE COPS WILL ONLY BE AFTER BEN AND ME. GREAT.
WHAT'S DONE IS DONE. LETS JUST KEEP MOVING. IT'S A LONG WAY TO MY PARENT'S HOUSE.

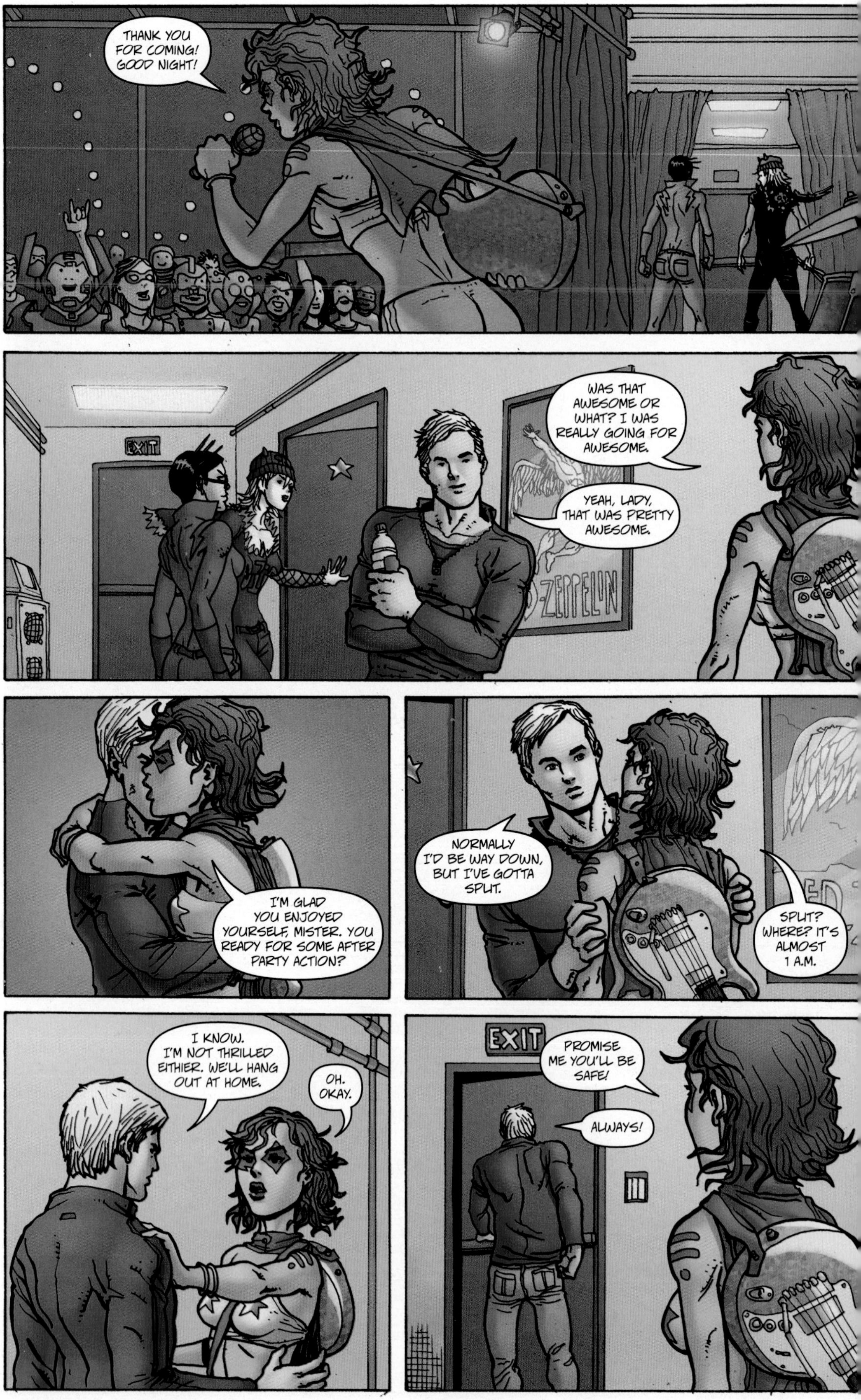
THANK YOU FOR COMING! GOOD NIGHT!
WAS THAT AWESOME OR WHAT? I WAS REALLY GOING FOR AWESOME.
YEAH, LADY, THAT WAS PRETTY AWESOME.
EXIT
ZEPPELIN
I'M GLAD YOU ENJOYED YOURSELF, MISTER. YOU READY FOR SOME AFTER PARTY ACTION?
NORMALLY I'D BE WAY DOWN, BUT I'VE GOTTA SPLIT.
SPLIT? WHERE? IT'S ALMOST 1 A.M.
I KNOW. I'M NOT THRILLED EITHER. WE'LL HANG OUT AT HOME.
OH. OKAY.
EXIT
PROMISE ME YOU'LL BE SAFE!
ALWAYS!

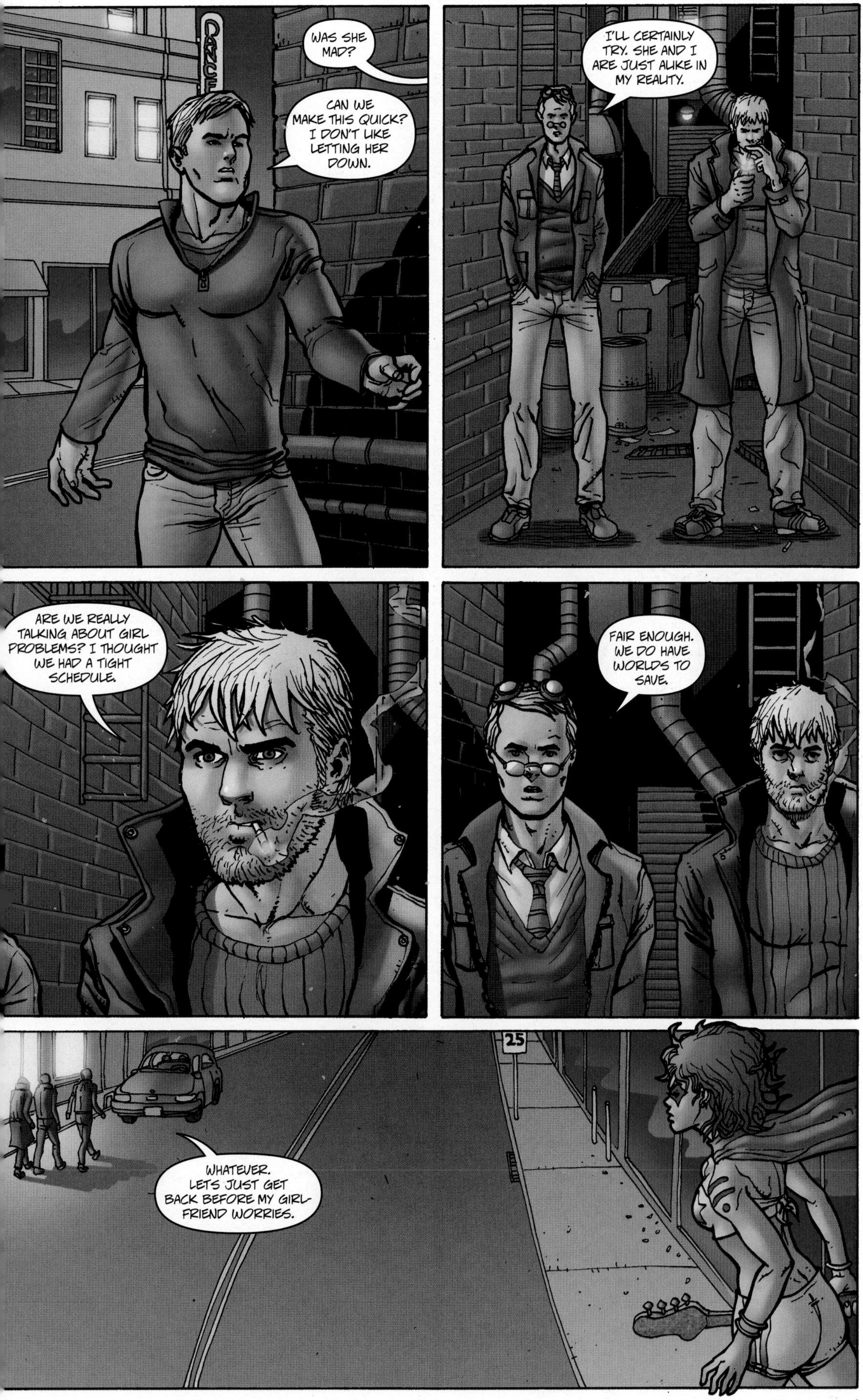
DANCE
WAS SHE MAD?
CAN WE MAKE THIS QUICK? I DON'T LIKE LETTING HER DOWN.
I'LL CERTAINLY TRY. SHE AND I ARE JUST ALIKE IN MY REALITY.
ARE WE REALLY TALKING ABOUT GIRL PROBLEMS? I THOUGHT WE HAD A TIGHT SCHEDULE.
FAIR ENOUGH. WE DO HAVE WORLDS TO SAVE.
25
WHATEVER. LET'S JUST GET BACK BEFORE MY GIRL-FRIEND WORRIES.

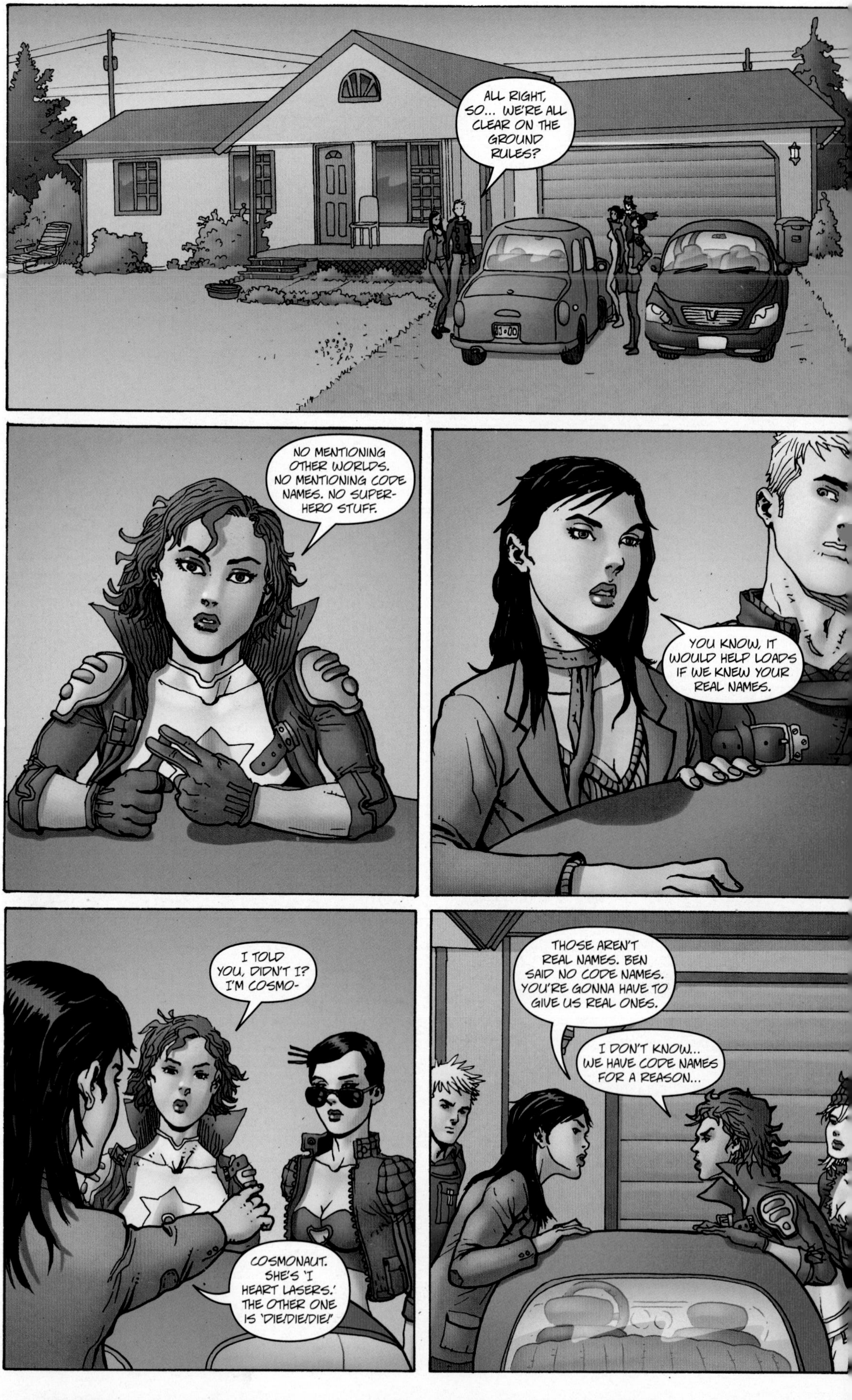
ALL RIGHT, SO... WE'RE ALL CLEAR ON THE GROUND RULES?
NO MENTIONING OTHER WORLDS. NO MENTIONING CODE NAMES. NO SUPER-HERO STUFF.
YOU KNOW, IT WOULD HELP LOADS IF WE KNEW YOUR REAL NAMES.
I TOLD YOU, DIDN'T I? I'M COSMO-
COSMONAUT. SHE'S 'I HEART LASERS.' THE OTHER ONE IS 'DIE!DIE!DIE!'
THOSE AREN'T REAL NAMES. BEN SAID NO CODE NAMES. YOU'RE GONNA HAVE TO GIVE US REAL ONES.
I DON'T KNOW... WE HAVE CODE NAMES FOR A REASON...

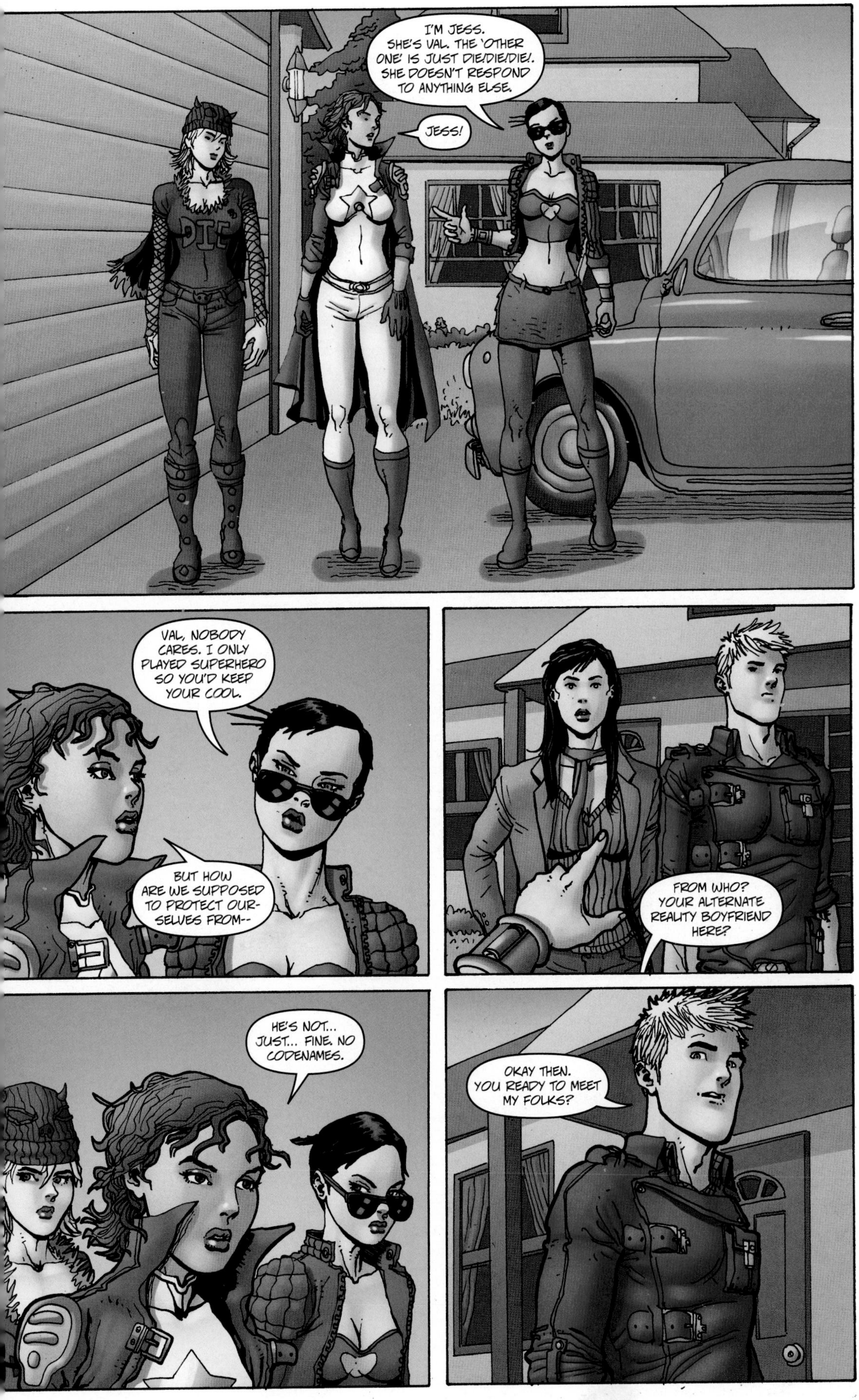
I'M JESS. SHE'S VAL. THE 'OTHER ONE' IS JUST DIE/DIE/DIE/. SHE DOESN'T RESPOND TO ANYTHING ELSE.
JESS!
VAL, NOBODY CARES. I ONLY PLAYED SUPERHERO SO YOU'D KEEP YOUR COOL.
BUT HOW ARE WE SUPPOSED TO PROTECT OUR-SELVES FROM--
FROM WHO? YOUR ALTERNATE REALITY BOYFRIEND HERE?
HE'S NOT... JUST... FINE. NO CODENAMES.
OKAY THEN. YOU READY TO MEET MY FOLKS?

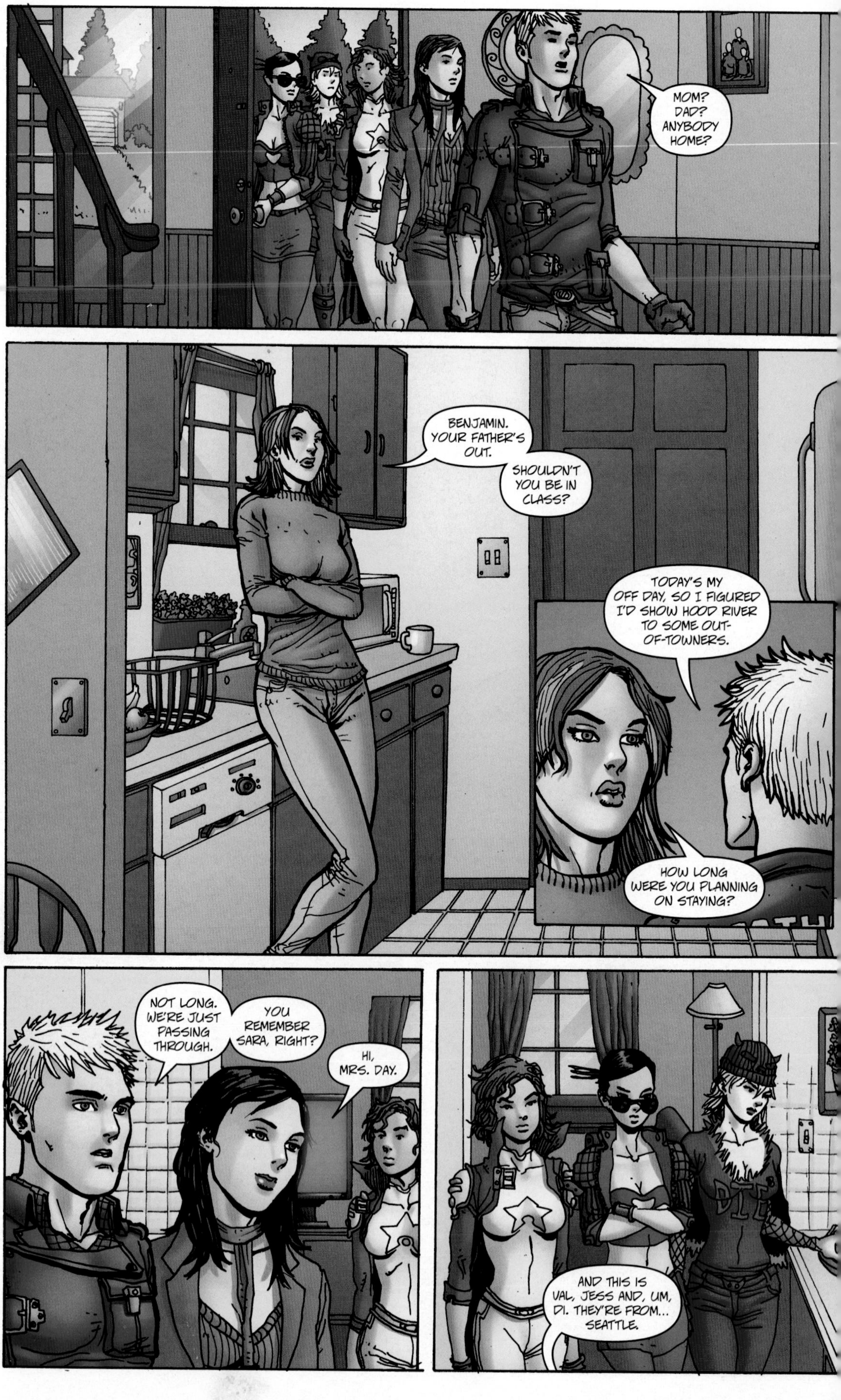
MOM? DAD? ANYBODY HOME?
BENJAMIN. YOUR FATHER'S OUT.
SHOULDN'T YOU BE IN CLASS?
TODAY'S MY OFF DAY, SO I FIGURED I'D SHOW HOOD RIVER TO SOME OUT-OF-TOWNERS.
HOW LONG WERE YOU PLANNING ON STAYING?
NOT LONG. WE'RE JUST PASSING THROUGH.
YOU REMEMBER SARA, RIGHT?
HI, MRS. DAY.
AND THIS IS VAL, JESS AND, UM, DI. THEY'RE FROM... SEATTLE.

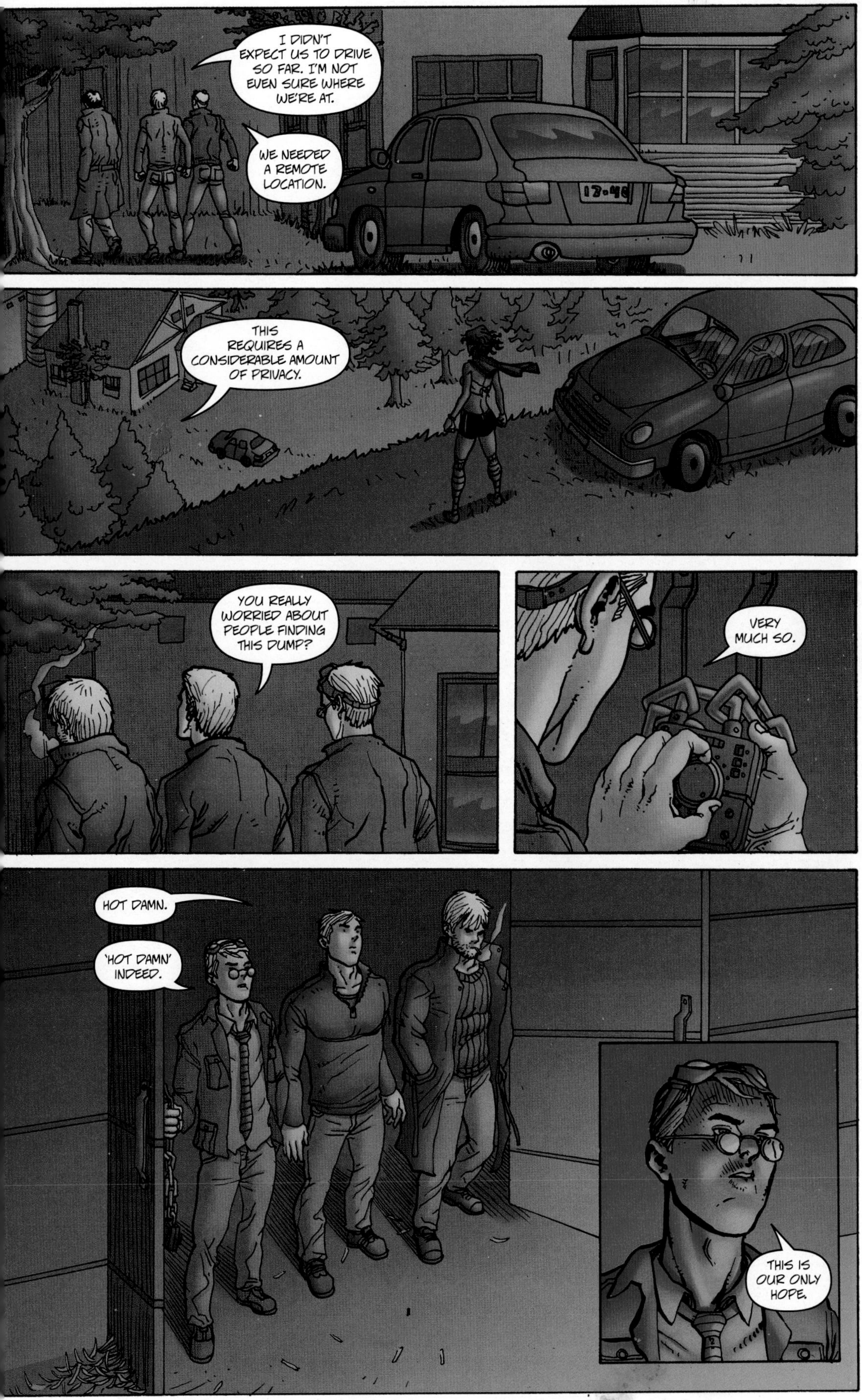
I DIDN'T EXPECT US TO DRIVE SO FAR. I'M NOT EVEN SURE WHERE WE'RE AT.
WE NEEDED A REMOTE LOCATION.
THIS REQUIRES A CONSIDERABLE AMOUNT OF PRIVACY.
YOU REALLY WORRIED ABOUT PEOPLE FINDING THIS DUMP?
VERY MUCH SO.
HOT DAMN.
'HOT DAMN' INDEED.
THIS IS OUR ONLY HOPE.

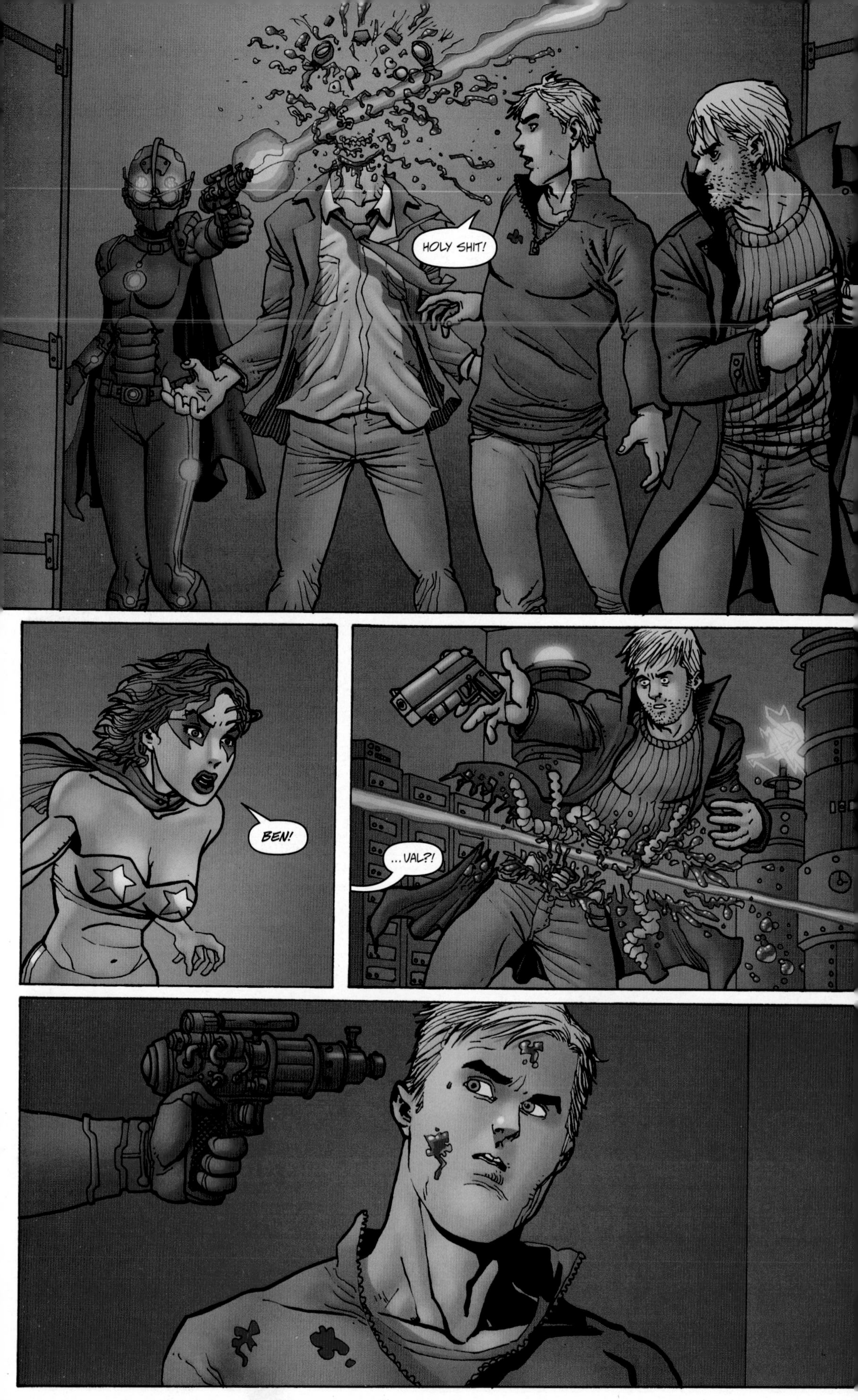
HOLY SHIT!
BEN!
...VAL?!

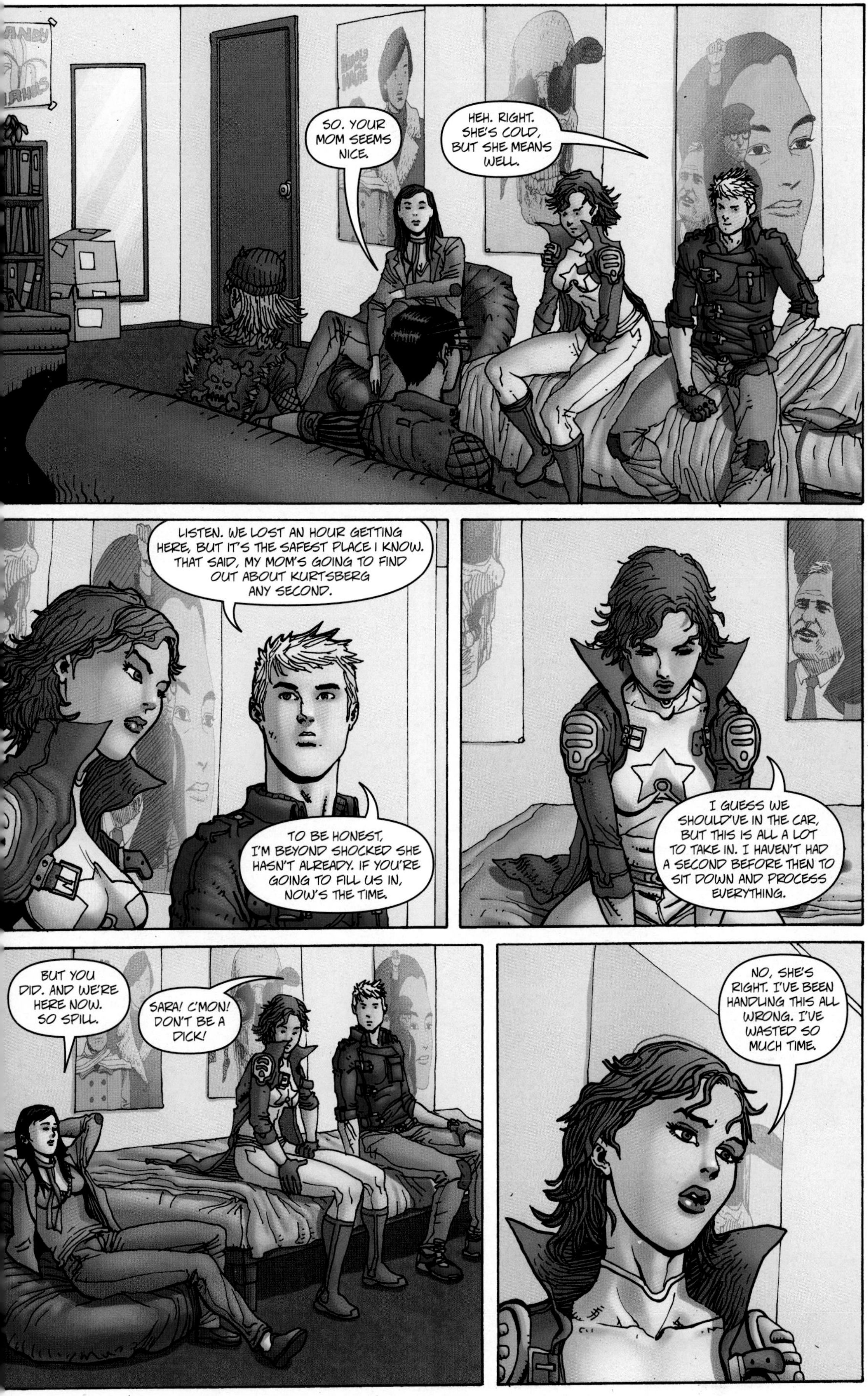
SO. YOUR MOM SEEMS NICE.
HEH. RIGHT. SHE'S COLD, BUT SHE MEANS WELL.
LISTEN. WE LOST AN HOUR GETTING HERE, BUT IT'S THE SAFEST PLACE I KNOW. THAT SAID, MY MOM'S GOING TO FIND OUT ABOUT KURTSBERG ANY SECOND.
TO BE HONEST, I'M BEYOND SHOCKED SHE HASN'T ALREADY. IF YOU'RE GOING TO FILL US IN, NOW'S THE TIME.
I GUESS WE SHOULD'VE IN THE CAR, BUT THIS IS ALL A LOT TO TAKE IN. I HAVEN'T HAD A SECOND BEFORE THEN TO SIT DOWN AND PROCESS EVERYTHING.
BUT YOU DID. AND WE'RE HERE NOW. SO SPILL.
SARA! C'MON! DON'T BE A DICK!
NO, SHE'S RIGHT. I'VE BEEN HANDLING THIS ALL WRONG. I'VE WASTED SO MUCH TIME.

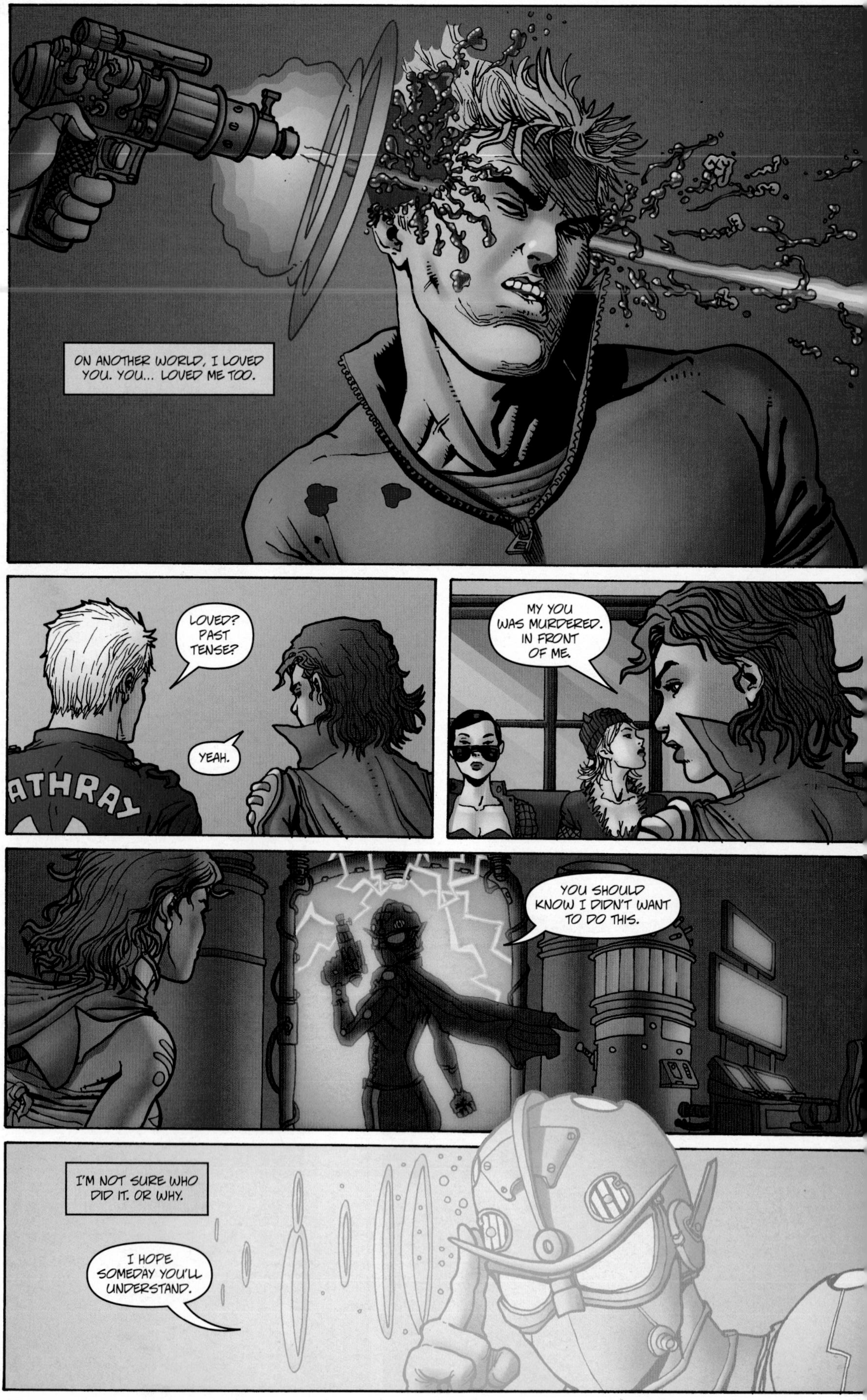

ON ANOTHER WORLD, I LOVED YOU. YOU... LOVED ME TOO.
LOVED? PAST TENSE?
YEAH.
ATHRAY
MY YOU WAS MURDERED. IN FRONT OF ME.
YOU SHOULD KNOW I DIDN'T WANT TO DO THIS.
I'M NOT SURE WHO DID IT. OR WHY.
I HOPE SOMEDAY YOU'LL UNDERSTAND.

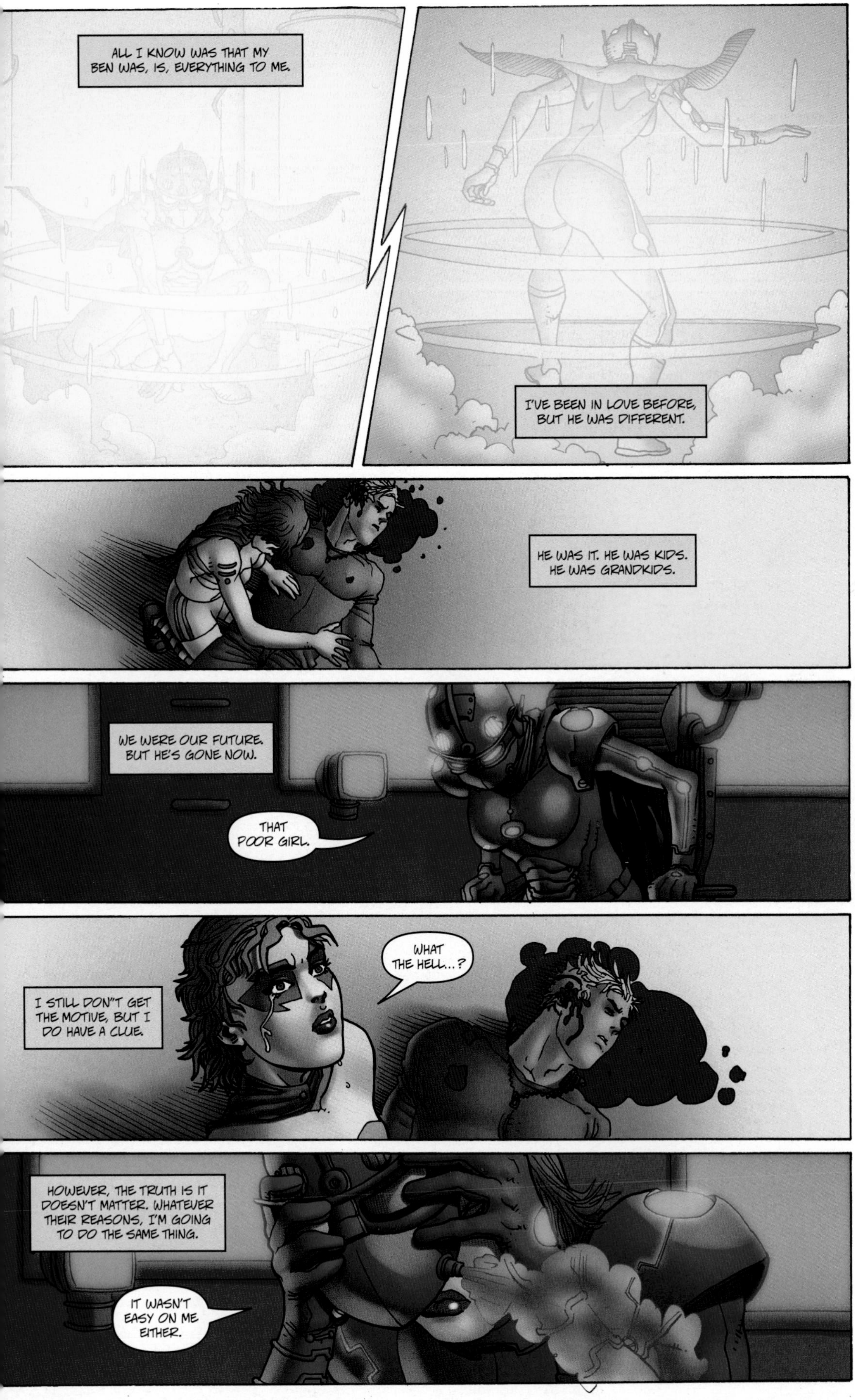

ALL I KNOW WAS THAT MY BEN WAS, IS, EVERYTHING TO ME.
I'VE BEEN IN LOVE BEFORE, BUT HE WAS DIFFERENT.
HE WAS IT. HE WAS KIDS. HE WAS GRANDKIDS.
WE WERE OUR FUTURE. BUT HE'S GONE NOW.
THAT POOR GIRL.
I STILL DON'T GET THE MOTIVE, BUT I DO HAVE A CLUE.
WHAT THE HELL...?
HOWEVER, THE TRUTH IS IT DOESN'T MATTER. WHATEVER THEIR REASONS, I'M GOING TO DO THE SAME THING.
IT WASN'T EASY ON ME EITHER.

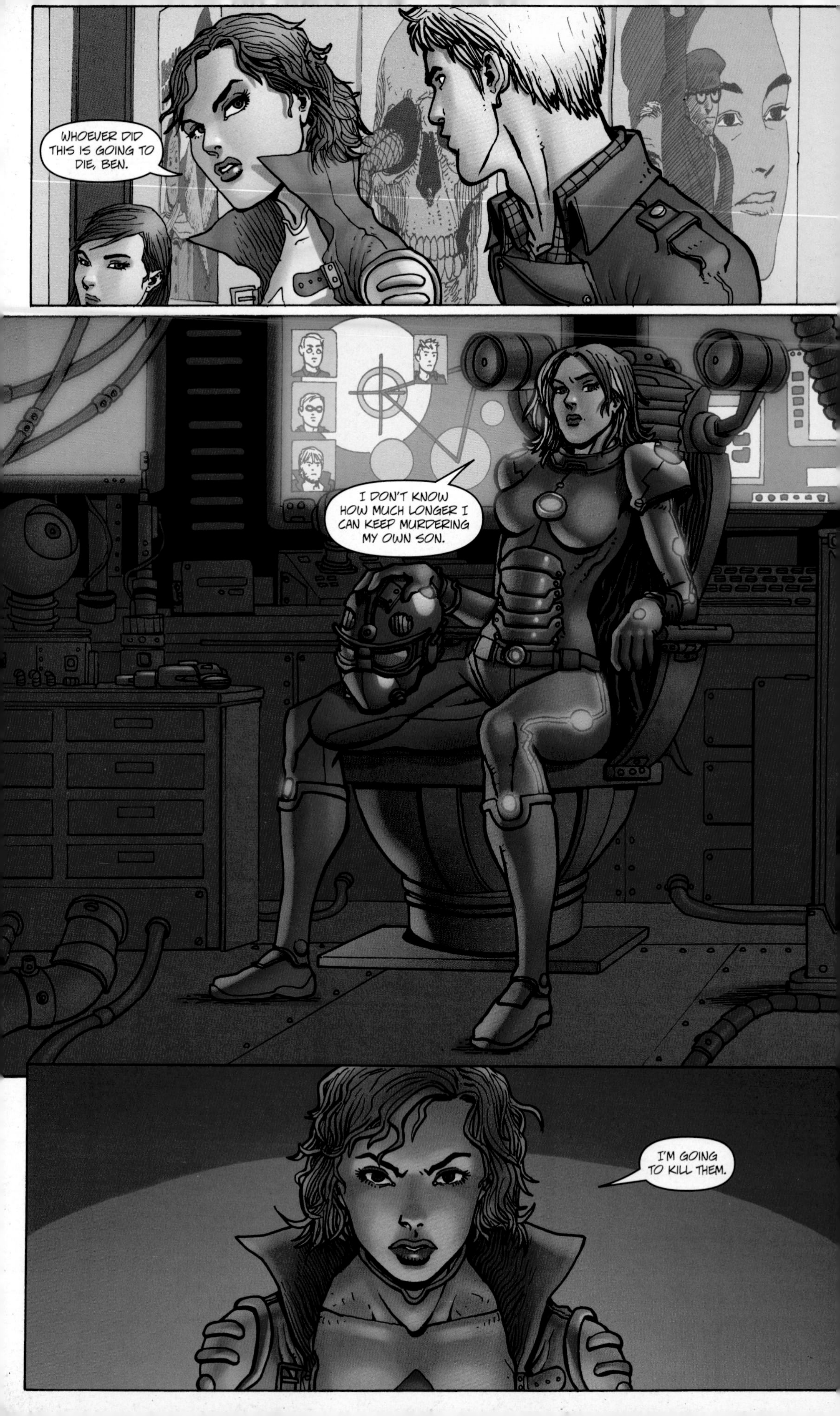
WHOEVER DID THIS IS GOING TO DIE, BEN.
I DON'T KNOW HOW MUCH LONGER I CAN KEEP MURDERING MY OWN SON.
I'M GOING TO KILL THEM.

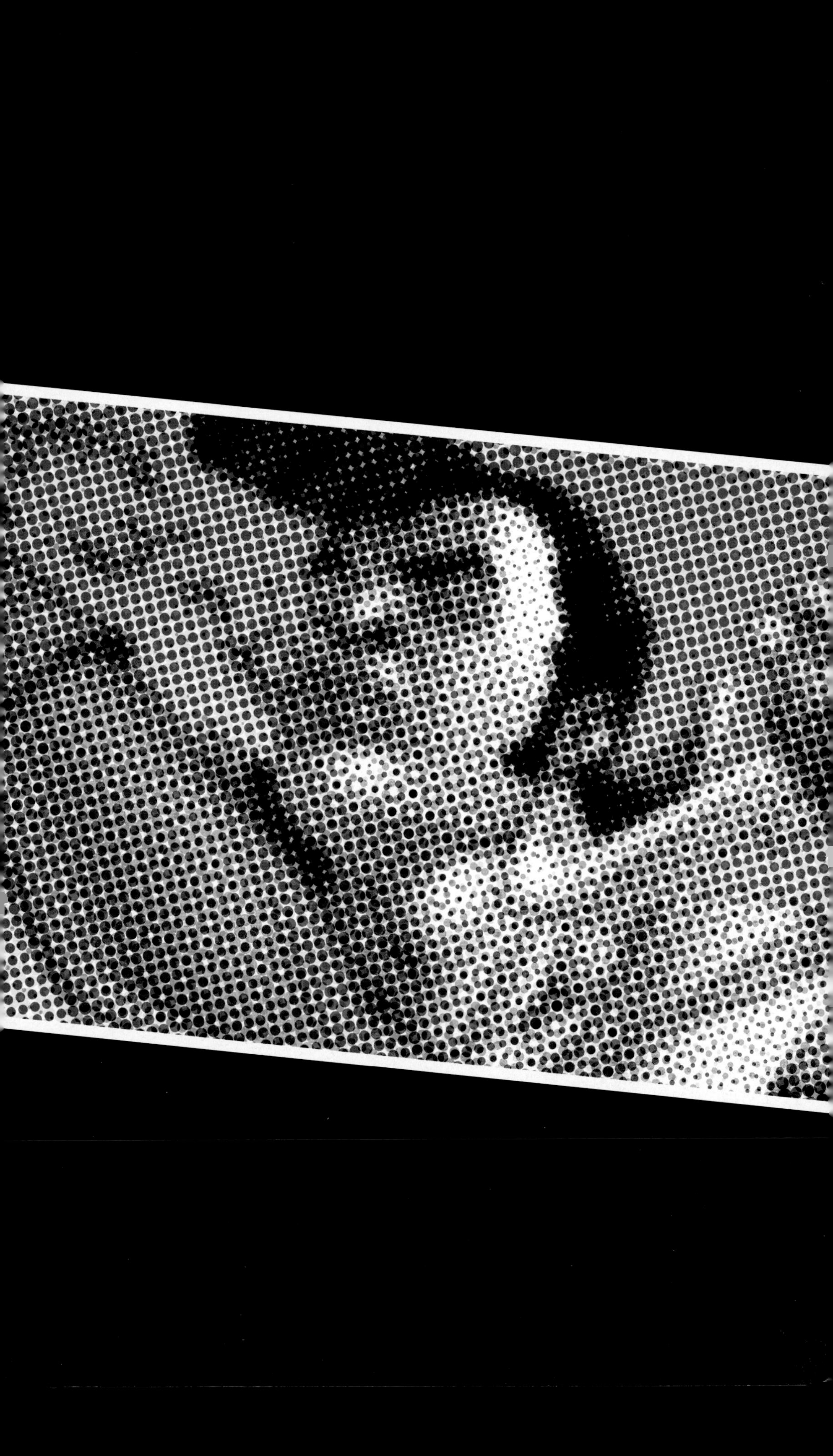

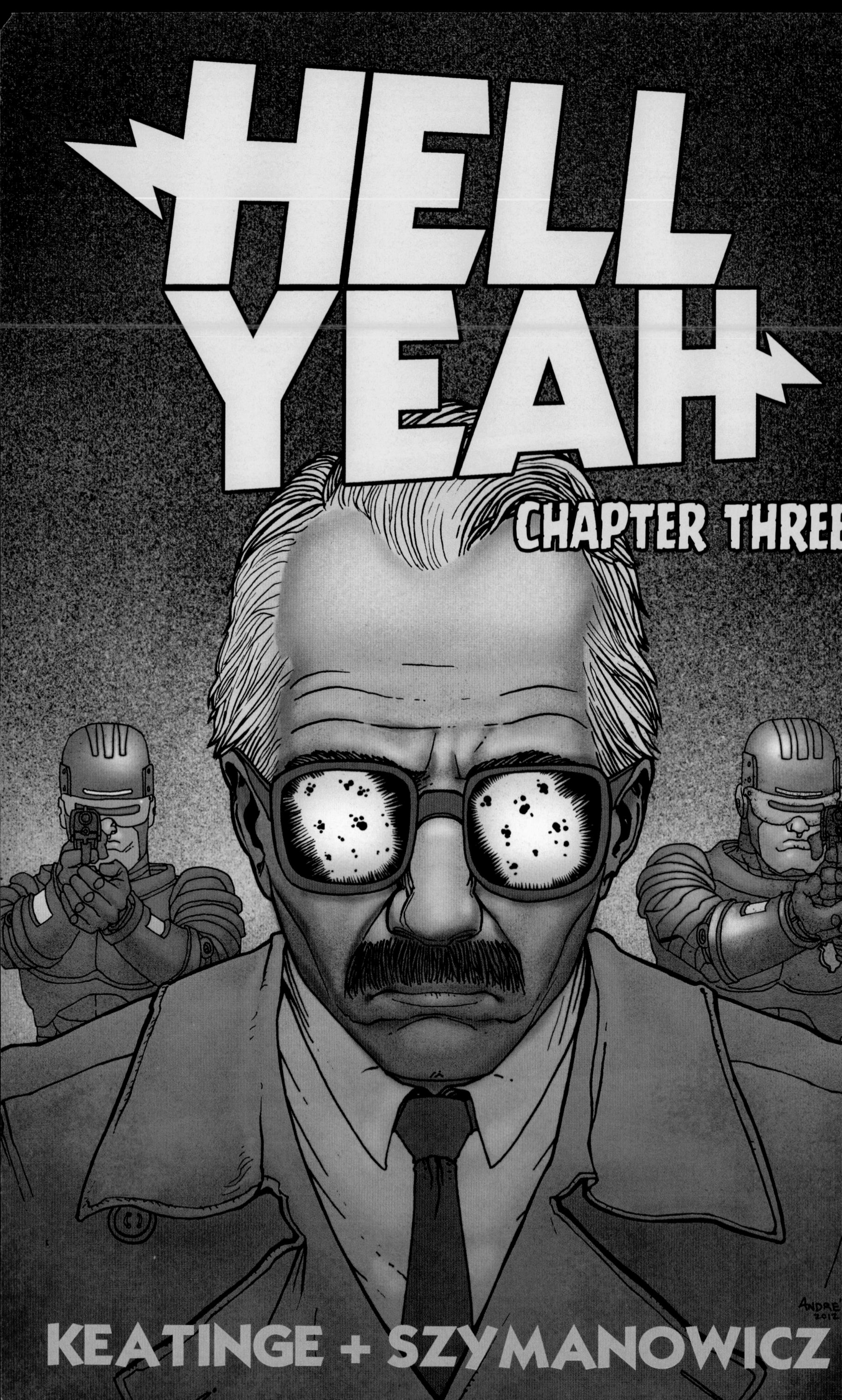
HELL YEAH
CHAPTER THREE
ANDRÉ 2012
KEATINGE + SZYMANOWICZ

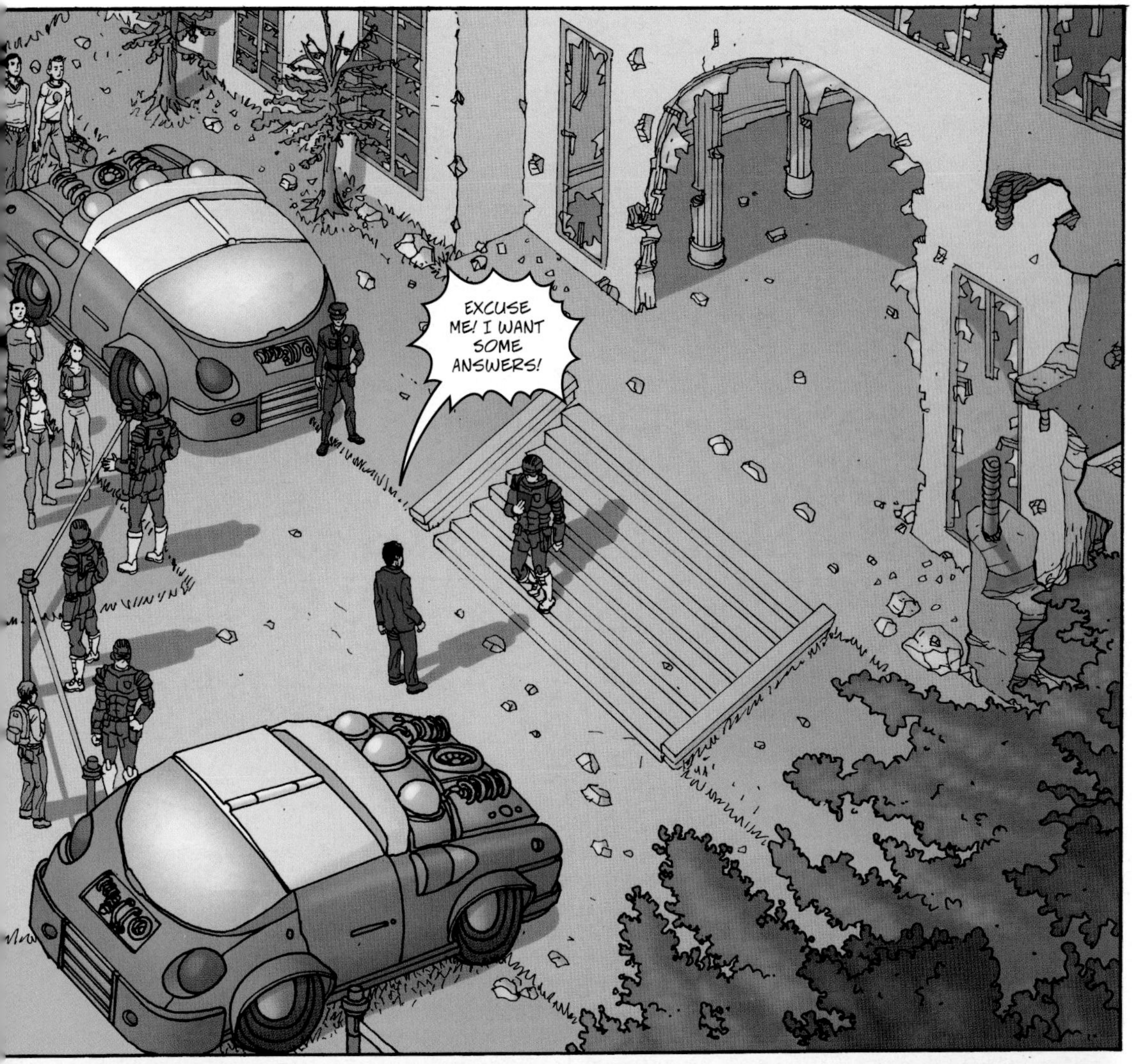
EXCUSE ME! I WANT SOME ANSWERS!

PORTLAND, OREGON
KURTZBERG UNIVERSITY

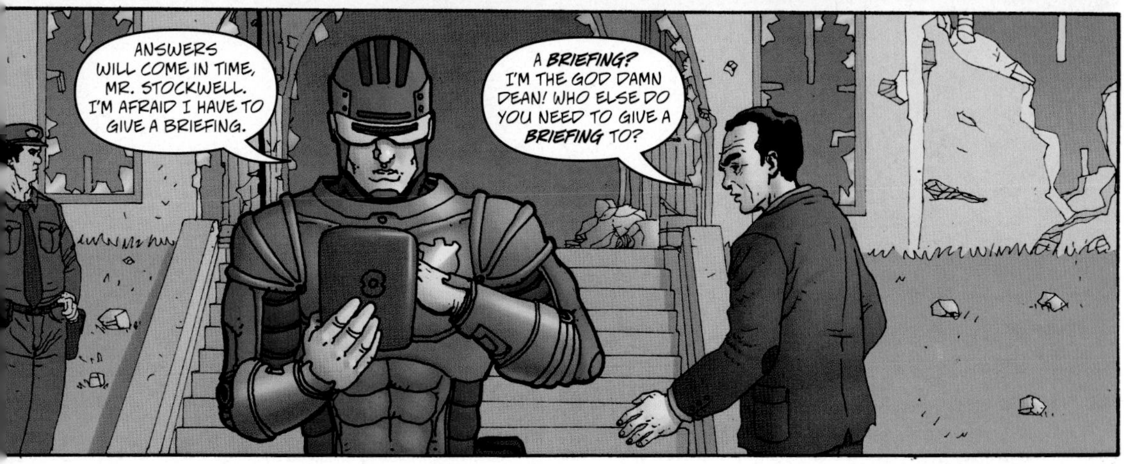
ANSWERS WILL COME IN TIME, MR. STOCKWELL. I'M AFRAID I HAVE TO GIVE A BRIEFING.
A *BRIEFING?* I'M THE GOD DAMN DEAN! WHO ELSE DO YOU NEED TO GIVE A *BRIEFING* TO?

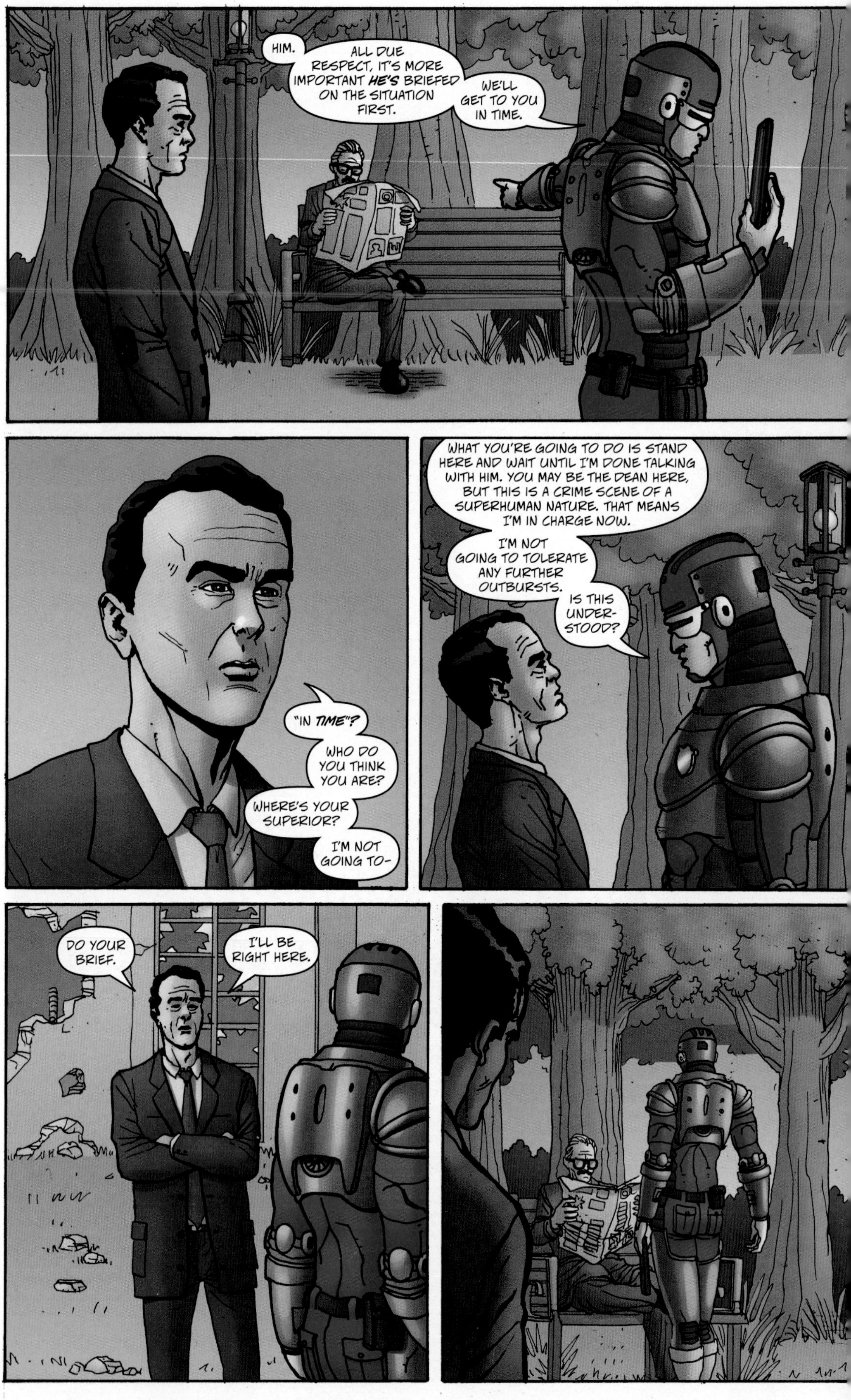
HIM.
ALL DUE RESPECT, IT'S MORE IMPORTANT HE'S BRIEFED ON THE SITUATION FIRST.
WE'LL GET TO YOU IN TIME.
"IN TIME"?
WHO DO YOU THINK YOU ARE?
WHERE'S YOUR SUPERIOR?
I'M NOT GOING TO-
WHAT YOU'RE GOING TO DO IS STAND HERE AND WAIT UNTIL I'M DONE TALKING WITH HIM. YOU MAY BE THE DEAN HERE, BUT THIS IS A CRIME SCENE OF A SUPERHUMAN NATURE. THAT MEANS I'M IN CHARGE NOW.
I'M NOT GOING TO TOLERATE ANY FURTHER OUTBURSTS.
IS THIS UNDERSTOOD?
DO YOUR BRIEF.
I'LL BE RIGHT HERE.

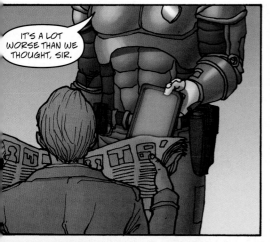

IT'S A LOT WORSE THAN WE THOUGHT, SIR.

KURTZBERG UNIVERSITY. ESTABLISHED 1961.

TOTAL CURRENT UNDERGRADUATES: 1,292

POST-GRADUATES: 29

IMAGE COMICS PRESENTS

UM. RIGHT.

WELL, THIS SHOULD SHOW YOU THE SITUATION.

WE THOUGHT THIS MIGHT BE AN ATTACK, POSSIBLE VIOLENT PROTEST, BUT THERE'S A FACTOR HERE WE DIDN'T PREDICT.

RESIDUE OF AN ALTERNATE EARTH.

THAT'S CORRECT. WHATEVER CAUSED THE EXPLOSION IS NOT FROM OUR REALITY.

I'M AFRAID THAT MAKES THIS IS OUT OF MY JURISDICTION. OF COURSE, YOU'RE FREE TO INVESTIGATE THIS FURTHER ON YOUR OWN, BUT I NEED TO EXTRACT MY CREW.

THIS JUST BECAME A SITUATION WELL BEYOND MY MEANS.

I TRUST YOU KNOW WHAT TO DO?

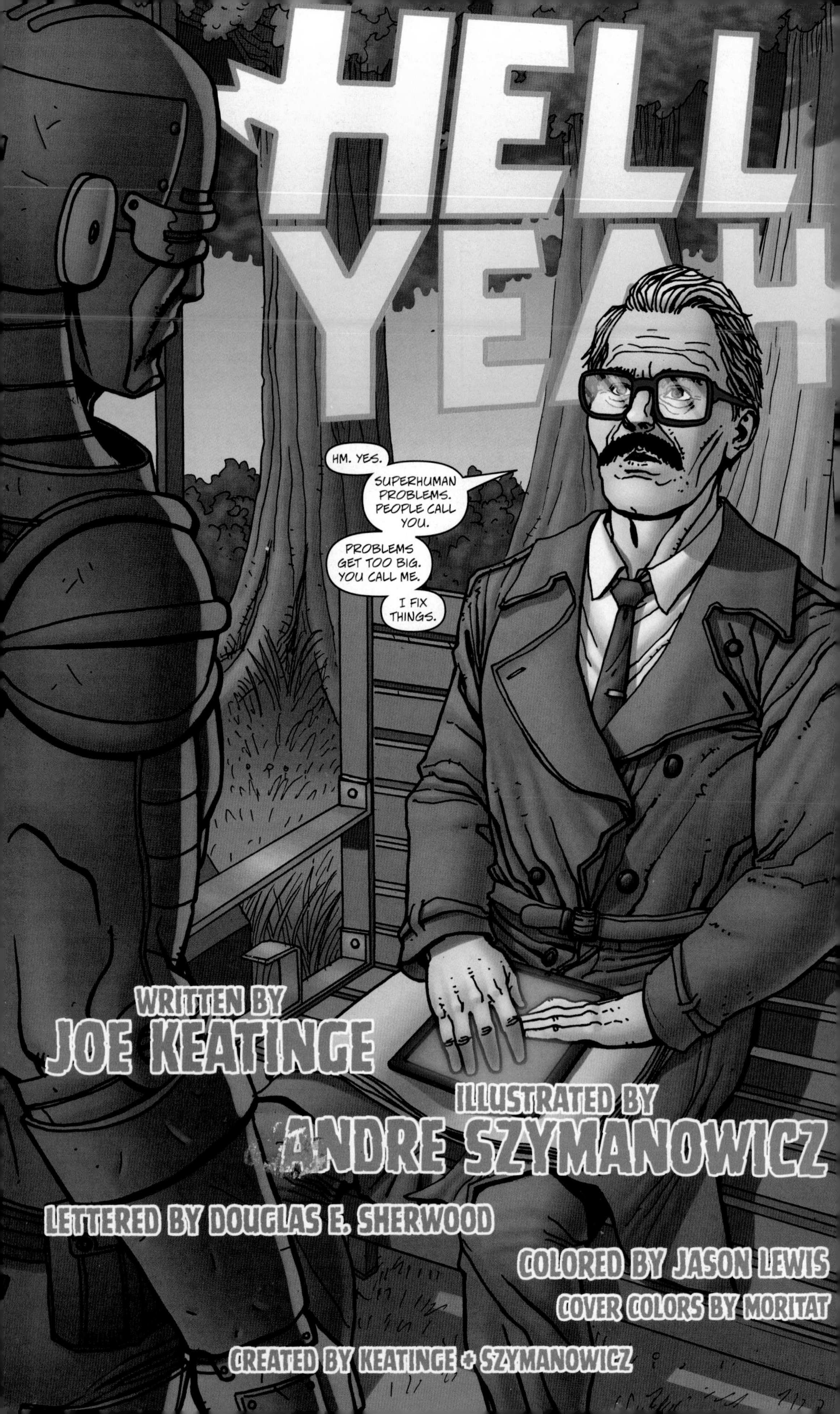
HELL YEAH
HM. YES.
SUPERHUMAN PROBLEMS. PEOPLE CALL YOU.
PROBLEMS GET TOO BIG. YOU CALL ME.
I FIX THINGS.
WRITTEN BY JOE KEATINGE
ILLUSTRATED BY ANDRE SZYMANOWICZ
LETTERED BY DOUGLAS E. SHERWOOD
COLORED BY JASON LEWIS
COVER COLORS BY MORITAT
CREATED BY KEATINGE + SZYMANOWICZ

BOOK ONE
LAST DAY ON EARTHS

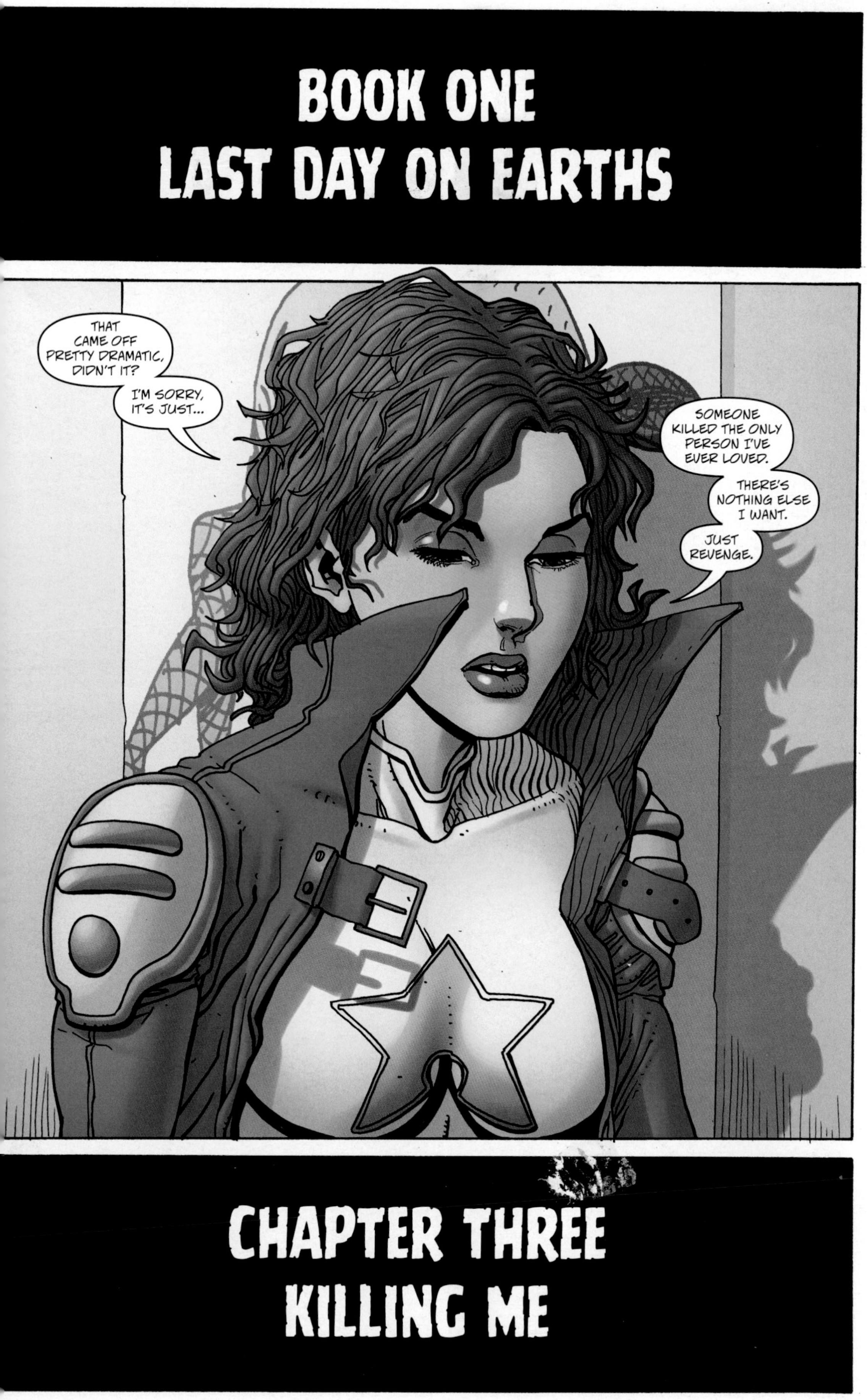

THAT CAME OFF PRETTY DRAMATIC, DIDN'T IT?
I'M SORRY, IT'S JUST...
SOMEONE KILLED THE ONLY PERSON I'VE EVER LOVED.
THERE'S NOTHING ELSE I WANT.
JUST REVENGE.

CHAPTER THREE
KILLING ME

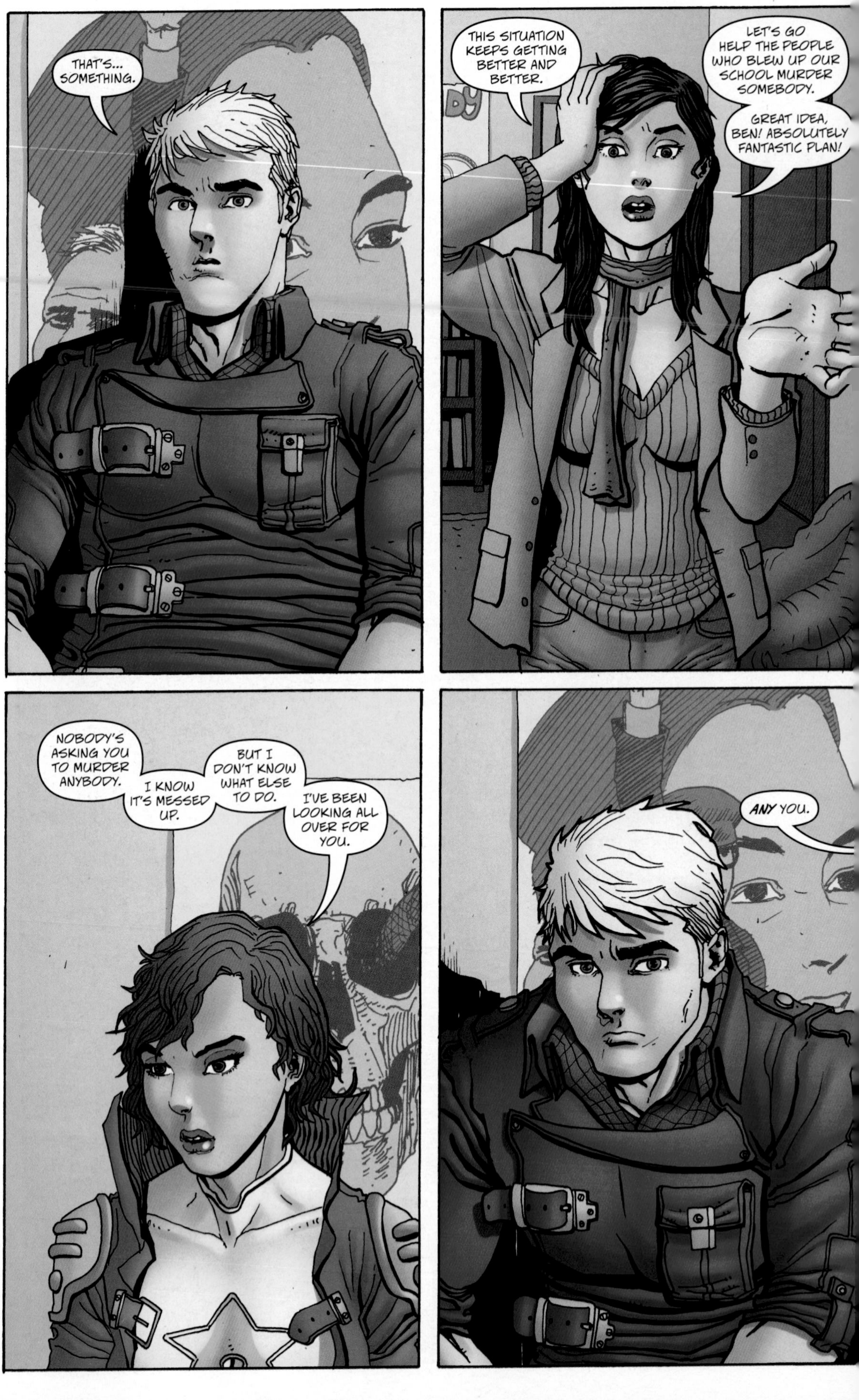
THAT'S... SOMETHING.
THIS SITUATION KEEPS GETTING BETTER AND BETTER.
LET'S GO HELP THE PEOPLE WHO BLEW UP OUR SCHOOL MURDER SOMEBODY.
GREAT IDEA, BEN! ABSOLUTELY FANTASTIC PLAN!
NOBODY'S ASKING YOU TO MURDER ANYBODY.
I KNOW IT'S MESSED UP.
BUT I DON'T KNOW WHAT ELSE TO DO.
I'VE BEEN LOOKING ALL OVER FOR YOU.
ANY YOU.

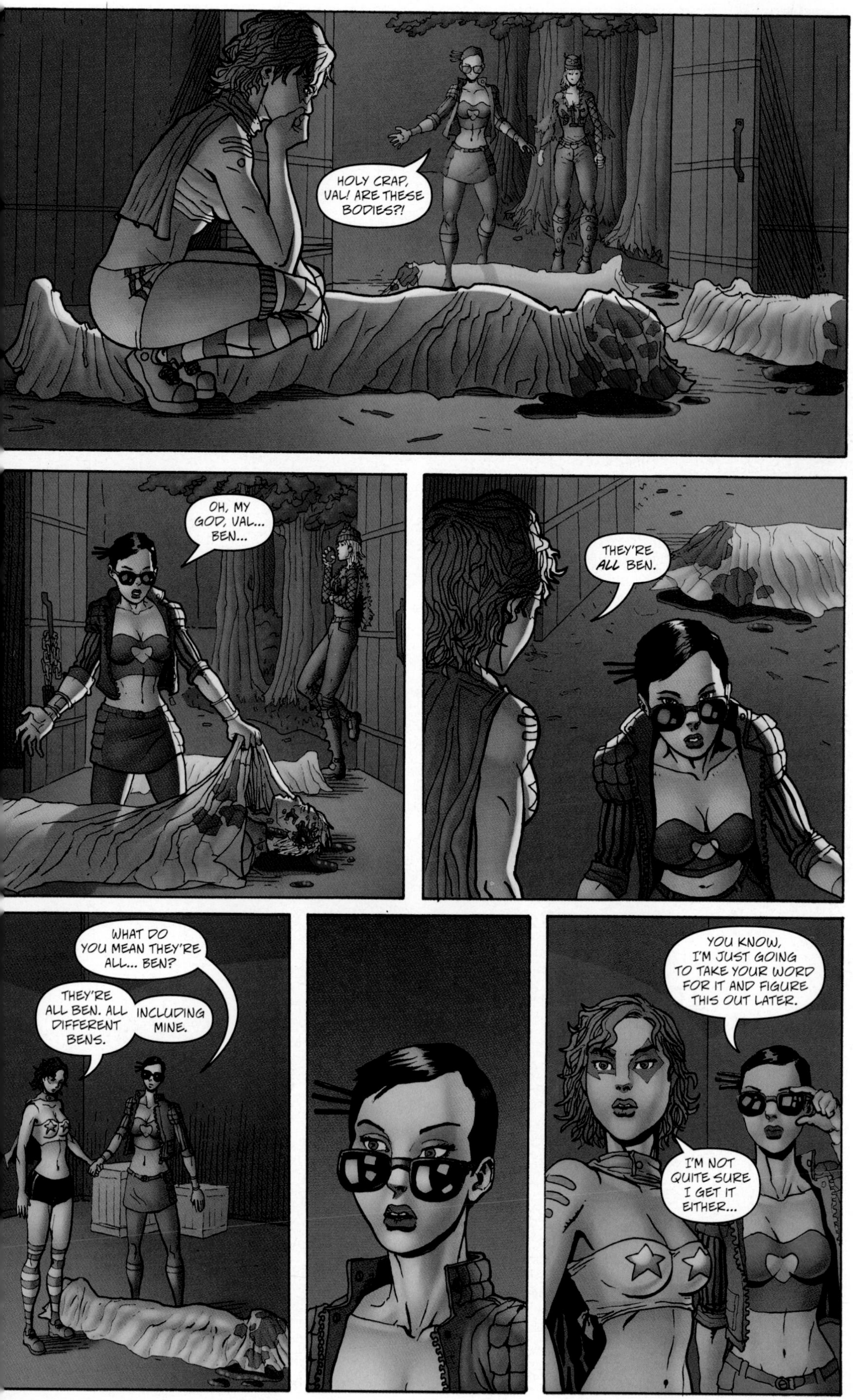
HOLY CRAP, VAL! ARE THESE BODIES?!
OH, MY GOD, VAL... BEN...
THEY'RE ALL BEN.
WHAT DO YOU MEAN THEY'RE ALL... BEN?
THEY'RE ALL BEN. ALL DIFFERENT BENS.
INCLUDING MINE.
YOU KNOW, I'M JUST GOING TO TAKE YOUR WORD FOR IT AND FIGURE THIS OUT LATER.
I'M NOT QUITE SURE I GET IT EITHER...

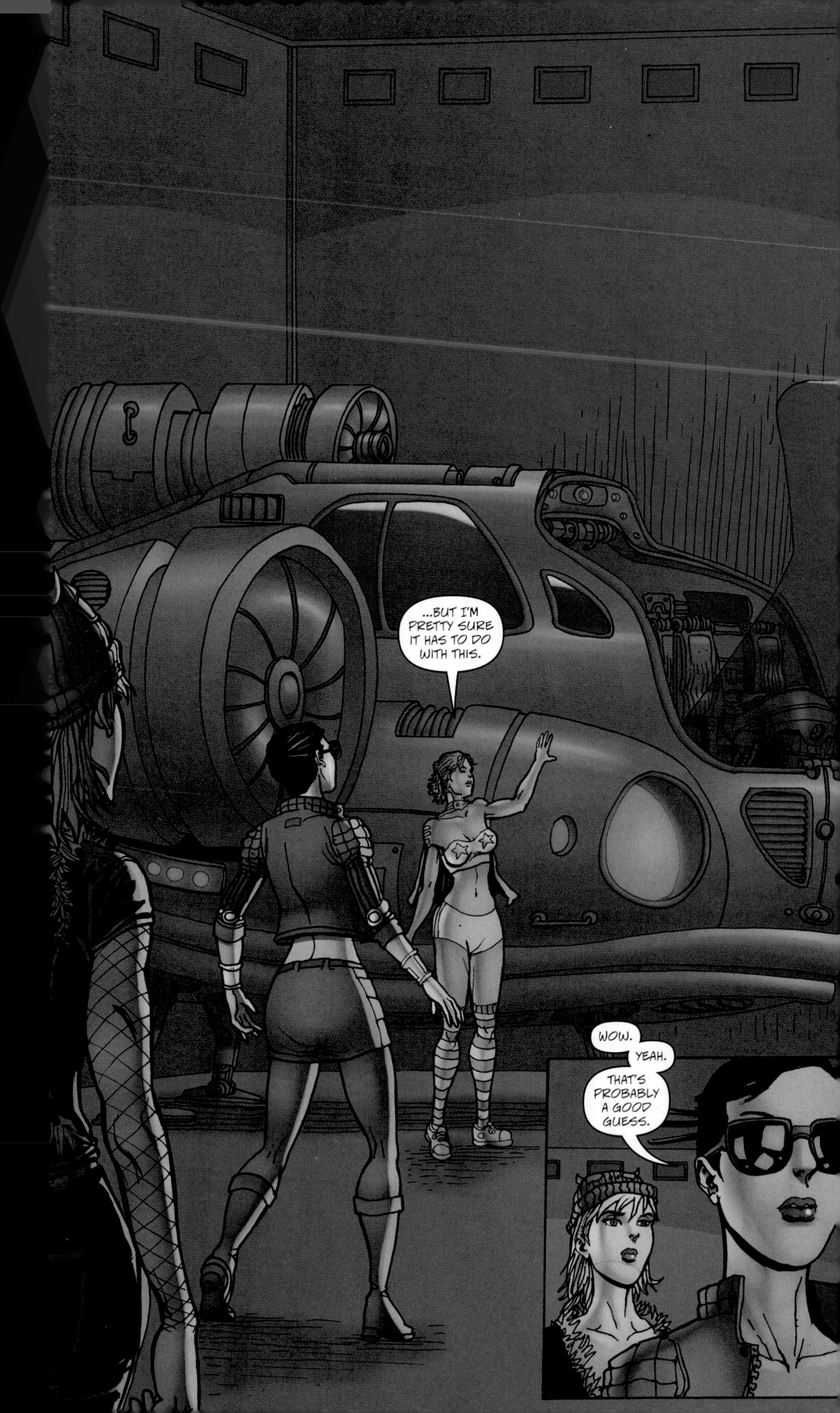
...BUT I'M PRETTY SURE IT HAS TO DO WITH THIS.
WOW.
YEAH.
THAT'S PROBABLY A GOOD GUESS.

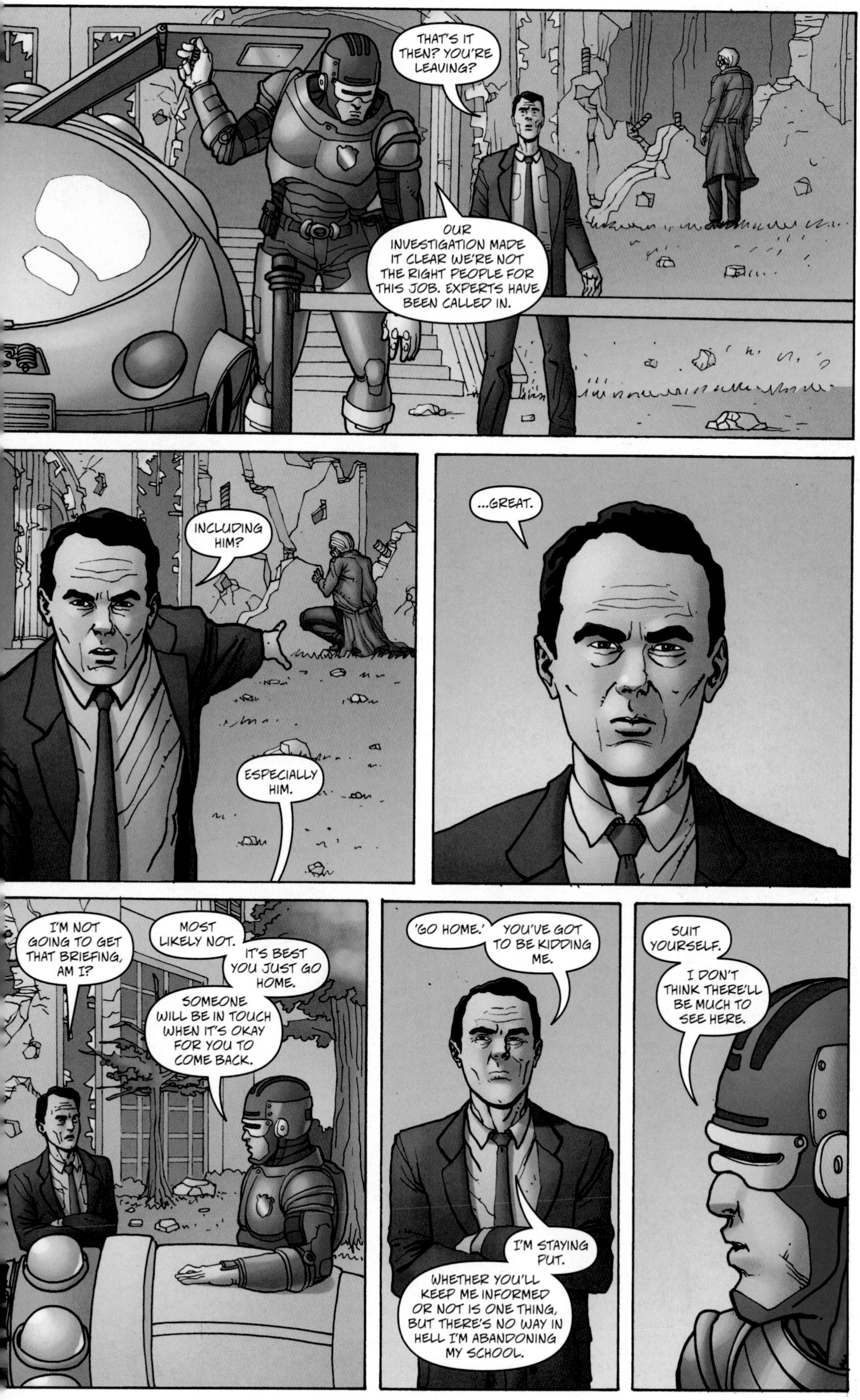
THAT'S IT THEN? YOU'RE LEAVING?
OUR INVESTIGATION MADE IT CLEAR WE'RE NOT THE RIGHT PEOPLE FOR THIS JOB. EXPERTS HAVE BEEN CALLED IN.
INCLUDING HIM?
ESPECIALLY HIM.
...GREAT.
I'M NOT GOING TO GET THAT BRIEFING, AM I?
MOST LIKELY NOT.
IT'S BEST YOU JUST GO HOME.
SOMEONE WILL BE IN TOUCH WHEN IT'S OKAY FOR YOU TO COME BACK.
'GO HOME.'
YOU'VE GOT TO BE KIDDING ME.
I'M STAYING PUT.
WHETHER YOU'LL KEEP ME INFORMED OR NOT IS ONE THING, BUT THERE'S NO WAY IN HELL I'M ABANDONING MY SCHOOL.
SUIT YOURSELF.
I DON'T THINK THERE'LL BE MUCH TO SEE HERE.

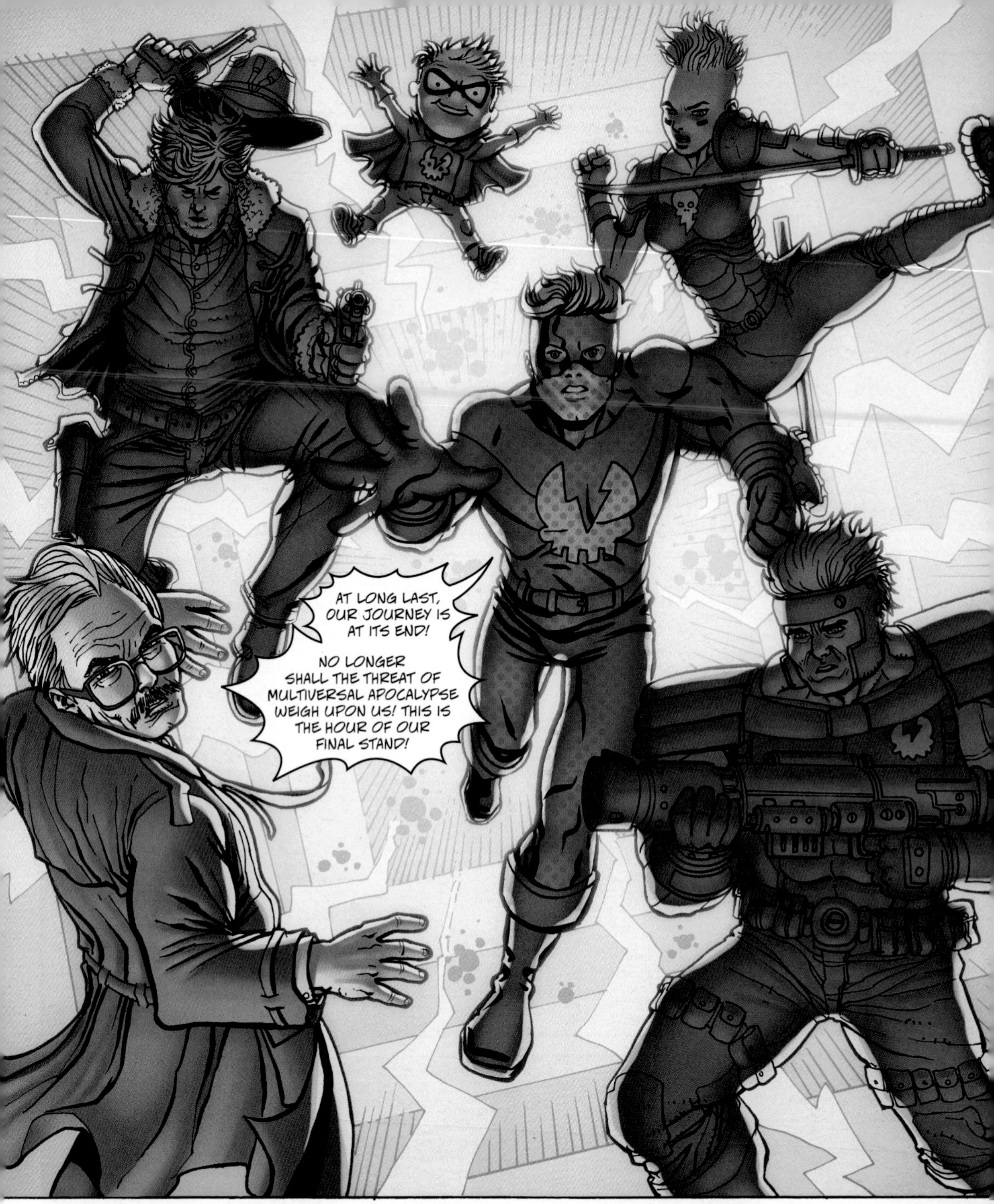
AT LONG LAST, OUR JOURNEY IS AT ITS END!
NO LONGER SHALL THE THREAT OF MULTIVERSAL APOCALYPSE WEIGH UPON US! THIS IS THE HOUR OF OUR FINAL STAND!

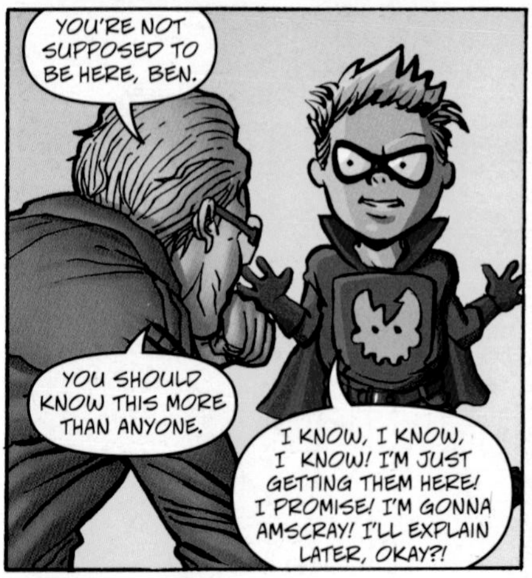
YOU'RE NOT SUPPOSED TO BE HERE, BEN.
YOU SHOULD KNOW THIS MORE THAN ANYONE.
I KNOW, I KNOW, I KNOW! I'M JUST GETTING THEM HERE! I PROMISE! I'M GONNA AMSCRAY! I'LL EXPLAIN LATER, OKAY?!

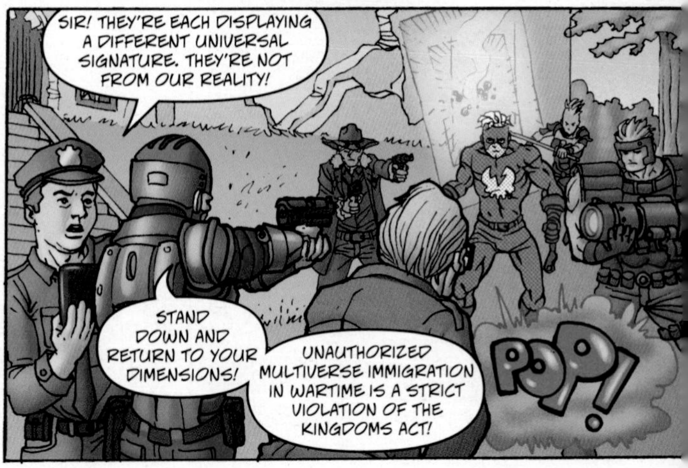
SIR! THEY'RE EACH DISPLAYING A DIFFERENT UNIVERSAL SIGNATURE. THEY'RE NOT FROM OUR REALITY!
STAND DOWN AND RETURN TO YOUR DIMENSIONS!
UNAUTHORIZED MULTIVERSE IMMIGRATION IN WARTIME IS A STRICT VIOLATION OF THE KINGDOMS ACT!
POP!

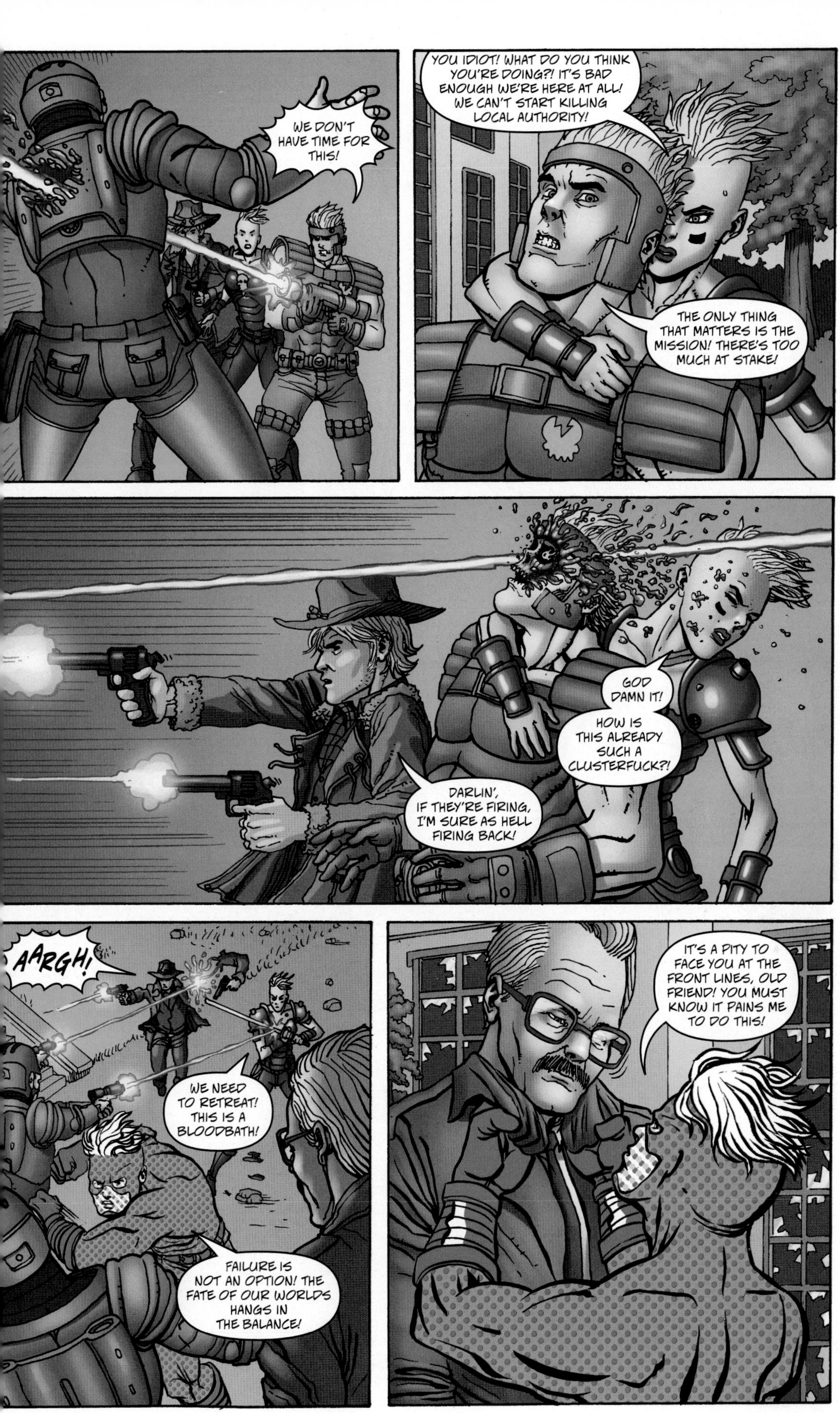
WE DON'T HAVE TIME FOR THIS!
YOU IDIOT! WHAT DO YOU THINK YOU'RE DOING?! IT'S BAD ENOUGH WE'RE HERE AT ALL! WE CAN'T START KILLING LOCAL AUTHORITY!
THE ONLY THING THAT MATTERS IS THE MISSION! THERE'S TOO MUCH AT STAKE!
GOD DAMN IT!
HOW IS THIS ALREADY SUCH A CLUSTERFUCK?!
DARLIN', IF THEY'RE FIRING, I'M SURE AS HELL FIRING BACK!
AARGH!
WE NEED TO RETREAT! THIS IS A BLOODBATH!
FAILURE IS NOT AN OPTION! THE FATE OF OUR WORLDS HANGS IN THE BALANCE!
IT'S A PITY TO FACE YOU AT THE FRONT LINES, OLD FRIEND! YOU MUST KNOW IT PAINS ME TO DO THIS!

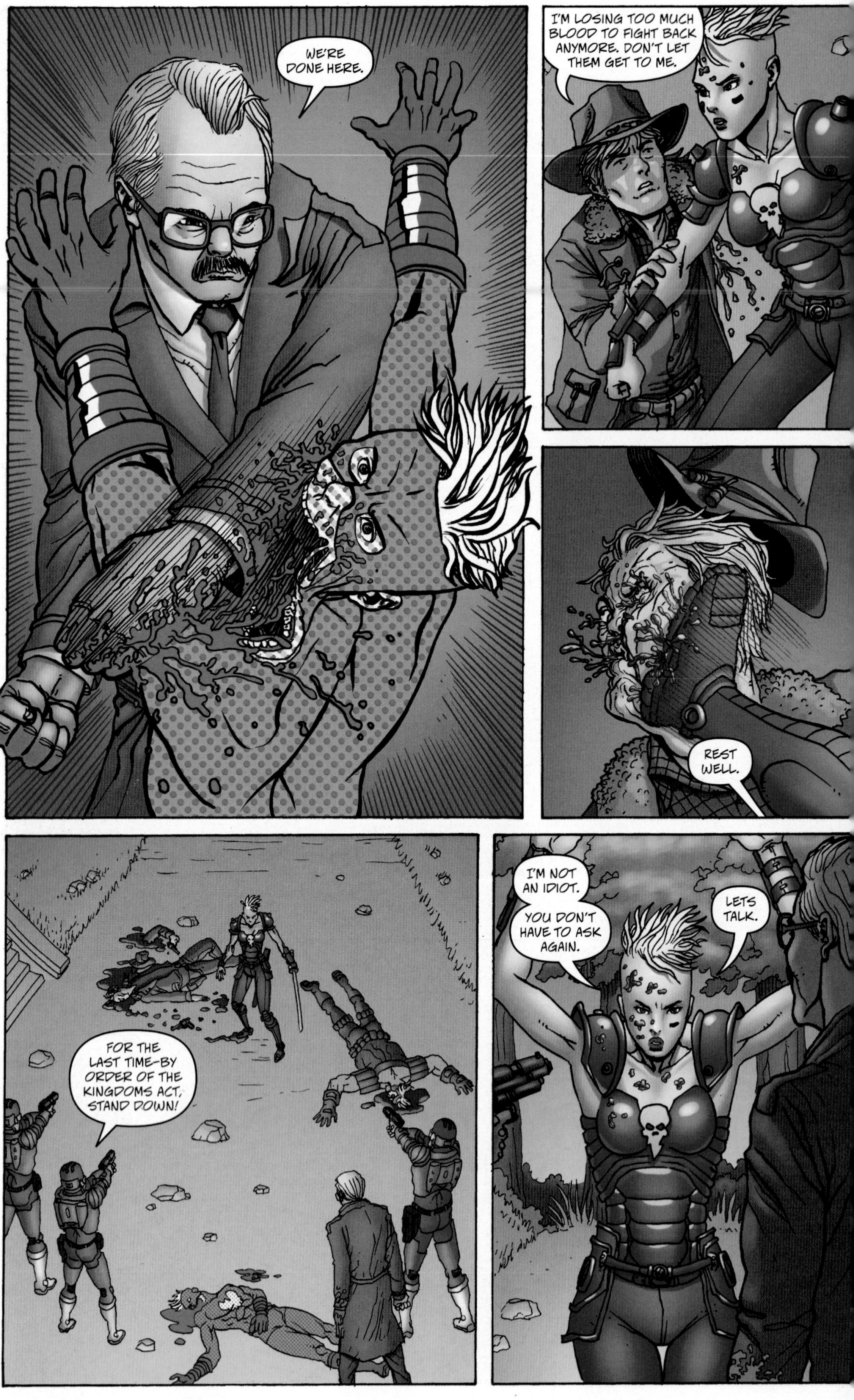
WE'RE DONE HERE.
I'M LOSING TOO MUCH BLOOD TO FIGHT BACK ANYMORE. DON'T LET THEM GET TO ME.
REST WELL.
FOR THE LAST TIME--BY ORDER OF THE KINGDOMS ACT, STAND DOWN!
I'M NOT AN IDIOT.
YOU DON'T HAVE TO ASK AGAIN.
LETS TALK.

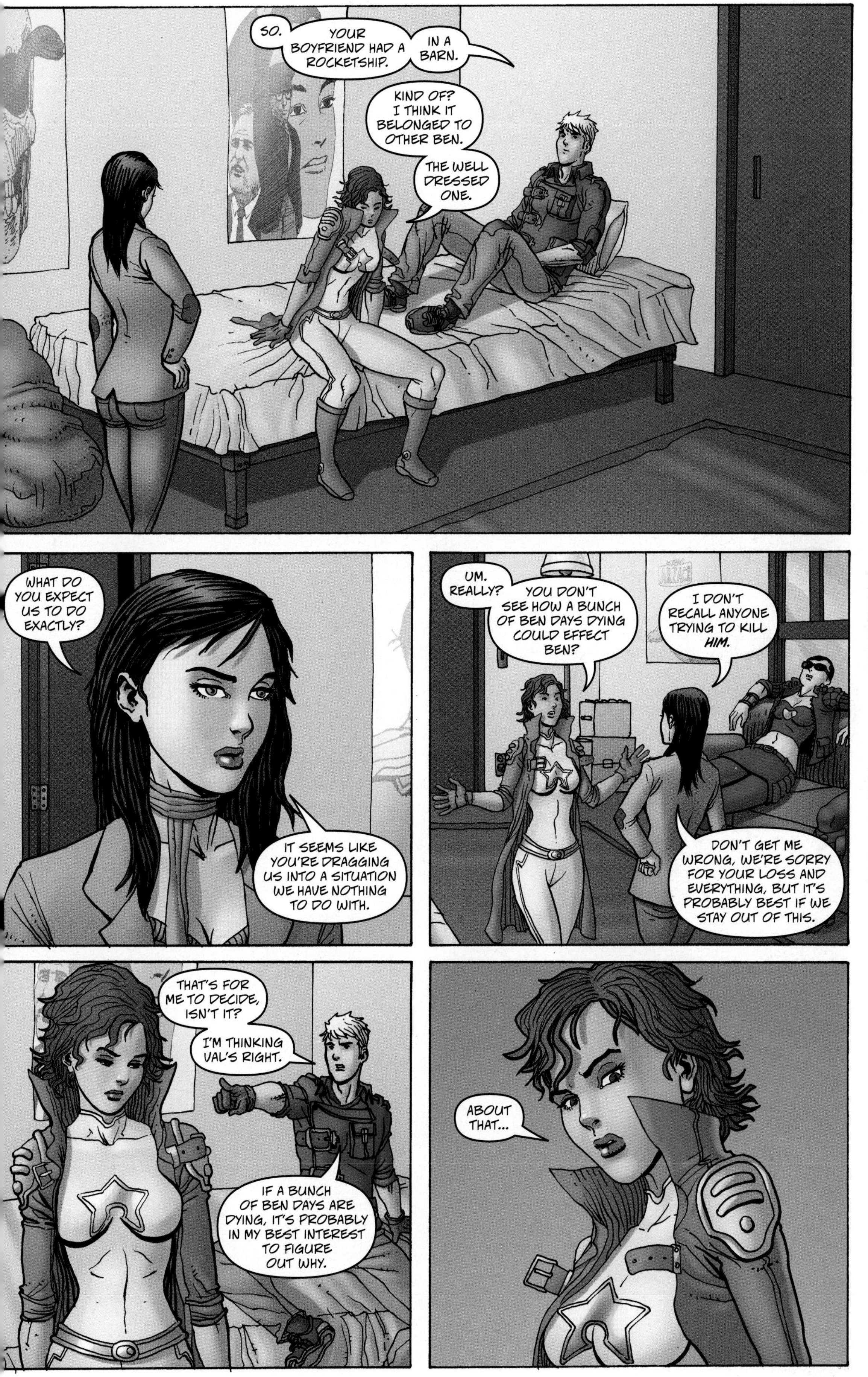
SO.
YOUR BOYFRIEND HAD A ROCKETSHIP.
IN A BARN.
KIND OF? I THINK IT BELONGED TO OTHER BEN.
THE WELL DRESSED ONE.
WHAT DO YOU EXPECT US TO DO EXACTLY?
IT SEEMS LIKE YOU'RE DRAGGING US INTO A SITUATION WE HAVE NOTHING TO DO WITH.
UM. REALLY?
YOU DON'T SEE HOW A BUNCH OF BEN DAYS DYING COULD EFFECT BEN?
I DON'T RECALL ANYONE TRYING TO KILL *HIM*.
DON'T GET ME WRONG, WE'RE SORRY FOR YOUR LOSS AND EVERYTHING, BUT IT'S PROBABLY BEST IF WE STAY OUT OF THIS.
THAT'S FOR ME TO DECIDE, ISN'T IT?
I'M THINKING VAL'S RIGHT.
IF A BUNCH OF BEN DAYS ARE DYING, IT'S PROBABLY IN MY BEST INTEREST TO FIGURE OUT WHY.
ABOUT THAT...

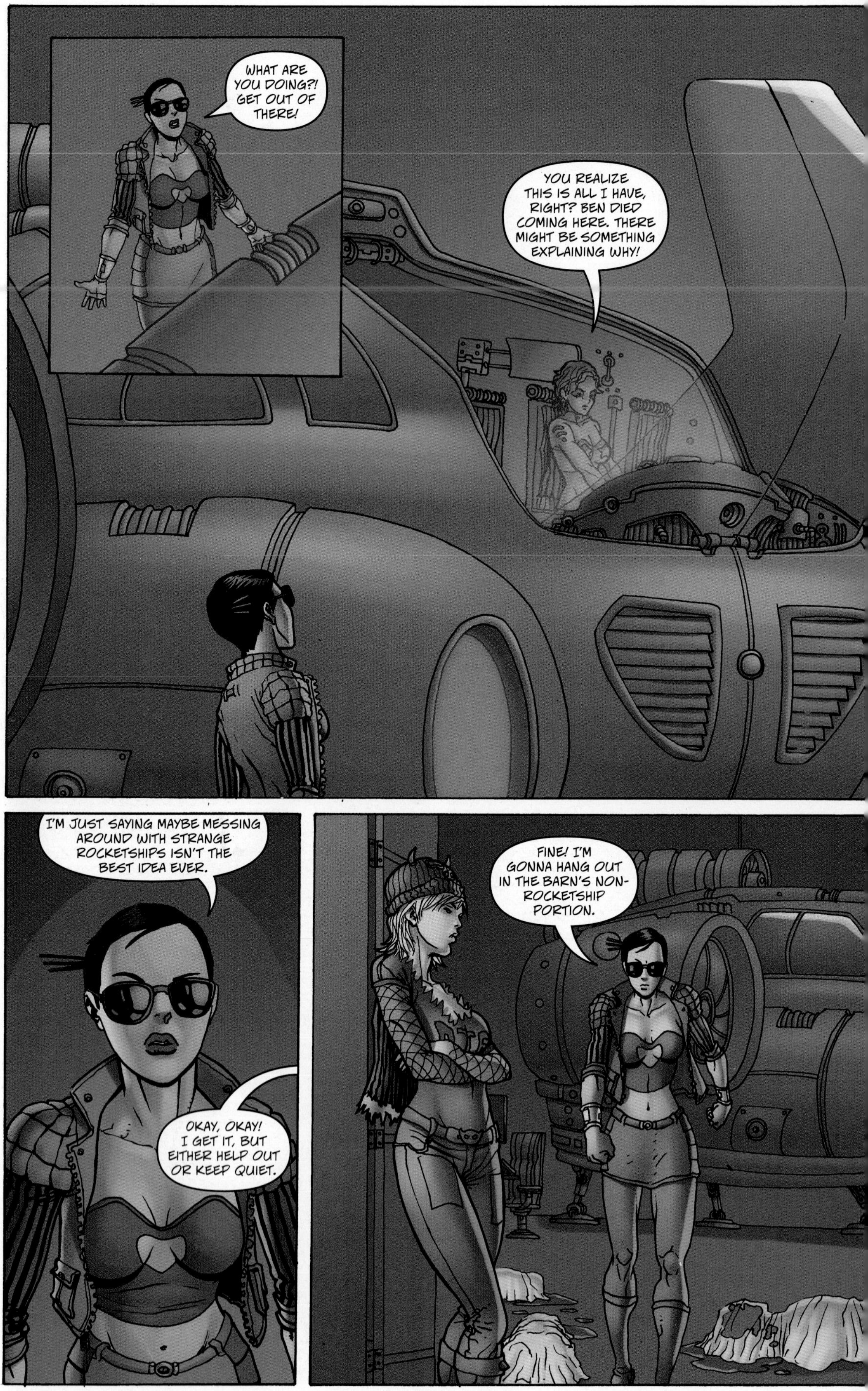
WHAT ARE YOU DOING?! GET OUT OF THERE!
YOU REALIZE THIS IS ALL I HAVE, RIGHT? BEN DIED COMING HERE. THERE MIGHT BE SOMETHING EXPLAINING WHY!
I'M JUST SAYING MAYBE MESSING AROUND WITH STRANGE ROCKETSHIPS ISN'T THE BEST IDEA EVER.
OKAY, OKAY! I GET IT, BUT EITHER HELP OUT OR KEEP QUIET.
FINE! I'M GONNA HANG OUT IN THE BARN'S NON-ROCKETSHIP PORTION.

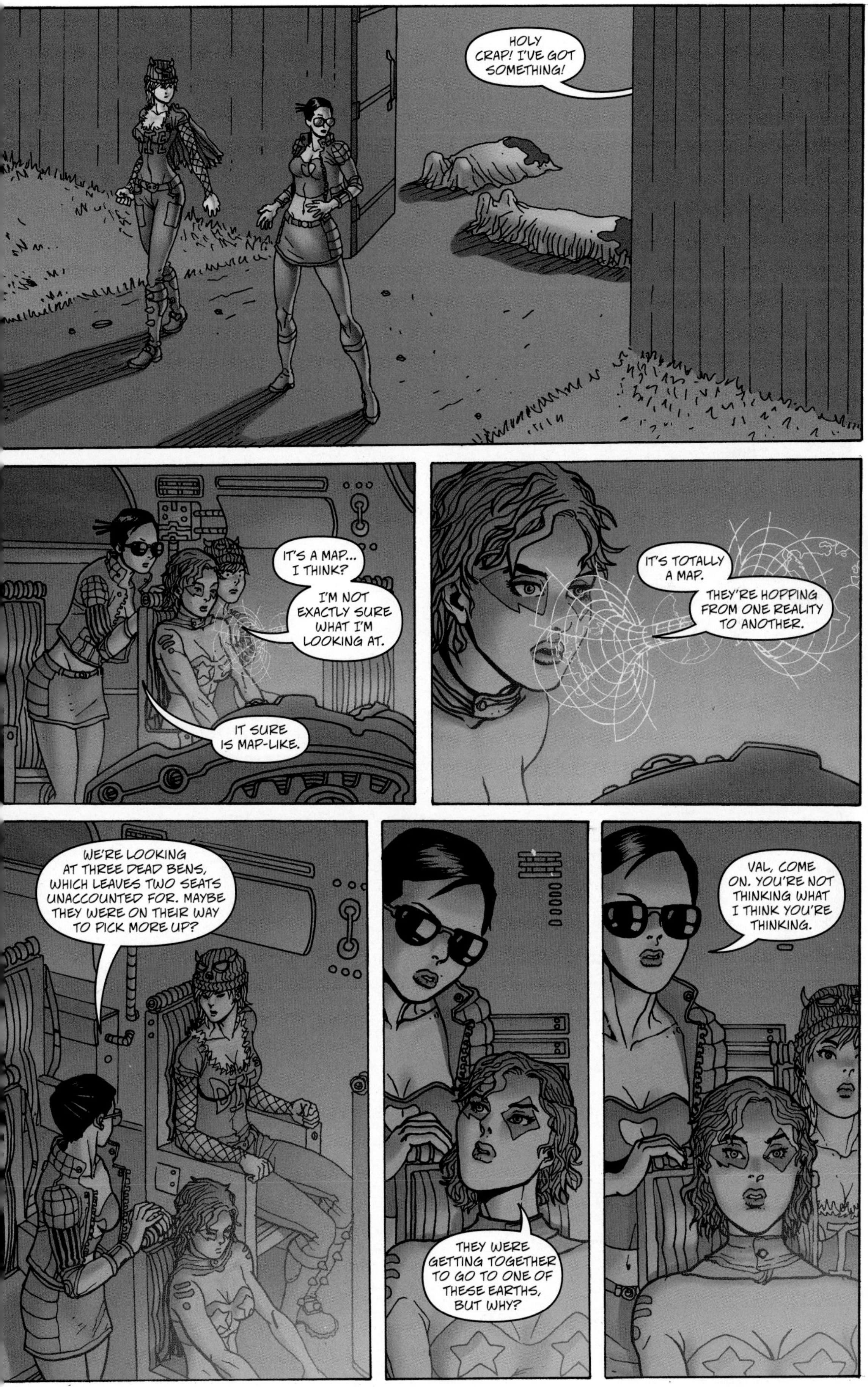
HOLY CRAP! I'VE GOT SOMETHING!
IT'S A MAP... I THINK?
I'M NOT EXACTLY SURE WHAT I'M LOOKING AT.
IT SURE IS MAP-LIKE.
IT'S TOTALLY A MAP.
THEY'RE HOPPING FROM ONE REALITY TO ANOTHER.
WE'RE LOOKING AT THREE DEAD BENS, WHICH LEAVES TWO SEATS UNACCOUNTED FOR. MAYBE THEY WERE ON THEIR WAY TO PICK MORE UP?
THEY WERE GETTING TOGETHER TO GO TO ONE OF THESE EARTHS, BUT WHY?
VAL, COME ON. YOU'RE NOT THINKING WHAT I THINK YOU'RE THINKING.

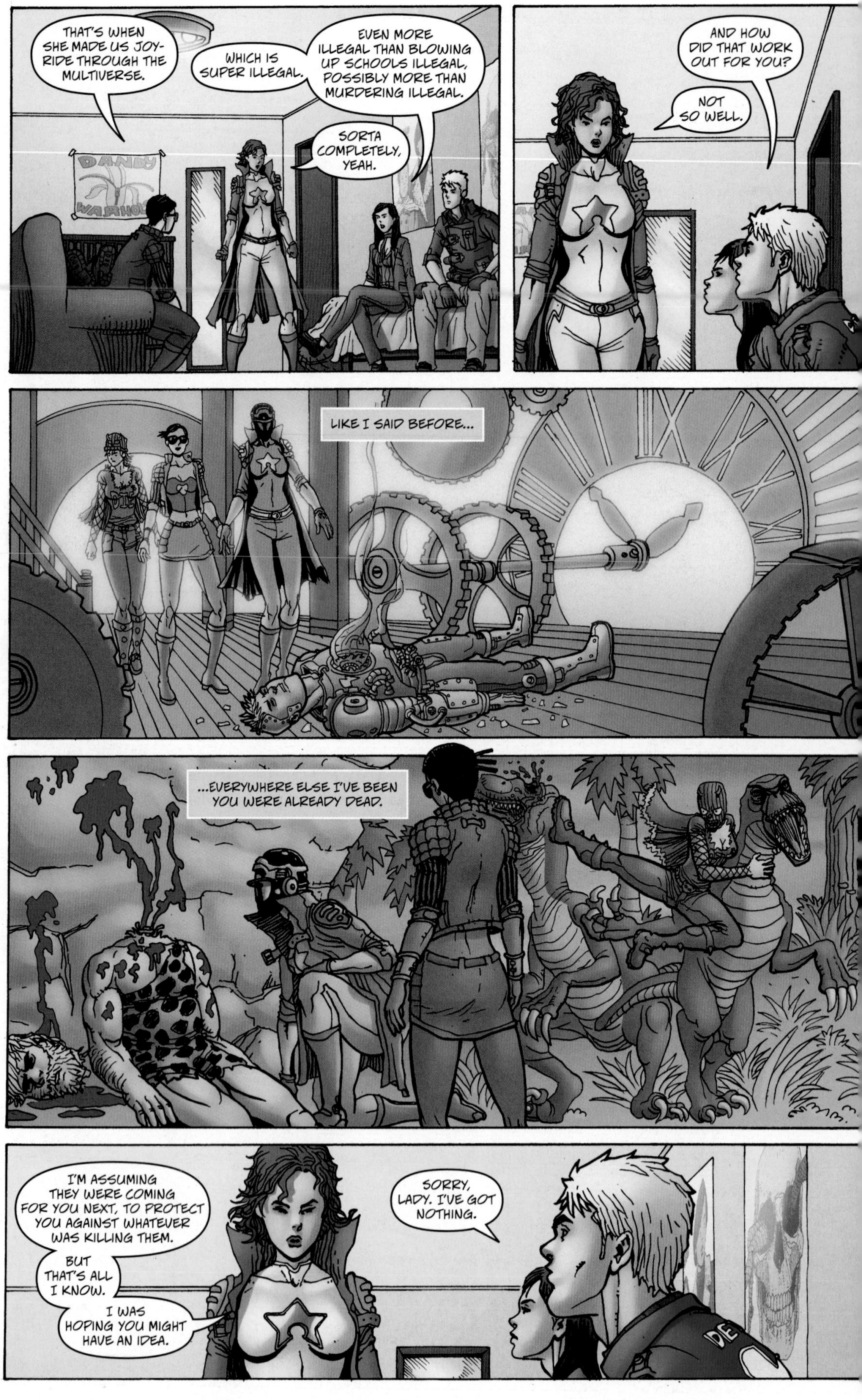
THAT'S WHEN SHE MADE US JOY-RIDE THROUGH THE MULTIVERSE.
WHICH IS SUPER ILLEGAL.
EVEN MORE ILLEGAL THAN BLOWING UP SCHOOLS ILLEGAL, POSSIBLY MORE THAN MURDERING ILLEGAL.
SORTA COMPLETELY, YEAH.
AND HOW DID THAT WORK OUT FOR YOU?
NOT SO WELL.
LIKE I SAID BEFORE...
...EVERYWHERE ELSE I'VE BEEN YOU WERE ALREADY DEAD.
I'M ASSUMING THEY WERE COMING FOR YOU NEXT, TO PROTECT YOU AGAINST WHATEVER WAS KILLING THEM.
BUT THAT'S ALL I KNOW.
I WAS HOPING YOU MIGHT HAVE AN IDEA.
SORRY, LADY. I'VE GOT NOTHING.

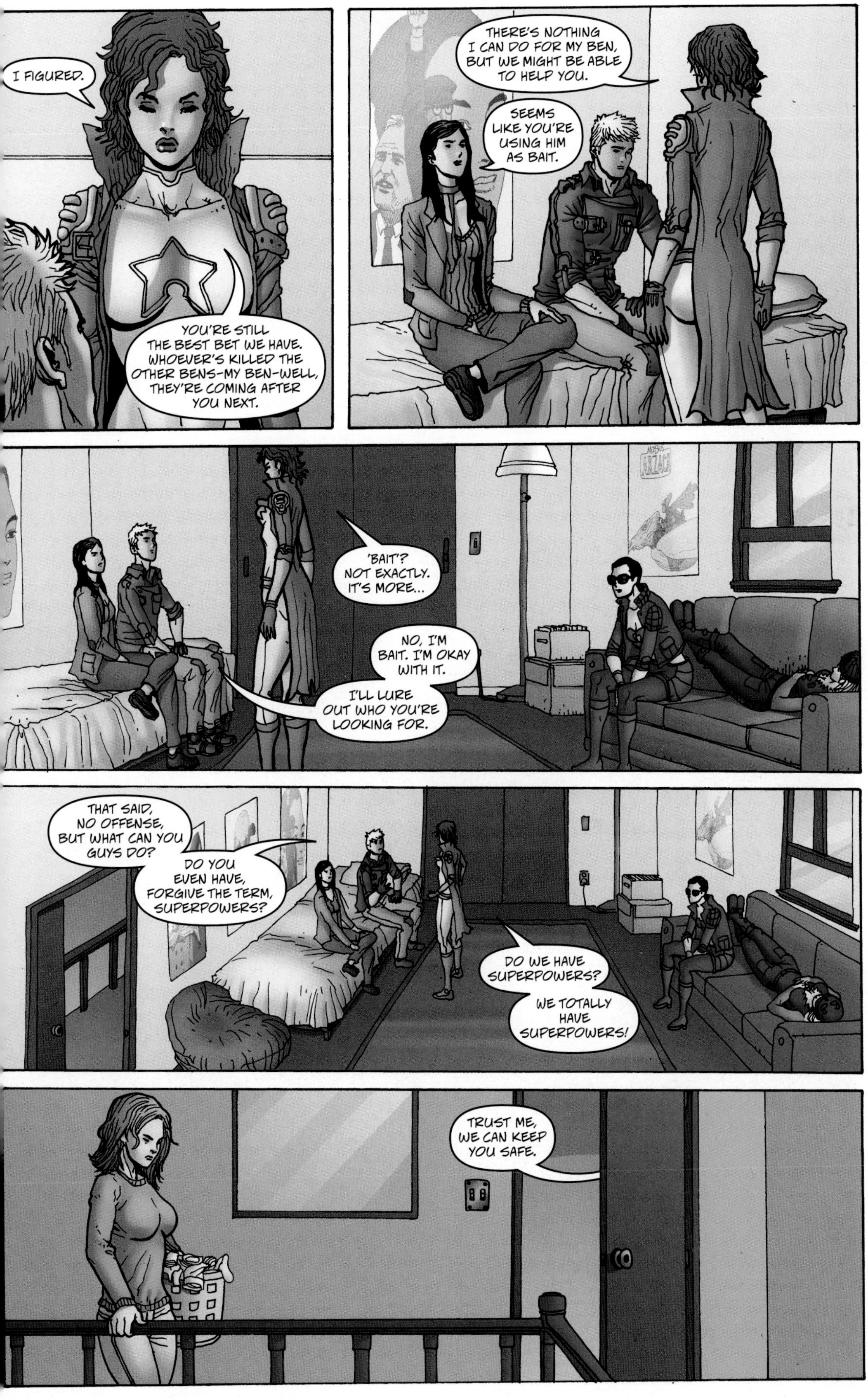
I FIGURED.
YOU'RE STILL THE BEST BET WE HAVE. WHOEVER'S KILLED THE OTHER BENS–MY BEN–WELL, THEY'RE COMING AFTER YOU NEXT.
THERE'S NOTHING I CAN DO FOR MY BEN, BUT WE MIGHT BE ABLE TO HELP YOU.
SEEMS LIKE YOU'RE USING HIM AS BAIT.
ARZACH
'BAIT'? NOT EXACTLY. IT'S MORE...
NO, I'M BAIT. I'M OKAY WITH IT.
I'LL LURE OUT WHO YOU'RE LOOKING FOR.
THAT SAID, NO OFFENSE, BUT WHAT CAN YOU GUYS DO?
DO YOU EVEN HAVE, FORGIVE THE TERM, SUPERPOWERS?
DO WE HAVE SUPERPOWERS?
WE TOTALLY HAVE SUPERPOWERS!
TRUST ME, WE CAN KEEP YOU SAFE.

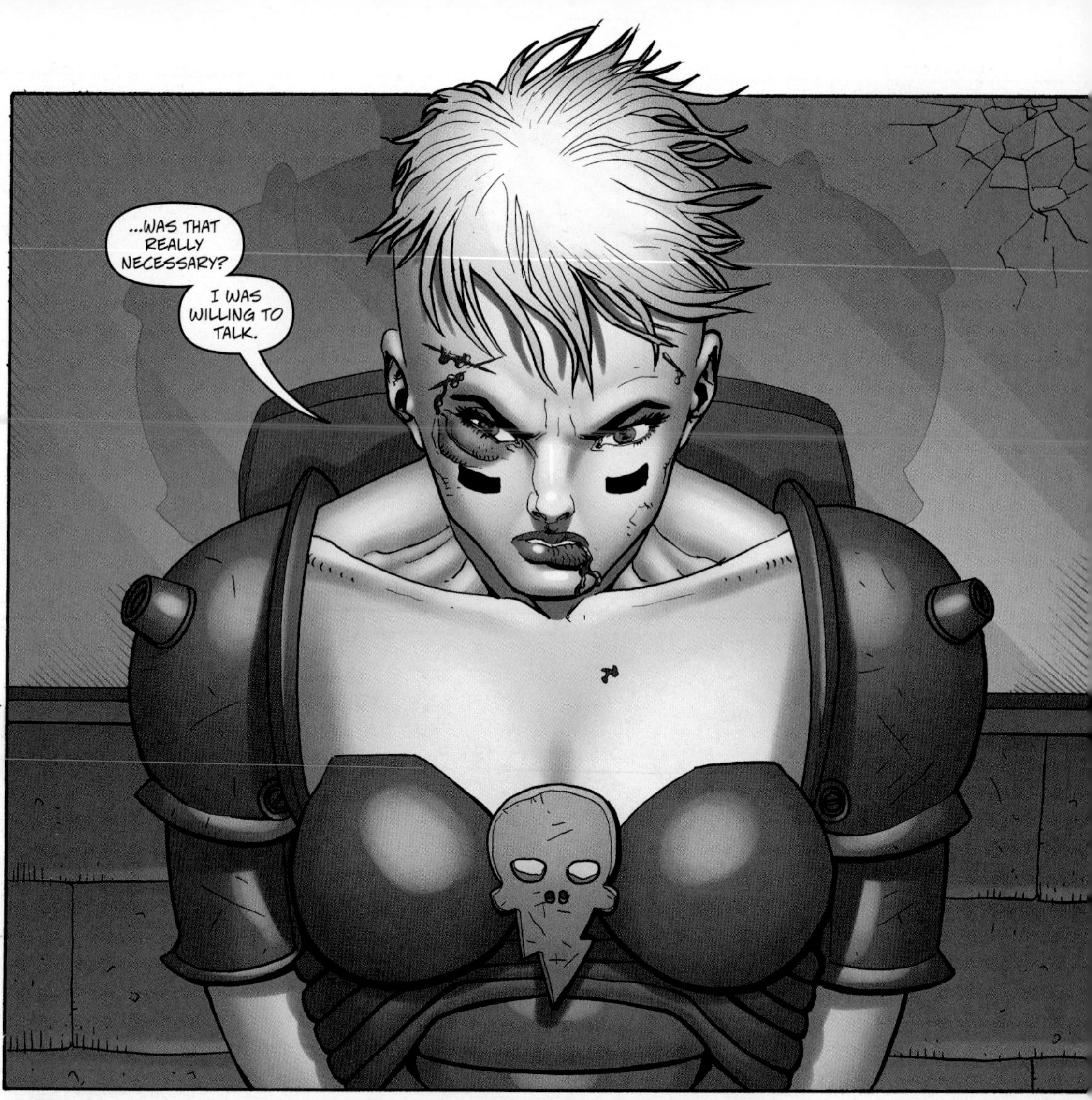
...WAS THAT REALLY NECESSARY?
I WAS WILLING TO TALK.

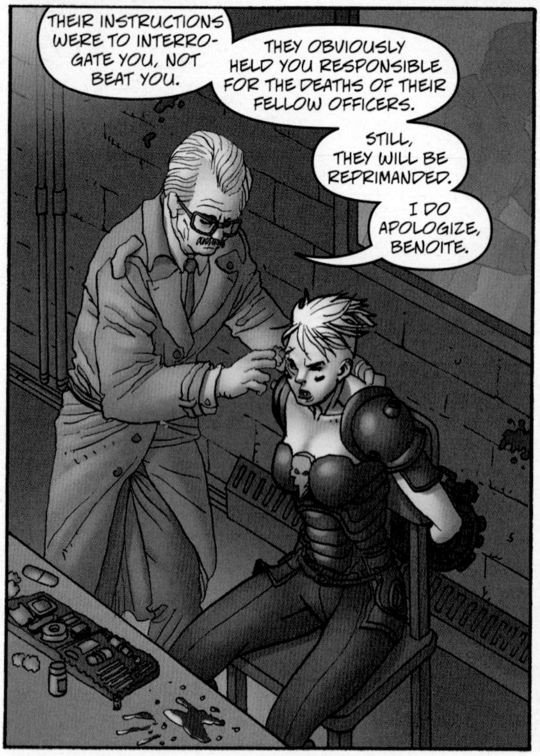
THEIR INSTRUCTIONS WERE TO INTERRO-GATE YOU, NOT BEAT YOU.
THEY OBVIOUSLY HELD YOU RESPONSIBLE FOR THE DEATHS OF THEIR FELLOW OFFICERS.
STILL, THEY WILL BE REPRIMANDED.
I DO APOLOGIZE, BENOITE.

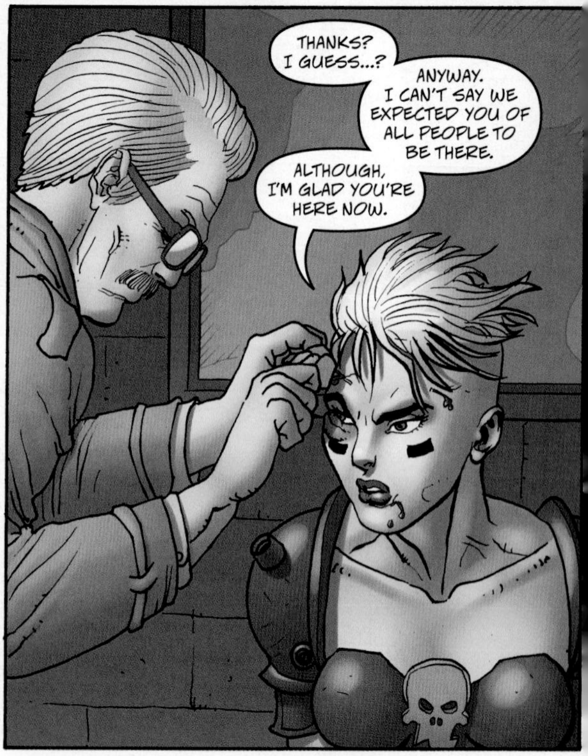
THANKS? I GUESS...?
ANYWAY. I CAN'T SAY WE EXPECTED YOU OF ALL PEOPLE TO BE THERE.
ALTHOUGH, I'M GLAD YOU'RE HERE NOW.

MM. TIMES ARE TOUGH ON THIS EARTH. I'M NEEDED.

OBVIOUSLY.

I DOUBT THAT BLOODBATH WOULD HAVE ENDED SO QUICKLY IF YOU DIDN'T INTERVENE.

IT DIDN'T NEED TO HAPPEN AT ALL.

NONE OF YOU SHOULD BE HERE.

SURE, NONE OF US 'SHOULD'. WE WOULDN'T HAVE ARGUED WITH YOU THERE.

THEN AGAIN, ALL OF US HAVE TO.

WE WEREN'T BREAKING INTER-DIMENSIONAL LAW BECAUSE OF A WHIM.

WE'RE HERE BECAUSE WE HAVE TO BE.

WE'RE THE ONLY ONES WHO CAN SAVE THE WORLDS. ALL OF OUR WORLDS.

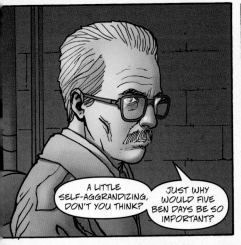

A LITTLE SELF-AGGRANDIZING, DON'T YOU THINK?

JUST WHY WOULD FIVE BEN DAYS BE SO IMPORTANT?

DON'T PLAY STUPID. I KNOW YOU KNOW WHAT WE KNOW. I'M SURE YOU KNOW IT EVEN BETTER THAN WE DO.

WE'RE THE ONLY ONES WHO CAN REALLY DO ANYTHING ABOUT IT.

YOU WON'T. YOU'RE TOO CLOSE TO THE SITUATION.

YOU PRESUME TOO MUCH.

NO, I DON'T.

IF YOU WERE GOING TO DO SOMETHING, YOU WOULD HAVE ALREADY. EVERY BEN DAY FROM EVERY DIMENSION NOW KNOWS THE TRUTH. WE ALSO KNOW WHAT WE HAVE TO DO AND HOW WE DO IT.

IT'S SIMPLE, REALLY.

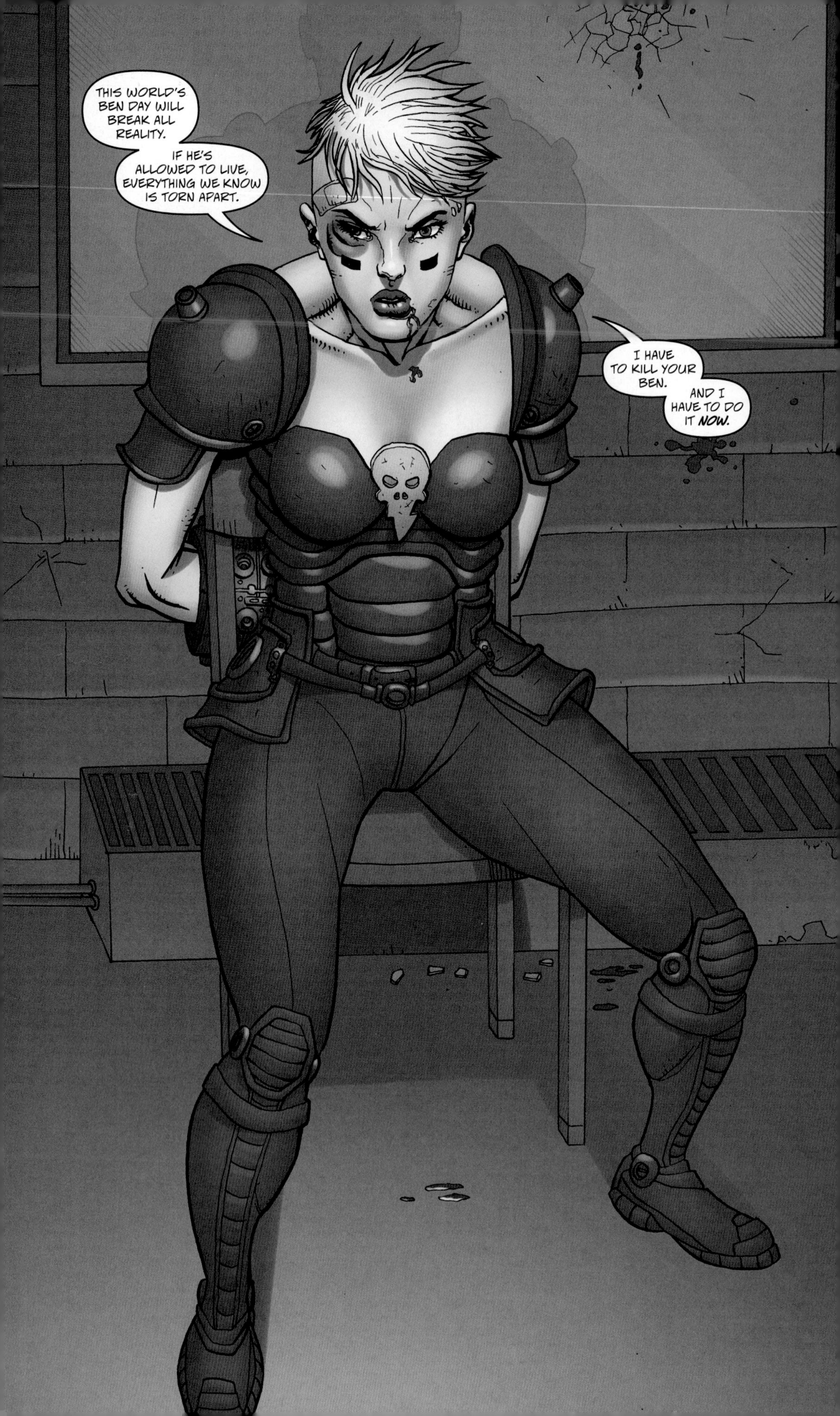
THIS WORLD'S BEN DAY WILL BREAK ALL REALITY.
IF HE'S ALLOWED TO LIVE, EVERYTHING WE KNOW IS TORN APART.
I HAVE TO KILL YOUR BEN.
AND I HAVE TO DO IT *NOW*.

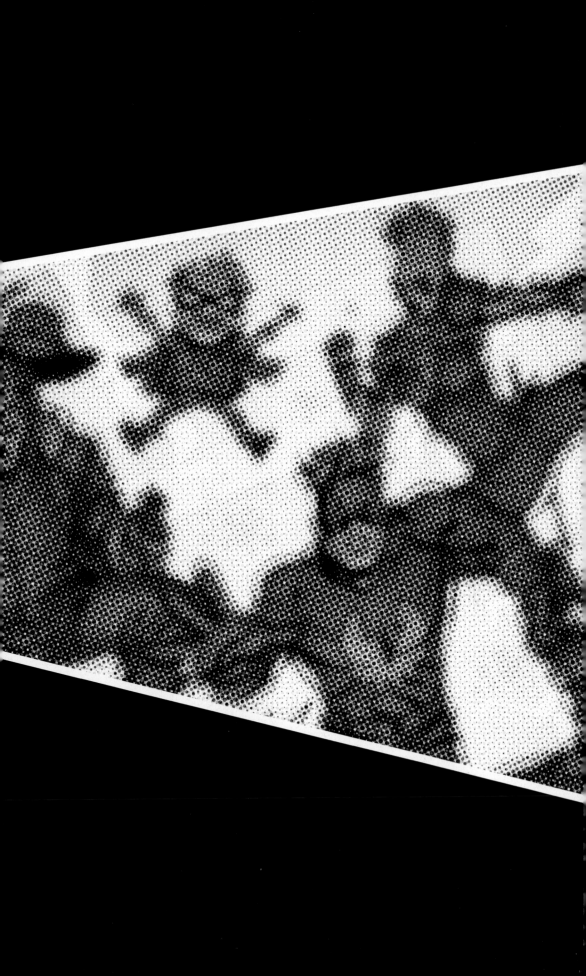

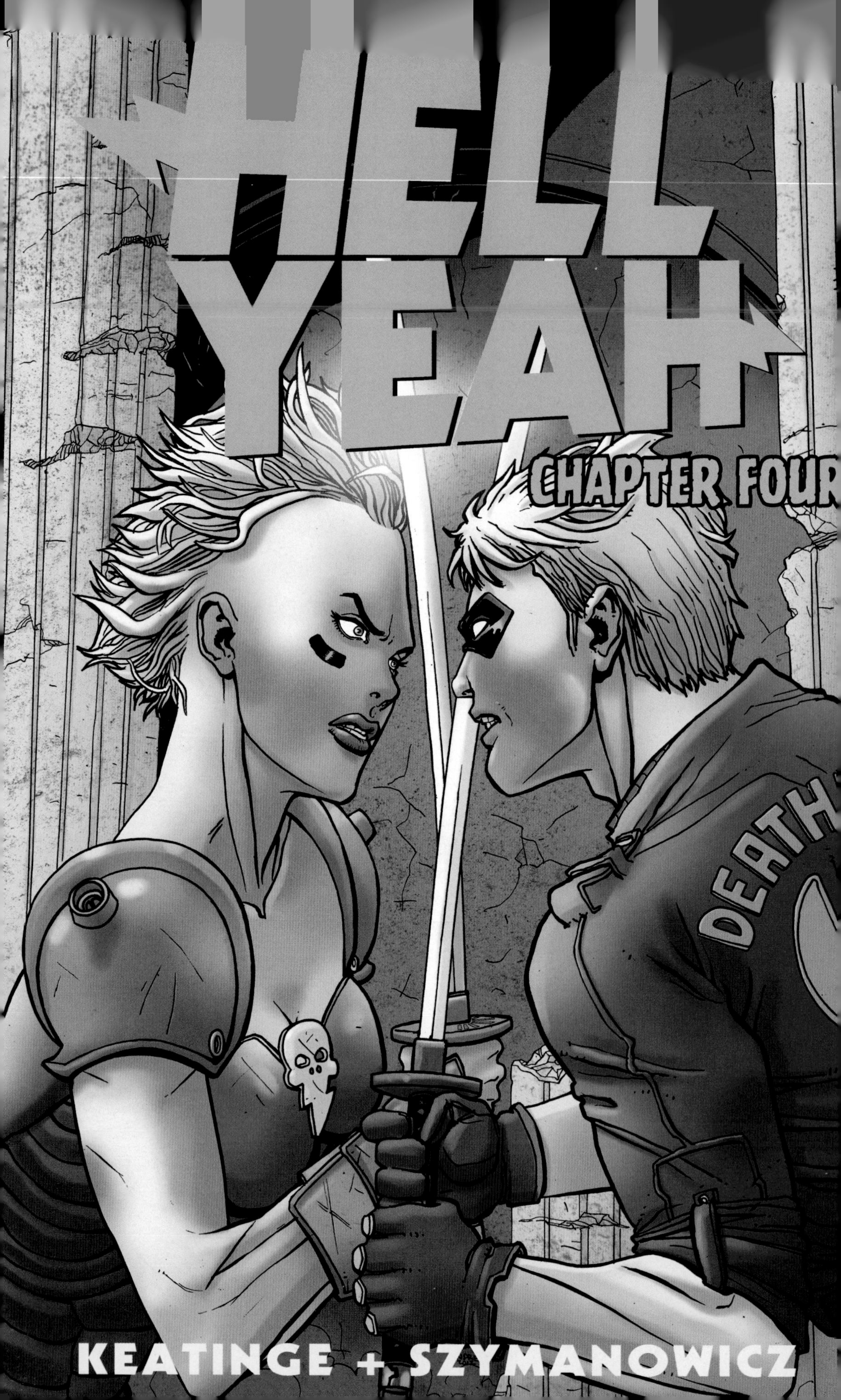
HELL YEAH
CHAPTER FOUR
DEATH
KEATINGE + SZYMANOWICZ

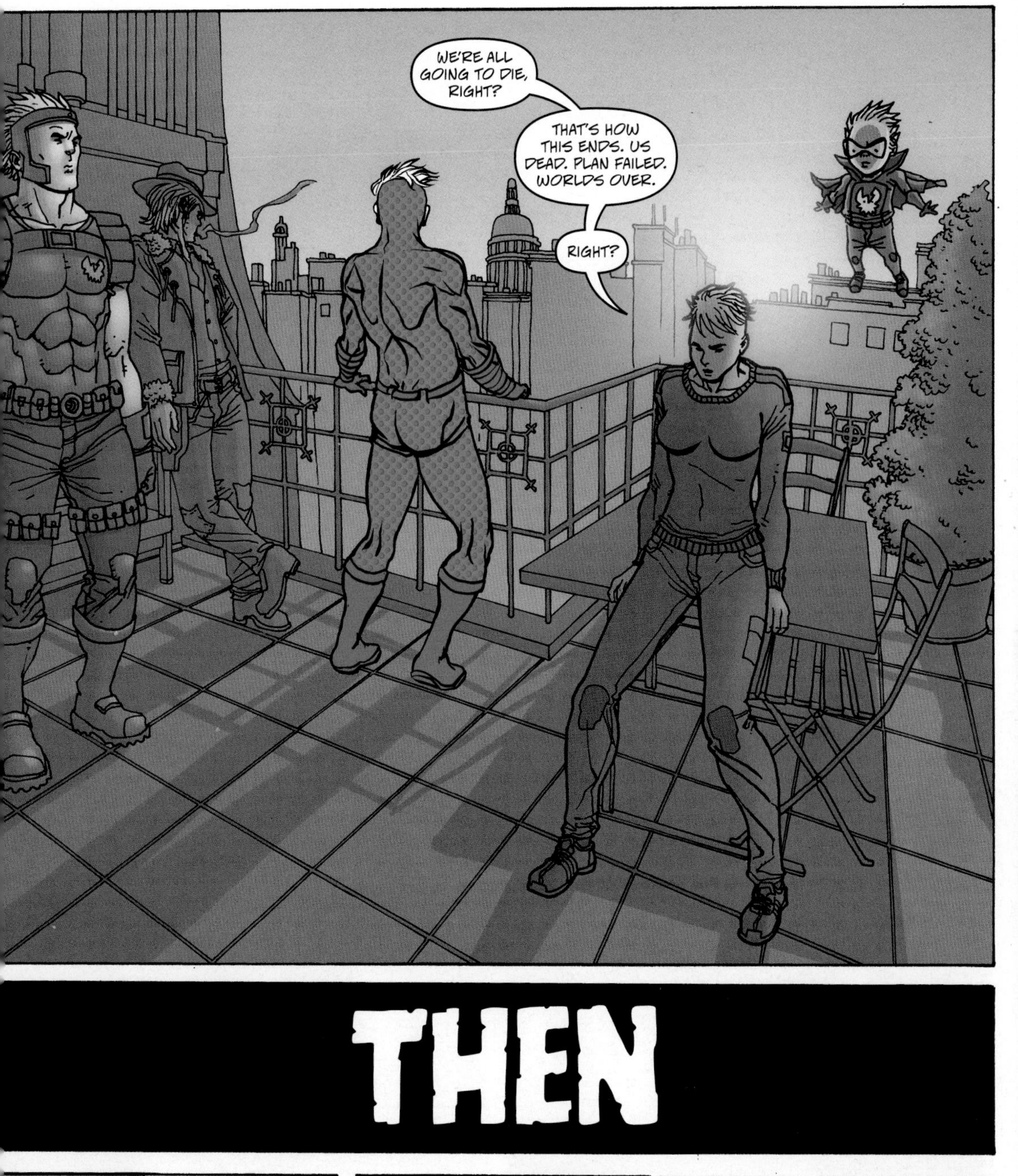
WE'RE ALL GOING TO DIE, RIGHT?
THAT'S HOW THIS ENDS. US DEAD. PLAN FAILED. WORLDS OVER.
RIGHT?

THEN

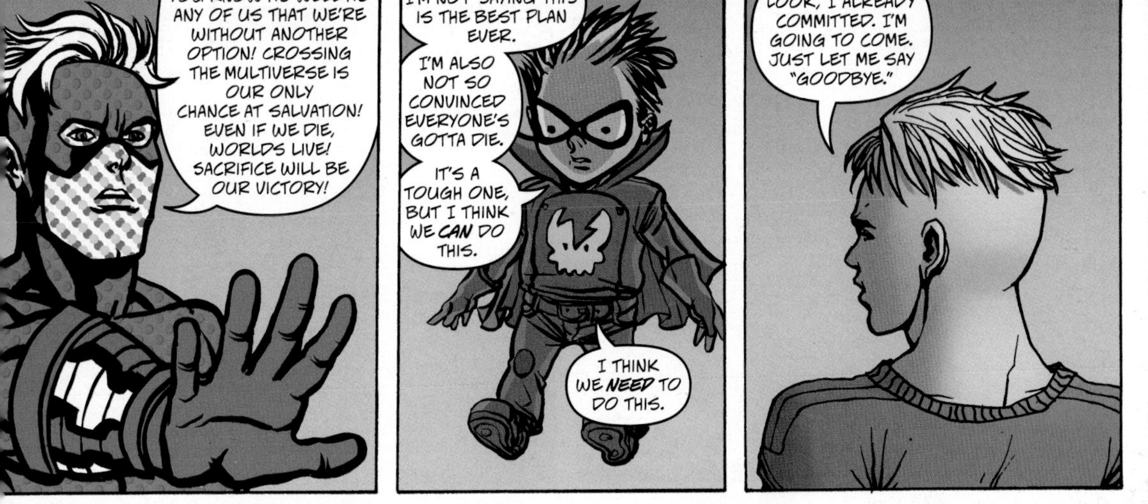
YOU KNOW AS WELL AS ANY OF US THAT WE'RE WITHOUT ANOTHER OPTION! CROSSING THE MULTIVERSE IS OUR ONLY CHANCE AT SALVATION! EVEN IF WE DIE, WORLDS LIVE! SACRIFICE WILL BE OUR VICTORY!
I'M NOT SAYING THIS IS THE BEST PLAN EVER.
I'M ALSO NOT SO CONVINCED EVERYONE'S GOTTA DIE.
IT'S A TOUGH ONE, BUT I THINK WE **CAN** DO THIS.
I THINK WE **NEED** TO DO THIS.
LOOK, I ALREADY COMMITTED. I'M GOING TO COME. JUST LET ME SAY "GOODBYE."

LOOKS LIKE YOUR MEETING WENT WELL.

IT'S THAT OBVIOUS, HUH?

MAMA!

YOU DON'T HIDE YOUR EMOTIONS.

IF IT MAKES YOU FEEL BETTER, *WE* HAD A GOOD TIME. DIDN'T WE?

WE PLAYED TRAINS ALL DAY THEN WE ATE FOOD THEN WE TOOK A NAP THEN WE PLAYED TRAINS ALL DAY AGAIN! DANNI WAS MEAN BUT THEN SHE SAID SORRY AND IT WAS OKAY!

I WAS MEAN, BUT I'M STILL SORRY!

SOUNDS LIKE A LONG DAY, BUT I'M GLAD YOU TWO WORKED IT OUT.

THEY DID. I'M IMPRESSED. OUR CHILDREN ACTUALLY SHOWED A LITTLE MATURITY.

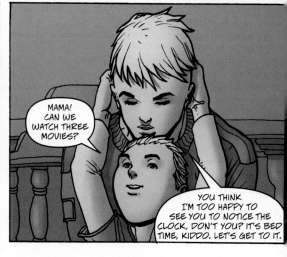

MAMA! CAN WE WATCH THREE MOVIES?

YOU THINK I'M TOO HAPPY TO SEE YOU TO NOTICE THE CLOCK, DON'T YOU? IT'S BED TIME, KIDDO. LET'S GET TO IT.

BENOITE? YOU COMING TO BED?

JESS, I DON'T KNOW HOW TO TELL YOU THIS...

THEN DON'T. I TRUST YOU. IF IT'S TOO HARD TO SAY NOW, THEN WAIT UNTIL IT'S EASIER.

THE PROBLEM IS THERE MAY NOT BE A LATER THIS TIME.

I'M GETTING INTO SOMETHING PRETTY BAD. SOMETHING REALLY PRETTY BAD.

THE WORST I'VE DEALT WITH.

AND? HOW'S THAT ANYTHING NEW? YOU REMEMBER HOW WE MET, RIGHT?

WE'VE BOTH BEEN GETTING INTO SOMETHING "PRETTY BAD" SINCE WELL BEFORE THEN.

WORSE AND WORSE EVERY TIME.

IT'S WHAT WE DO.

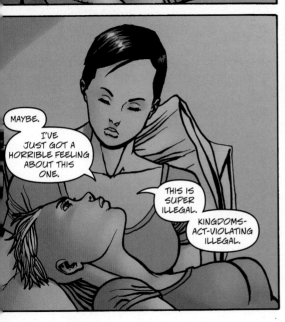

MAYBE. I'VE JUST GOT A HORRIBLE FEELING ABOUT THIS ONE.

THIS IS SUPER ILLEGAL. KINGDOMS-ACT-VIOLATING ILLEGAL.

OH. OH, HONEY, NO. WHAT HAVE YOU GOTTEN YOURSELF INTO?

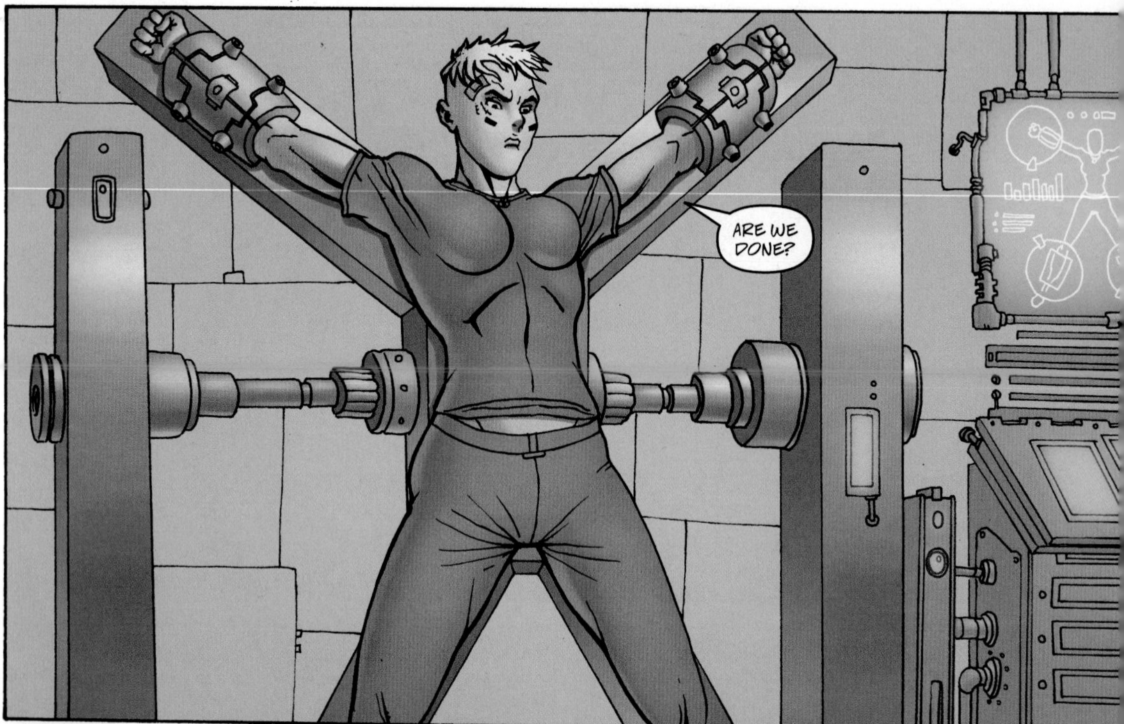
ARE WE DONE?

NOW

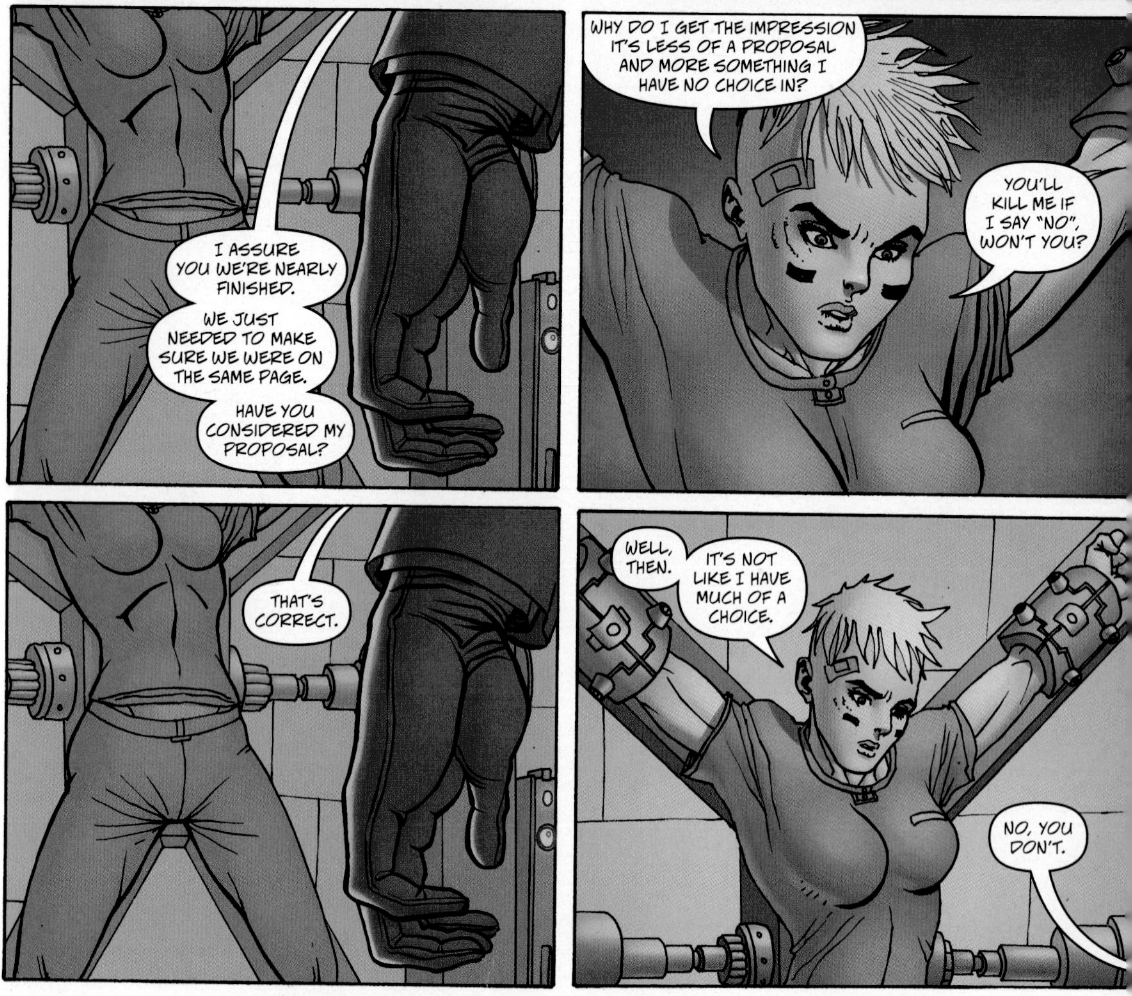
I ASSURE YOU WE'RE NEARLY FINISHED.
WE JUST NEEDED TO MAKE SURE WE WERE ON THE SAME PAGE.
HAVE YOU CONSIDERED MY PROPOSAL?
WHY DO I GET THE IMPRESSION IT'S LESS OF A PROPOSAL AND MORE SOMETHING I HAVE NO CHOICE IN?
YOU'LL KILL ME IF I SAY "NO", WON'T YOU?
THAT'S CORRECT.
WELL, THEN.
IT'S NOT LIKE I HAVE MUCH OF A CHOICE.
NO, YOU DON'T.

IMAGE COMICS PRESENTS

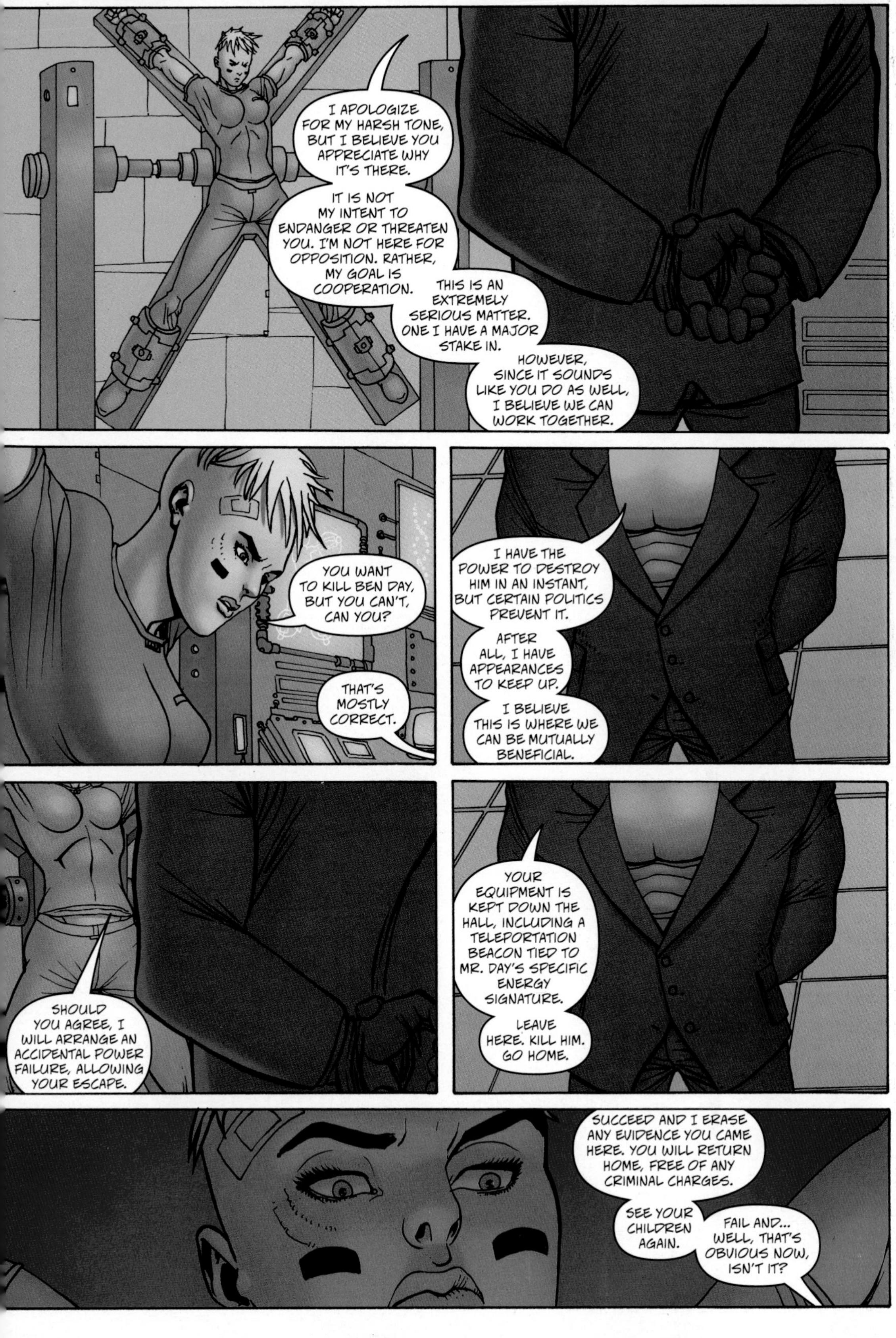

I APOLOGIZE FOR MY HARSH TONE, BUT I BELIEVE YOU APPRECIATE WHY IT'S THERE.
IT IS NOT MY INTENT TO ENDANGER OR THREATEN YOU. I'M NOT HERE FOR OPPOSITION. RATHER, MY GOAL IS COOPERATION.
THIS IS AN EXTREMELY SERIOUS MATTER. ONE I HAVE A MAJOR STAKE IN.
HOWEVER, SINCE IT SOUNDS LIKE YOU DO AS WELL, I BELIEVE WE CAN WORK TOGETHER.
YOU WANT TO KILL BEN DAY, BUT YOU CAN'T, CAN YOU?
THAT'S MOSTLY CORRECT.
I HAVE THE POWER TO DESTROY HIM IN AN INSTANT, BUT CERTAIN POLITICS PREVENT IT.
AFTER ALL, I HAVE APPEARANCES TO KEEP UP.
I BELIEVE THIS IS WHERE WE CAN BE MUTUALLY BENEFICIAL.
SHOULD YOU AGREE, I WILL ARRANGE AN ACCIDENTAL POWER FAILURE, ALLOWING YOUR ESCAPE.
YOUR EQUIPMENT IS KEPT DOWN THE HALL, INCLUDING A TELEPORTATION BEACON TIED TO MR. DAY'S SPECIFIC ENERGY SIGNATURE.
LEAVE HERE. KILL HIM. GO HOME.
SUCCEED AND I ERASE ANY EVIDENCE YOU CAME HERE. YOU WILL RETURN HOME, FREE OF ANY CRIMINAL CHARGES.
SEE YOUR CHILDREN AGAIN.
FAIL AND... WELL, THAT'S OBVIOUS NOW, ISN'T IT?

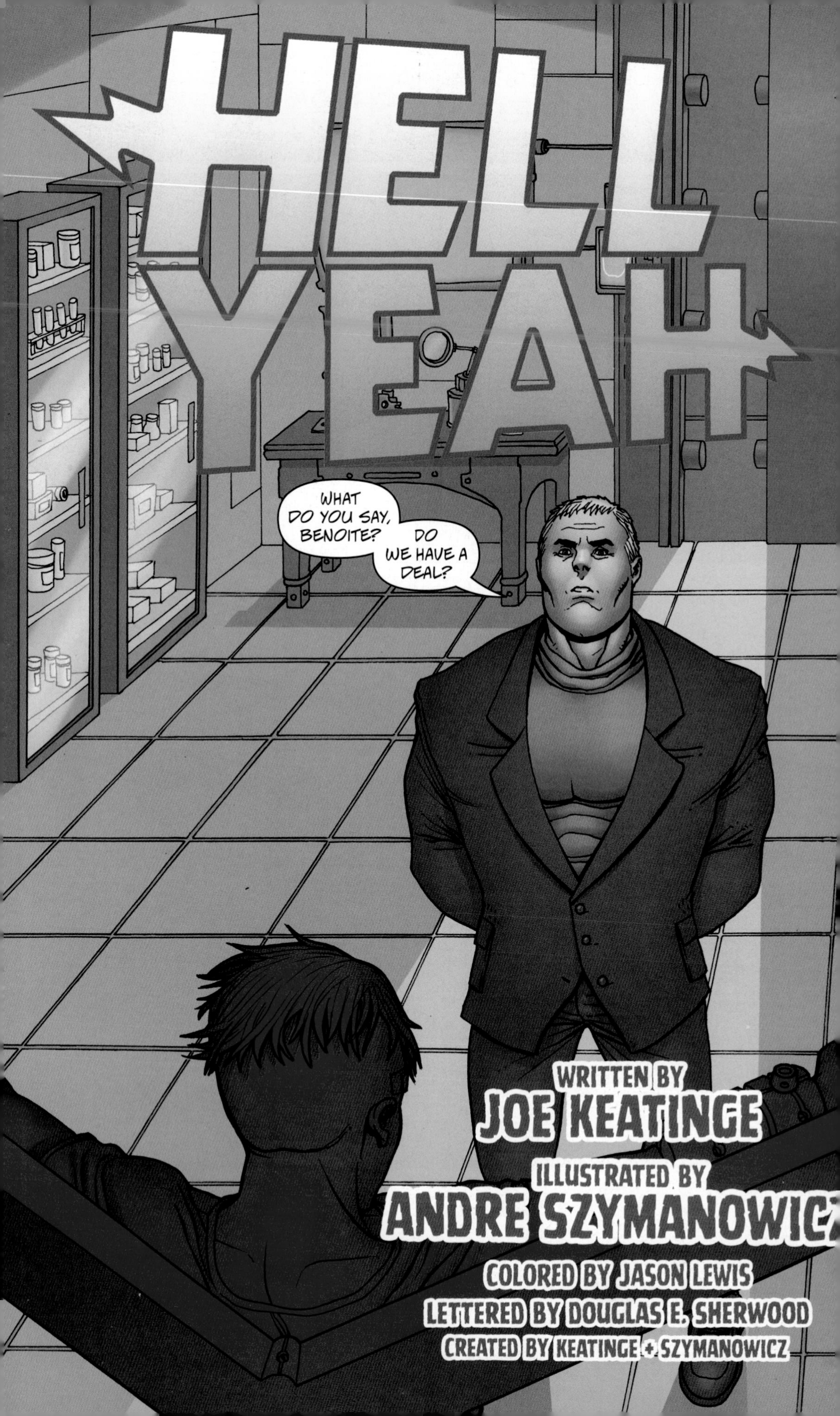
HELL YEAH
WHAT DO YOU SAY, BENOITE?
DO WE HAVE A DEAL?
WRITTEN BY
JOE KEATINGE
ILLUSTRATED BY
ANDRE SZYMANOWICZ
COLORED BY JASON LEWIS
LETTERED BY DOUGLAS E. SHERWOOD
CREATED BY KEATINGE + SZYMANOWICZ

BOOK ONE
LAST DAY ON EARTHS

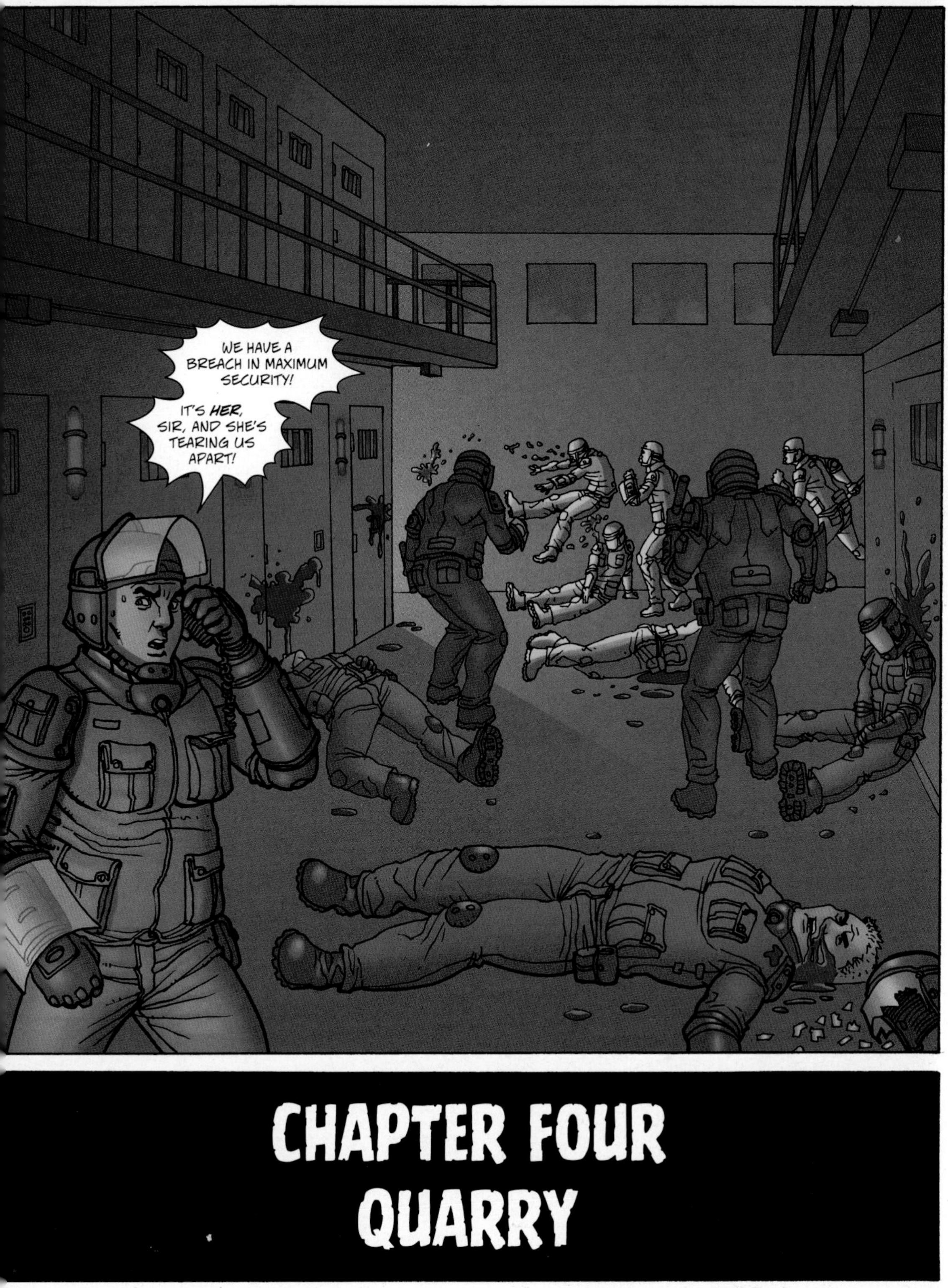

WE HAVE A BREACH IN MAXIMUM SECURITY!
IT'S **HER**, SIR, AND SHE'S TEARING US APART!

CHAPTER FOUR
QUARRY

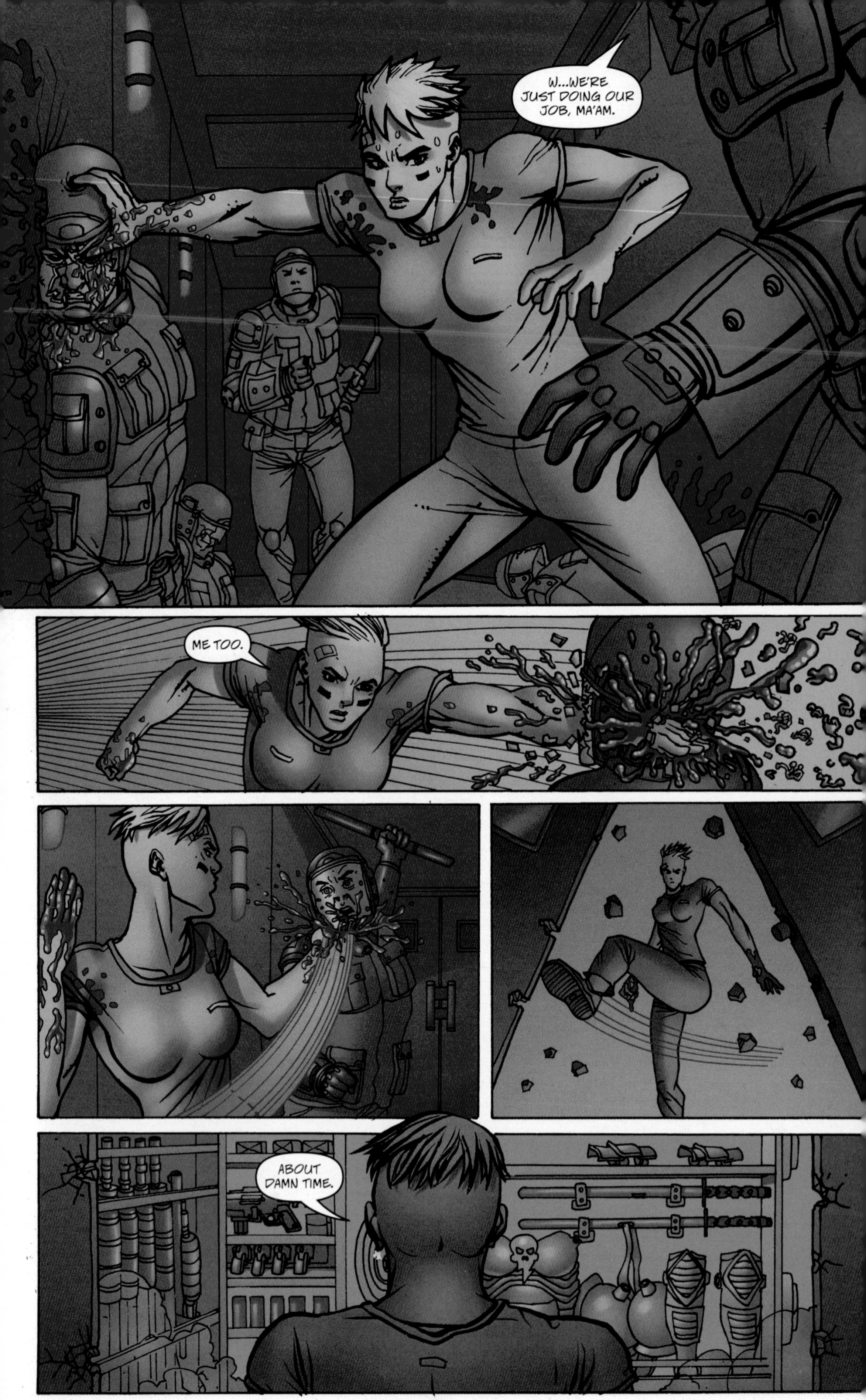
W...WE'RE JUST DOING OUR JOB, MA'AM.
ME TOO.
ABOUT DAMN TIME.

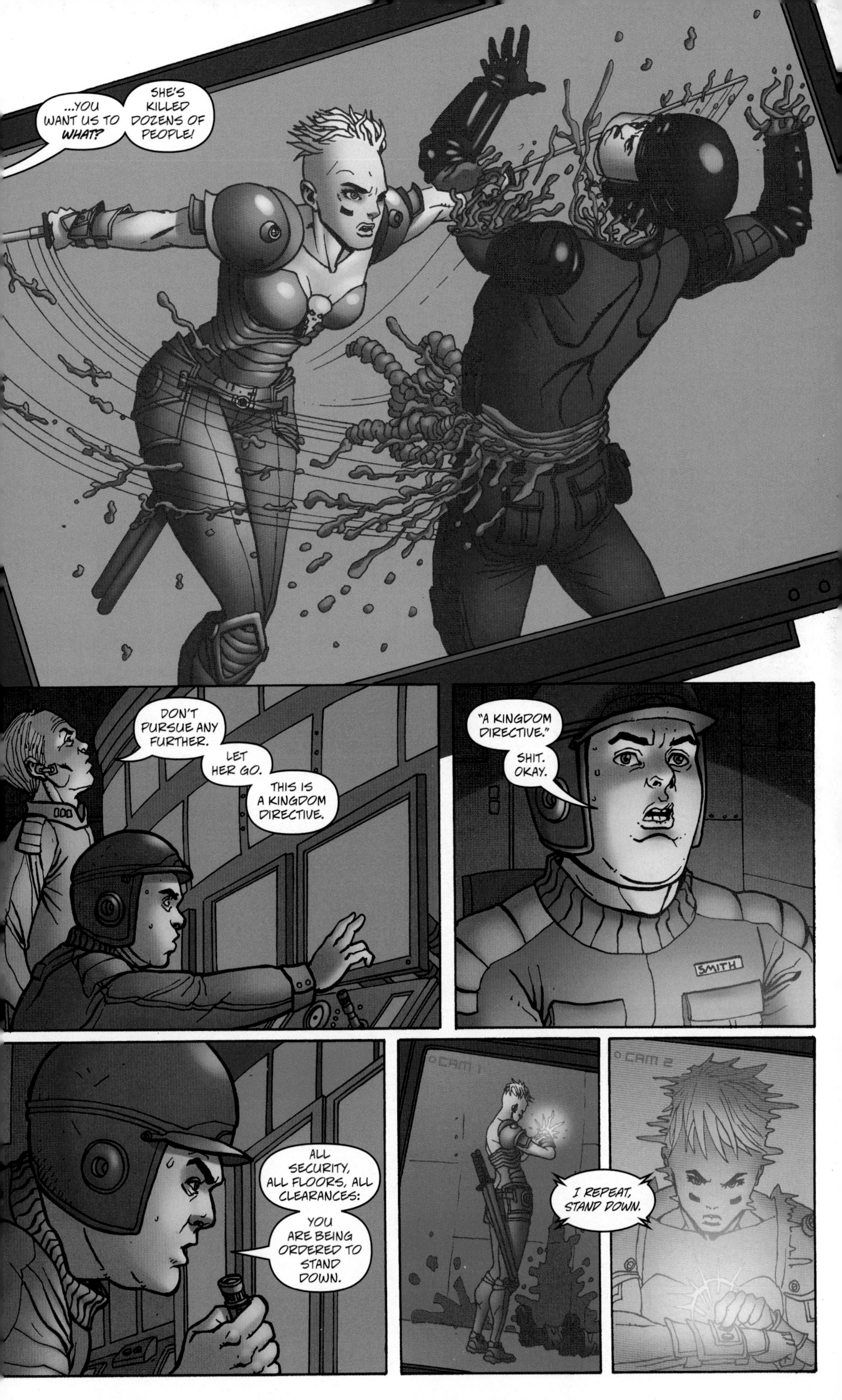

...YOU WANT US TO *WHAT?*
SHE'S KILLED DOZENS OF PEOPLE!
DON'T PURSUE ANY FURTHER.
LET HER GO.
THIS IS A KINGDOM DIRECTIVE.
"A KINGDOM DIRECTIVE."
SHIT. OKAY.
SMITH
ALL SECURITY, ALL FLOORS, ALL CLEARANCES:
YOU ARE BEING ORDERED TO STAND DOWN.
CAM 1
I REPEAT, STAND DOWN.
CAM 2

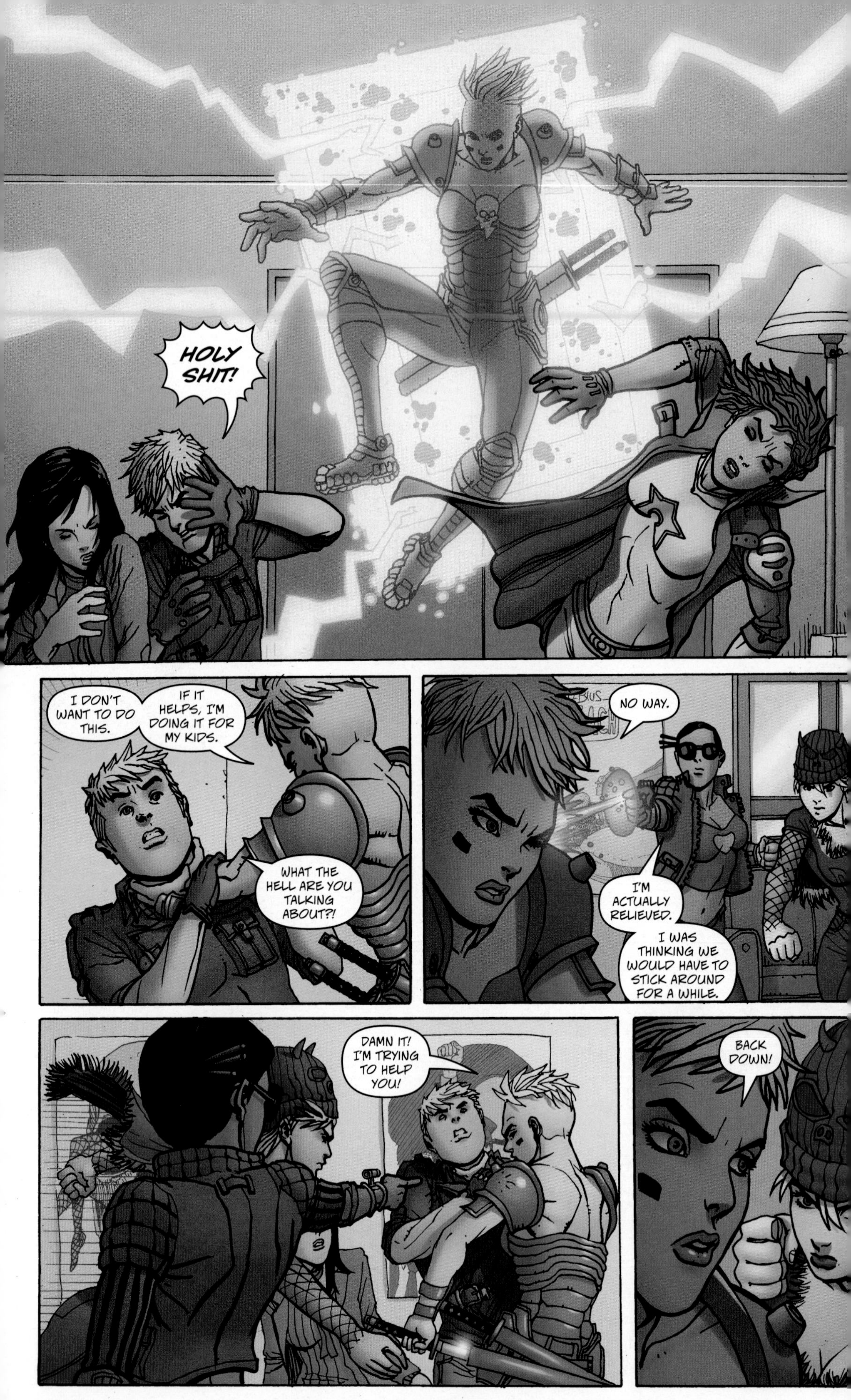
HOLY SHIT!
I DON'T WANT TO DO THIS.
IF IT HELPS, I'M DOING IT FOR MY KIDS.
WHAT THE HELL ARE YOU TALKING ABOUT?!
NO WAY.
I'M ACTUALLY RELIEVED.
I WAS THINKING WE WOULD HAVE TO STICK AROUND FOR A WHILE.
DAMN IT! I'M TRYING TO HELP YOU!
BACK DOWN!

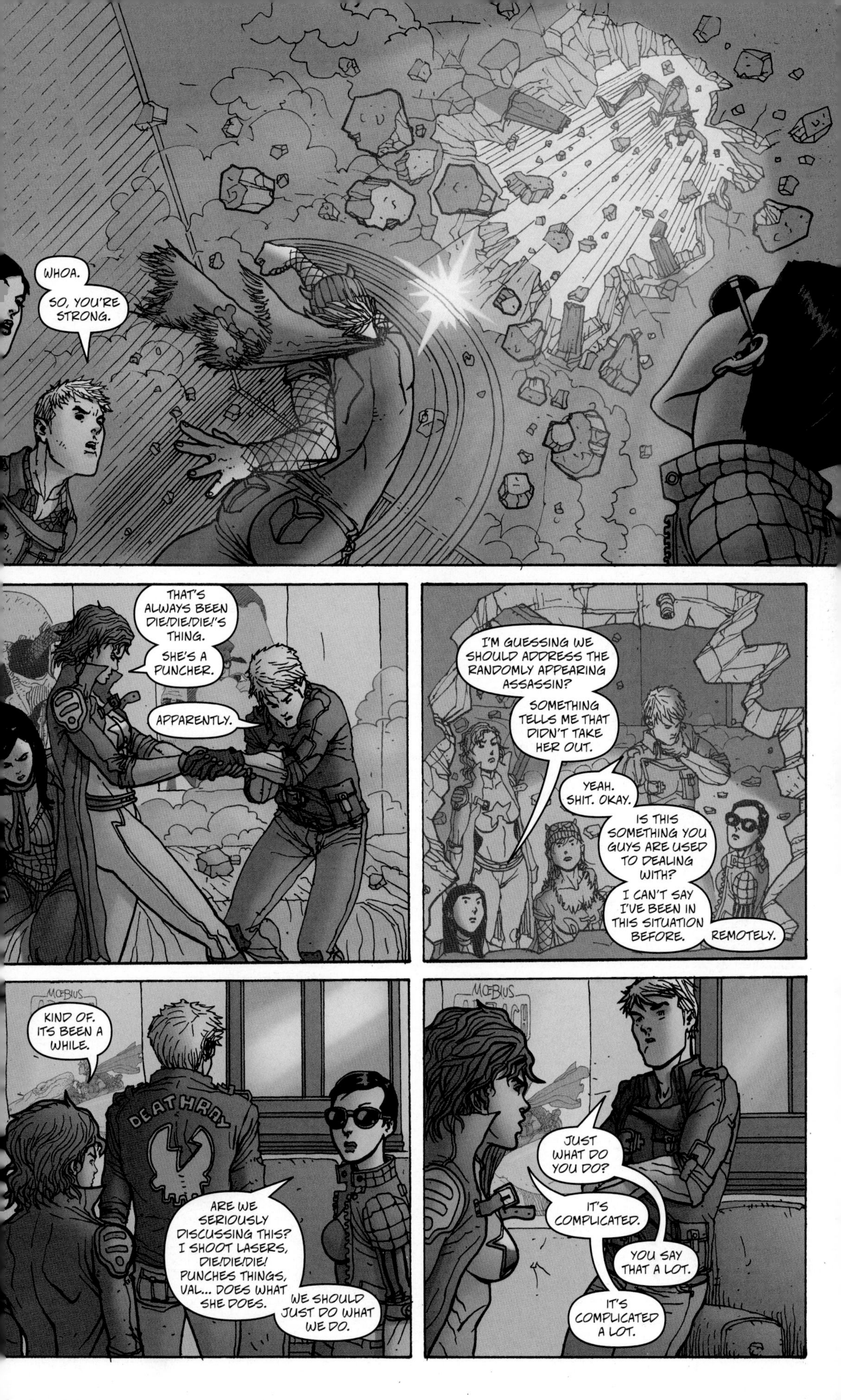
WHOA.
SO, YOU'RE STRONG.
THAT'S ALWAYS BEEN DIE!DIE!DIE!'S THING.
SHE'S A PUNCHER.
APPARENTLY.
I'M GUESSING WE SHOULD ADDRESS THE RANDOMLY APPEARING ASSASSIN?
SOMETHING TELLS ME THAT DIDN'T TAKE HER OUT.
YEAH. SHIT. OKAY.
IS THIS SOMETHING YOU GUYS ARE USED TO DEALING WITH?
I CAN'T SAY I'VE BEEN IN THIS SITUATION BEFORE.
REMOTELY.
MOEBIUS
KIND OF. ITS BEEN A WHILE.
DEATHRAY
ARE WE SERIOUSLY DISCUSSING THIS? I SHOOT LASERS, DIE!DIE!DIE! PUNCHES THINGS, VAL... DOES WHAT SHE DOES.
WE SHOULD JUST DO WHAT WE DO.
MOEBIUS
JUST WHAT DO YOU DO?
IT'S COMPLICATED.
YOU SAY THAT A LOT.
IT'S COMPLICATED A LOT.

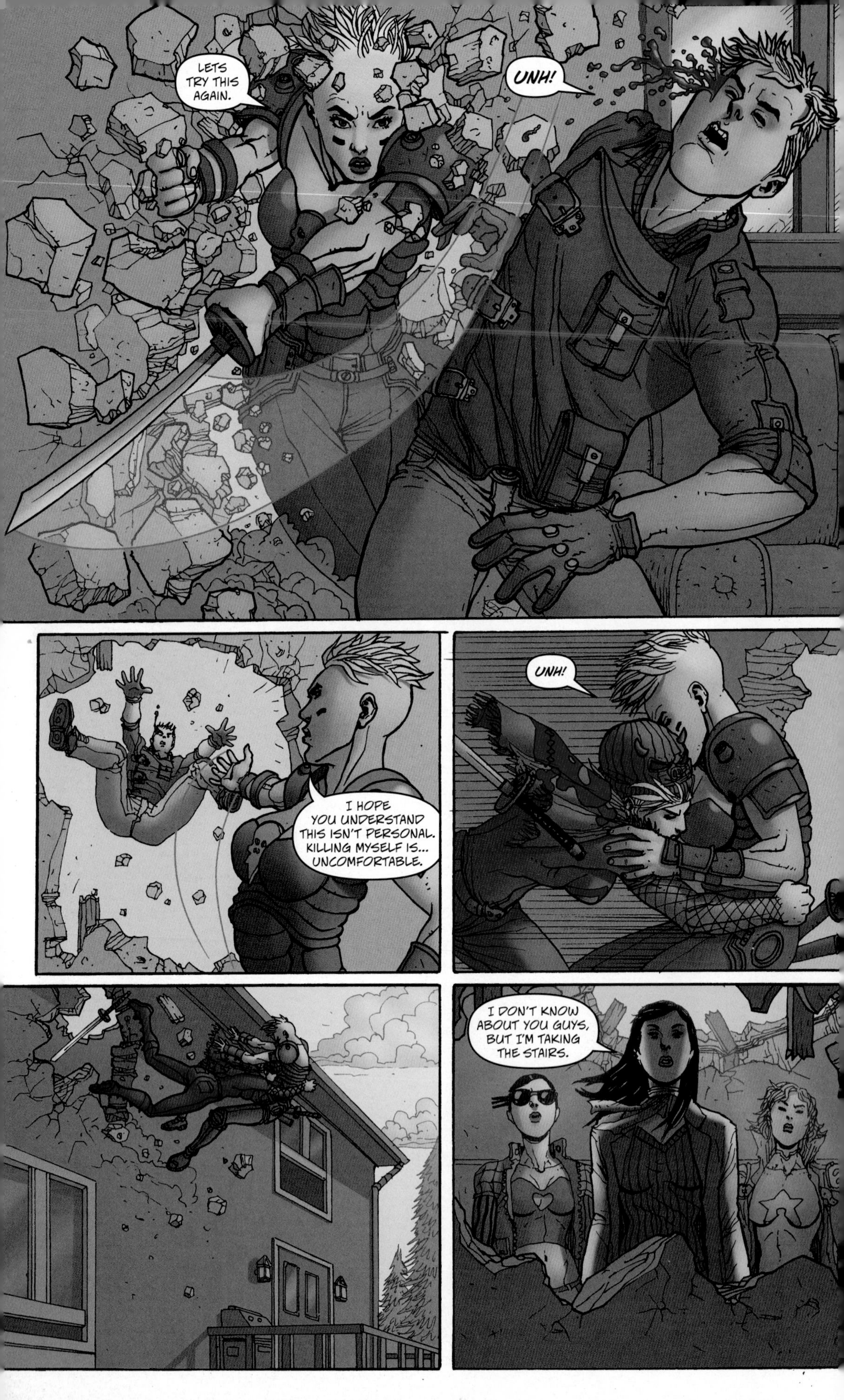
LETS TRY THIS AGAIN.
UNH!
I HOPE YOU UNDERSTAND THIS ISN'T PERSONAL. KILLING MYSELF IS... UNCOMFORTABLE.
UNH!
I DON'T KNOW ABOUT YOU GUYS, BUT I'M TAKING THE STAIRS.

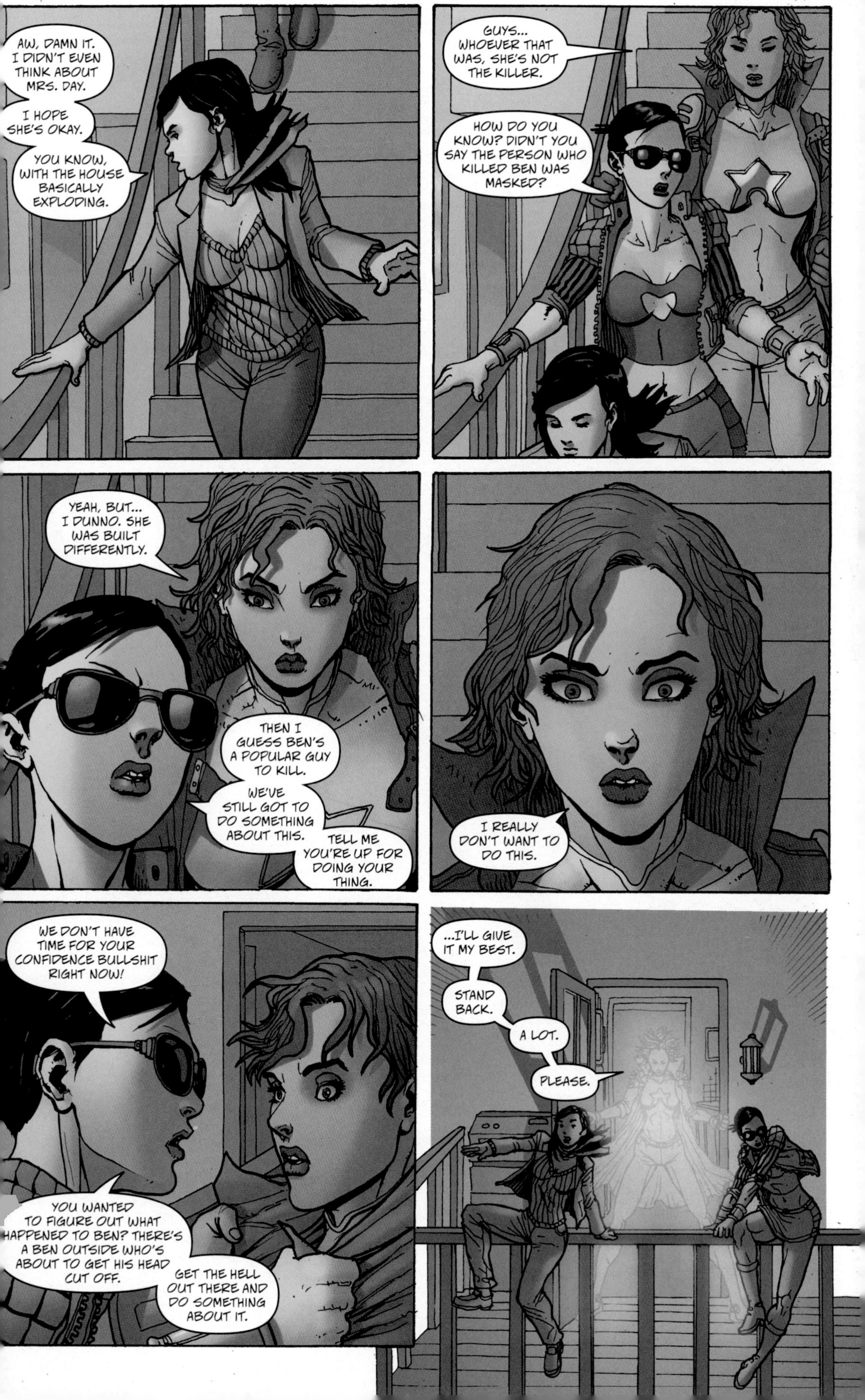
AW, DAMN IT. I DIDN'T EVEN THINK ABOUT MRS. DAY.
I HOPE SHE'S OKAY.
YOU KNOW, WITH THE HOUSE BASICALLY EXPLODING.
GUYS... WHOEVER THAT WAS, SHE'S NOT THE KILLER.
HOW DO YOU KNOW? DIDN'T YOU SAY THE PERSON WHO KILLED BEN WAS MASKED?
YEAH, BUT... I DUNNO. SHE WAS BUILT DIFFERENTLY.
THEN I GUESS BEN'S A POPULAR GUY TO KILL.
WE'VE STILL GOT TO DO SOMETHING ABOUT THIS.
TELL ME YOU'RE UP FOR DOING YOUR THING.
I REALLY DON'T WANT TO DO THIS.
WE DON'T HAVE TIME FOR YOUR CONFIDENCE BULLSHIT RIGHT NOW!
YOU WANTED TO FIGURE OUT WHAT HAPPENED TO BEN? THERE'S A BEN OUTSIDE WHO'S ABOUT TO GET HIS HEAD CUT OFF.
GET THE HELL OUT THERE AND DO SOMETHING ABOUT IT.
...I'LL GIVE IT MY BEST.
STAND BACK.
A LOT.
PLEASE.

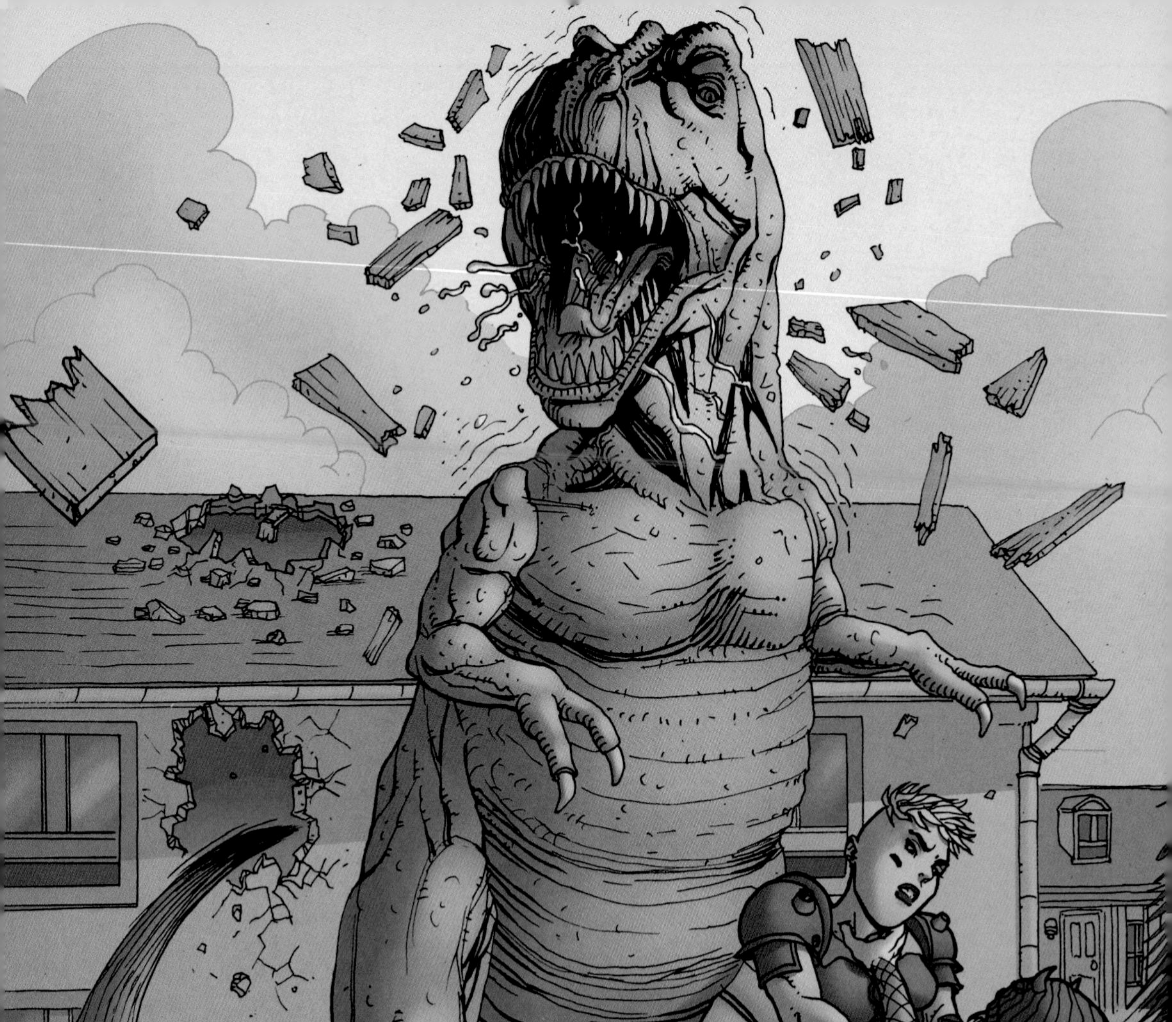
FUUU-
UUUUUUU-
UUUCK.

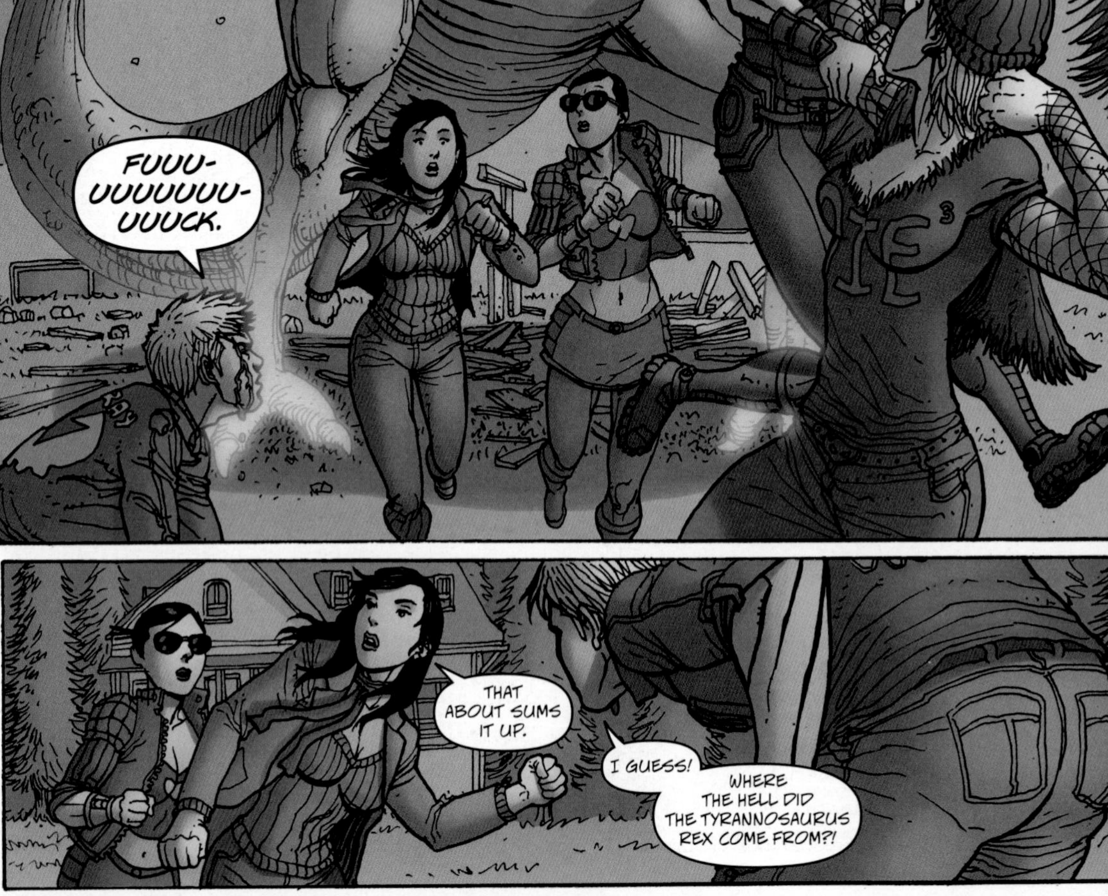
THAT ABOUT SUMS IT UP.
I GUESS!
WHERE THE HELL DID THE TYRANNOSAURUS REX COME FROM?!

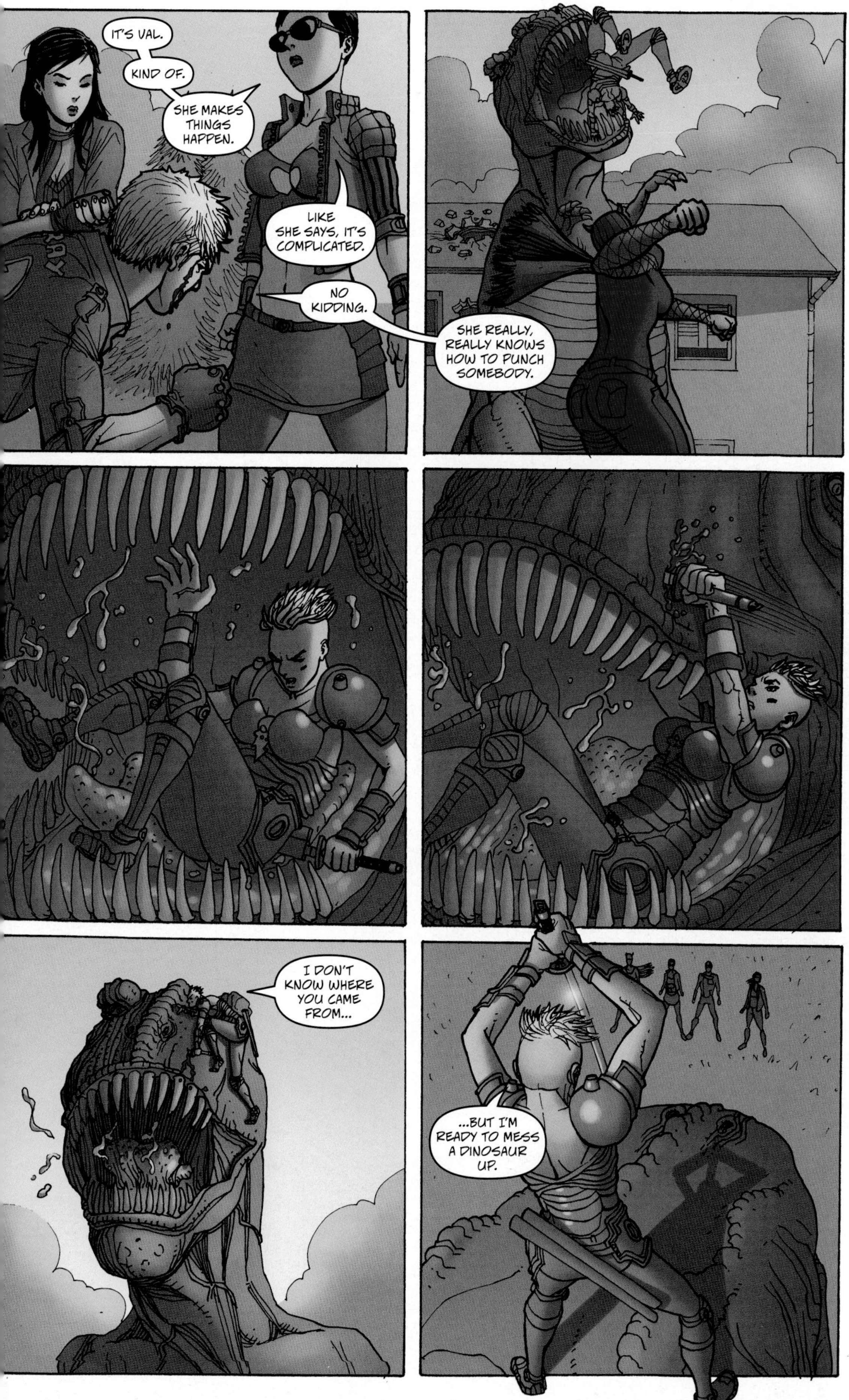
IT'S VAL.
KIND OF.
SHE MAKES THINGS HAPPEN.
LIKE SHE SAYS, IT'S COMPLICATED.
NO KIDDING.
SHE REALLY, REALLY KNOWS HOW TO PUNCH SOMEBODY.
I DON'T KNOW WHERE YOU CAME FROM...
...BUT I'M READY TO MESS A DINOSAUR UP.

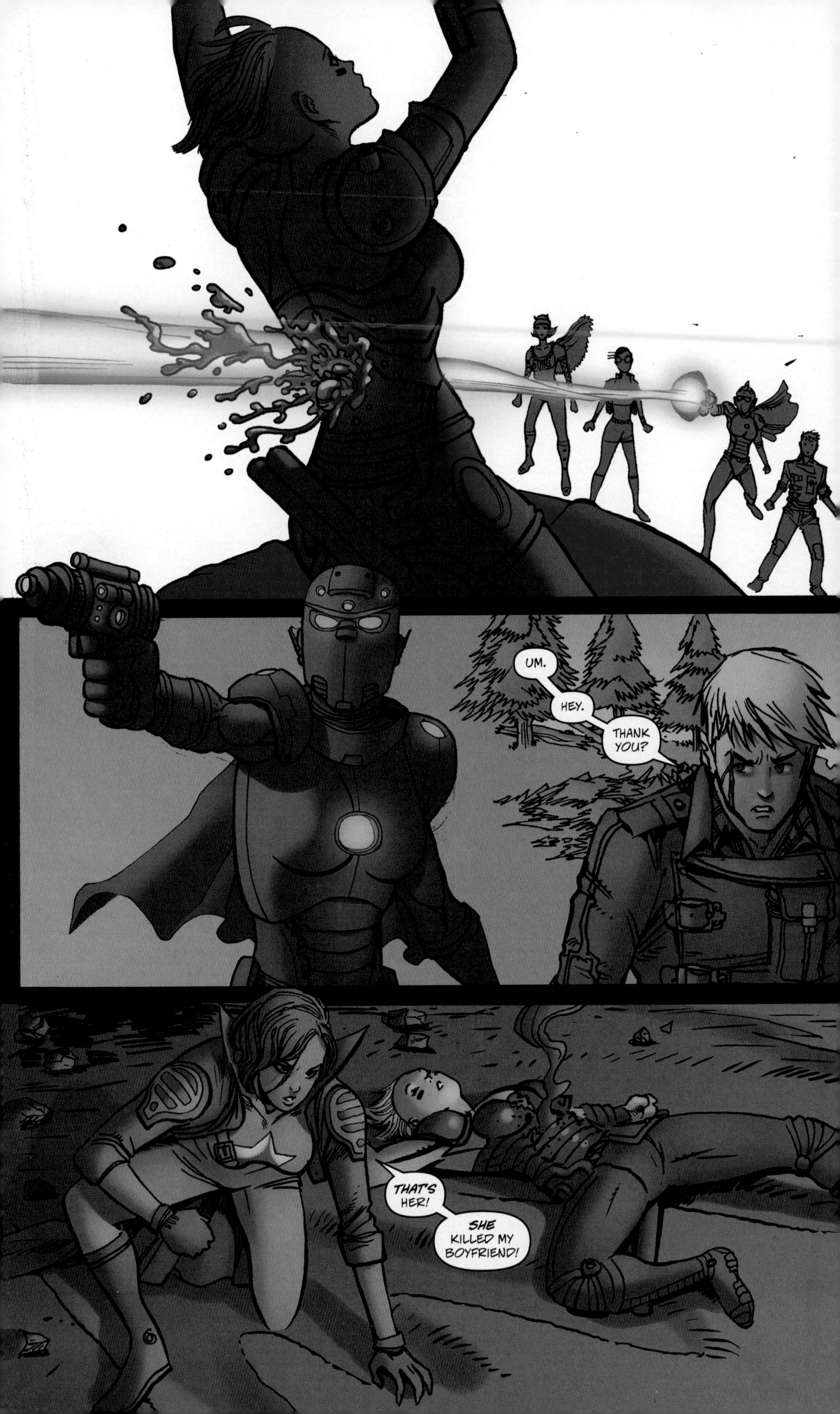
UM.
HEY.
THANK YOU?
THAT'S HER!
SHE KILLED MY BOYFRIEND!

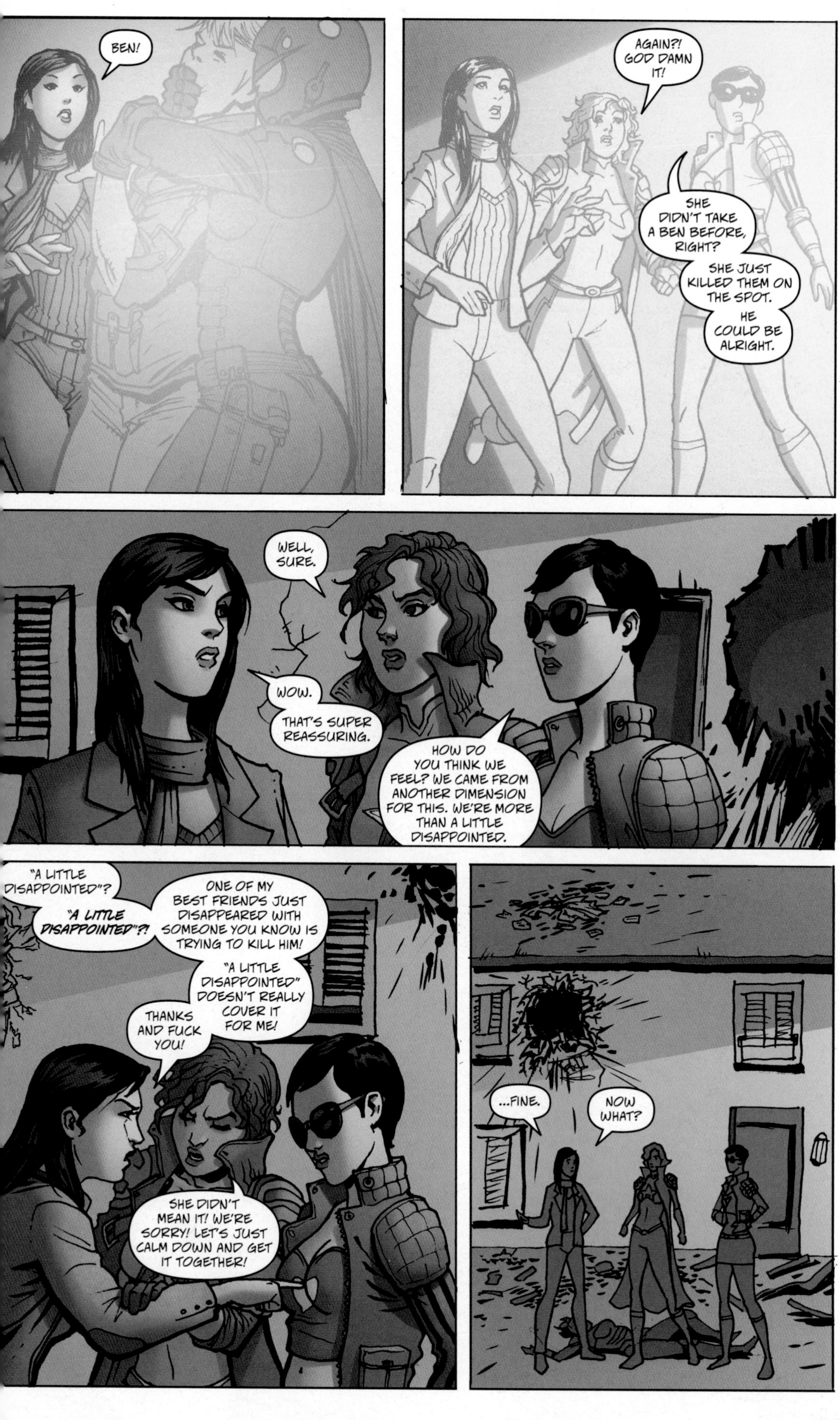
BEN!
AGAIN?! GOD DAMN IT!
SHE DIDN'T TAKE A BEN BEFORE, RIGHT?
SHE JUST KILLED THEM ON THE SPOT.
HE COULD BE ALRIGHT.
WELL, SURE.
WOW.
THAT'S SUPER REASSURING.
HOW DO YOU THINK WE FEEL? WE CAME FROM ANOTHER DIMENSION FOR THIS. WE'RE MORE THAN A LITTLE DISAPPOINTED.
"A LITTLE DISAPPOINTED"?
"A LITTLE DISAPPOINTED"?!
ONE OF MY BEST FRIENDS JUST DISAPPEARED WITH SOMEONE YOU KNOW IS TRYING TO KILL HIM!
"A LITTLE DISAPPOINTED" DOESN'T REALLY COVER IT FOR ME!
THANKS AND FUCK YOU!
SHE DIDN'T MEAN IT! WE'RE SORRY! LET'S JUST CALM DOWN AND GET IT TOGETHER!
...FINE.
NOW WHAT?

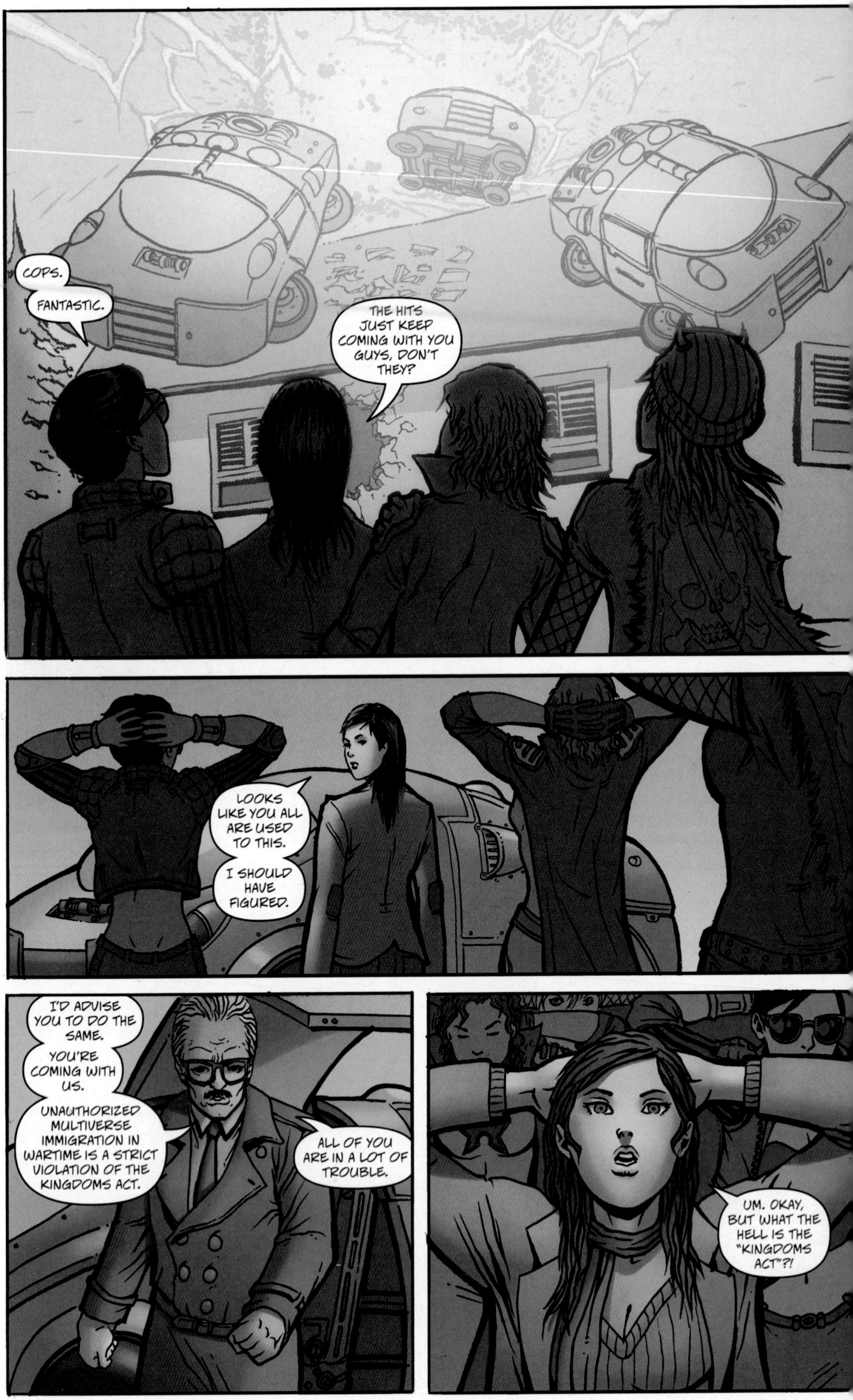
COPS.
FANTASTIC.
THE HITS JUST KEEP COMING WITH YOU GUYS, DON'T THEY?
LOOKS LIKE YOU ALL ARE USED TO THIS.
I SHOULD HAVE FIGURED.
I'D ADVISE YOU TO DO THE SAME.
YOU'RE COMING WITH US.
UNAUTHORIZED MULTIVERSE IMMIGRATION IN WARTIME IS A STRICT VIOLATION OF THE KINGDOMS ACT.
ALL OF YOU ARE IN A LOT OF TROUBLE.
UM. OKAY, BUT WHAT THE HELL IS THE "KINGDOMS ACT"?!

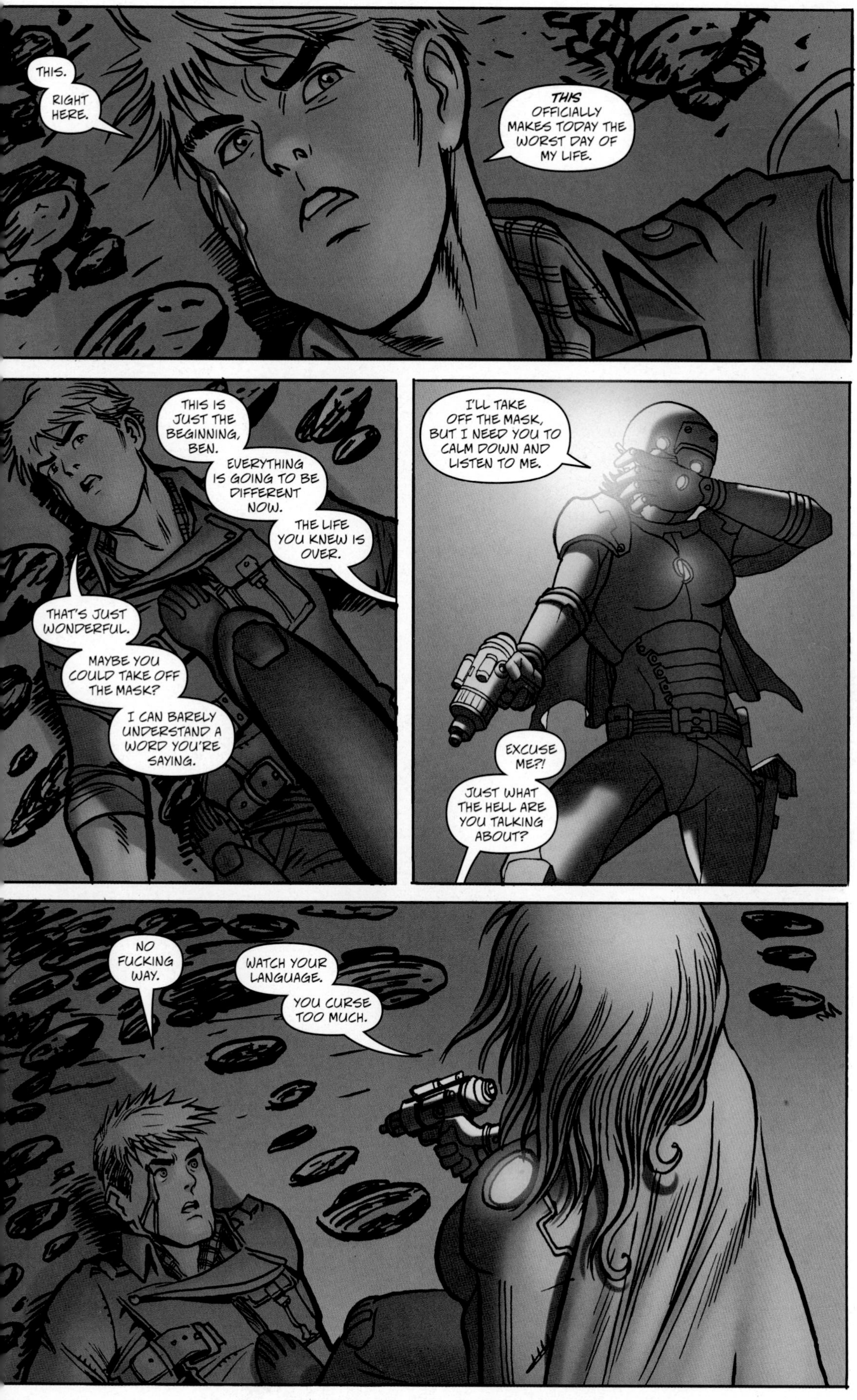

THIS.
RIGHT HERE.
THIS OFFICIALLY MAKES TODAY THE WORST DAY OF MY LIFE.
THIS IS JUST THE BEGINNING, BEN.
EVERYTHING IS GOING TO BE DIFFERENT NOW.
THE LIFE YOU KNEW IS OVER.
THAT'S JUST WONDERFUL.
MAYBE YOU COULD TAKE OFF THE MASK?
I CAN BARELY UNDERSTAND A WORD YOU'RE SAYING.
I'LL TAKE OFF THE MASK, BUT I NEED YOU TO CALM DOWN AND LISTEN TO ME.
EXCUSE ME?!
JUST WHAT THE HELL ARE YOU TALKING ABOUT?
NO FUCKING WAY.
WATCH YOUR LANGUAGE.
YOU CURSE TOO MUCH.

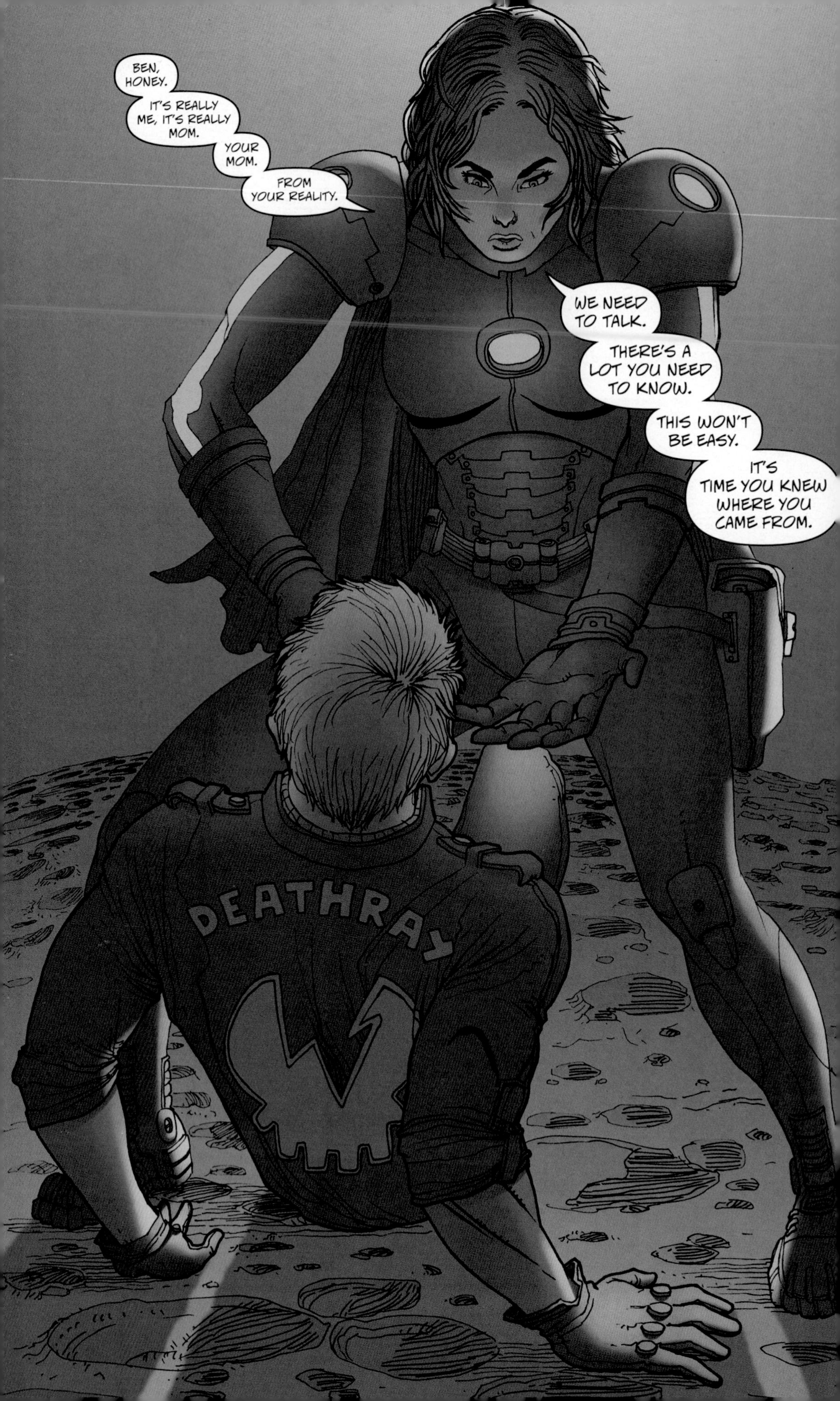
BEN, HONEY.
IT'S REALLY ME, IT'S REALLY MOM.
YOUR MOM.
FROM YOUR REALITY.
WE NEED TO TALK.
THERE'S A LOT YOU NEED TO KNOW.
THIS WON'T BE EASY.
IT'S TIME YOU KNEW WHERE YOU CAME FROM.
DEATHRAY

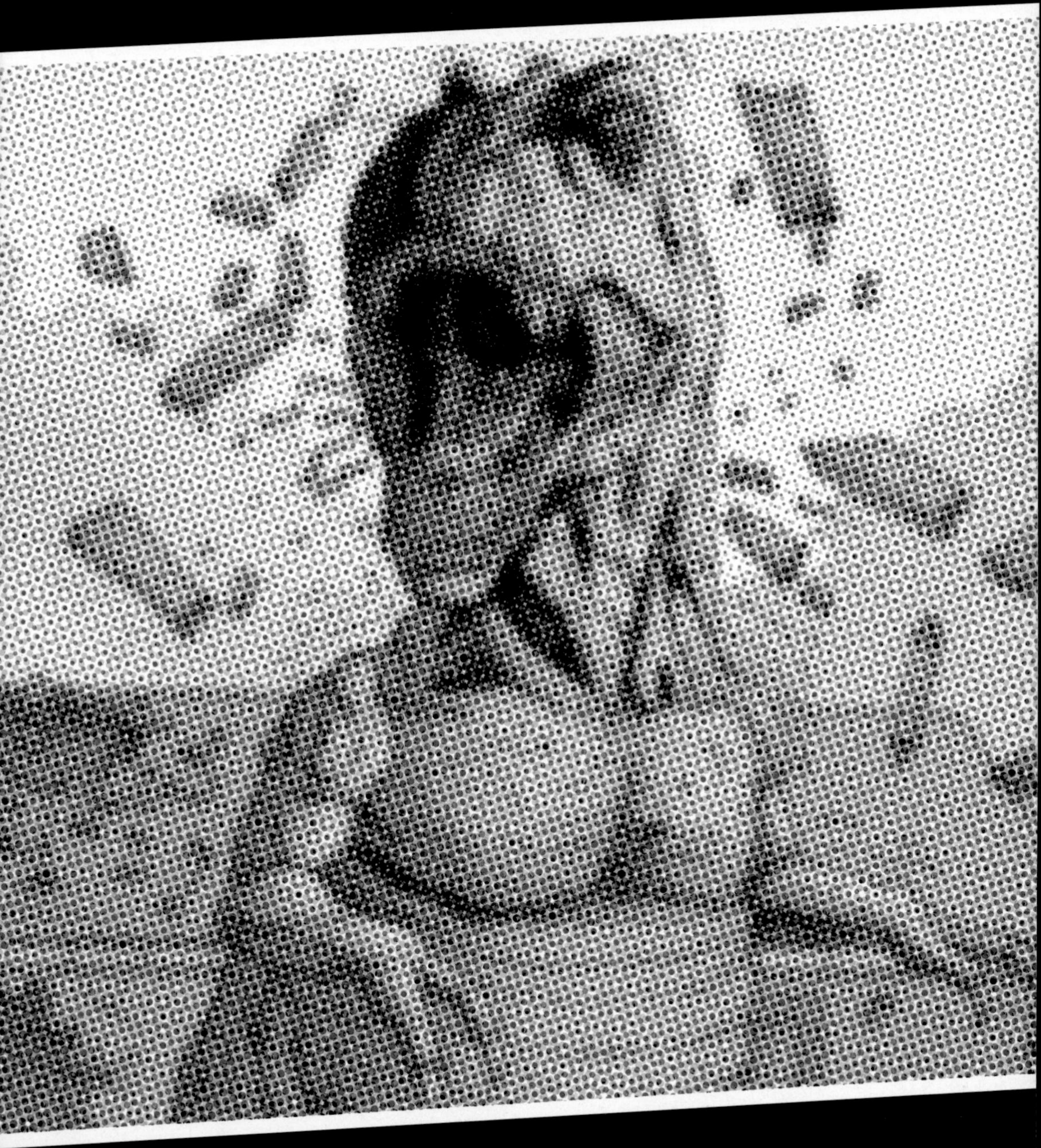

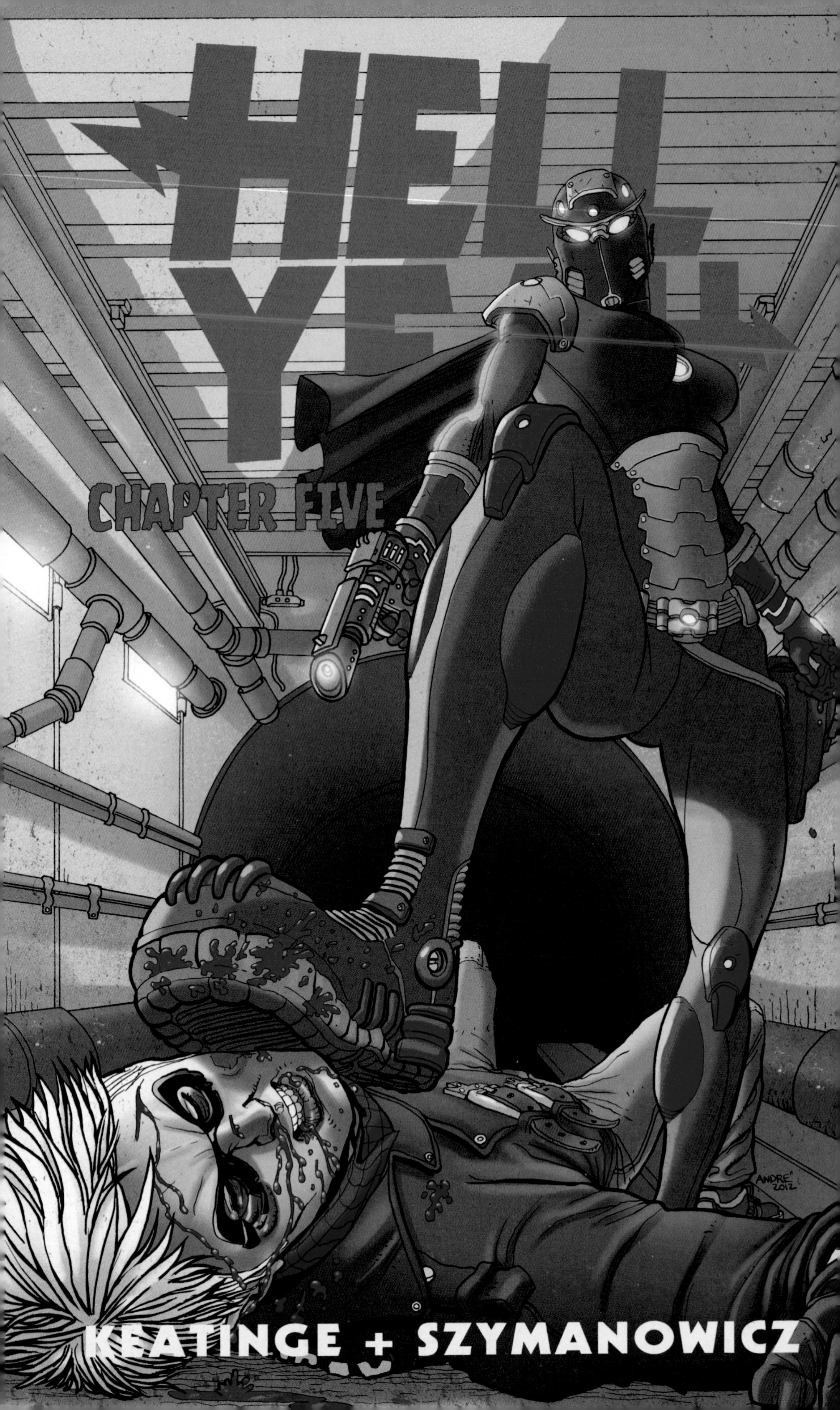
HELL YEAH
CHAPTER FIVE
ANDRÉ 2012
KEATINGE + SZYMANOWICZ

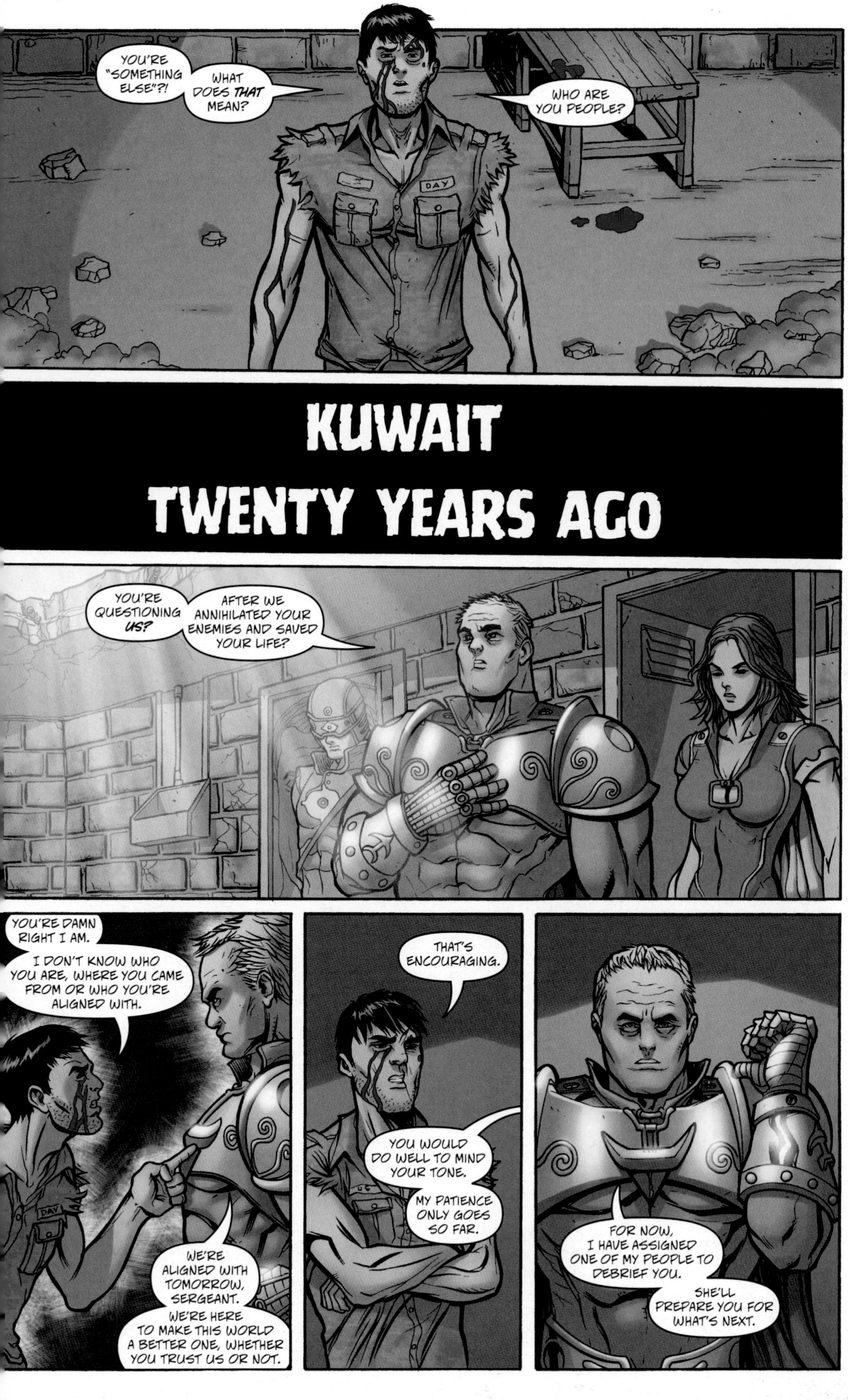
YOU'RE "SOMETHING ELSE"?!
WHAT DOES THAT MEAN?
WHO ARE YOU PEOPLE?
KUWAIT
TWENTY YEARS AGO
YOU'RE QUESTIONING US?
AFTER WE ANNIHILATED YOUR ENEMIES AND SAVED YOUR LIFE?
YOU'RE DAMN RIGHT I AM.
I DON'T KNOW WHO YOU ARE, WHERE YOU CAME FROM OR WHO YOU'RE ALIGNED WITH.
WE'RE ALIGNED WITH TOMORROW, SERGEANT.
WE'RE HERE TO MAKE THIS WORLD A BETTER ONE, WHETHER YOU TRUST US OR NOT.
THAT'S ENCOURAGING.
YOU WOULD DO WELL TO MIND YOUR TONE.
MY PATIENCE ONLY GOES SO FAR.
FOR NOW, I HAVE ASSIGNED ONE OF MY PEOPLE TO DEBRIEF YOU.
SHE'LL PREPARE YOU FOR WHAT'S NEXT.

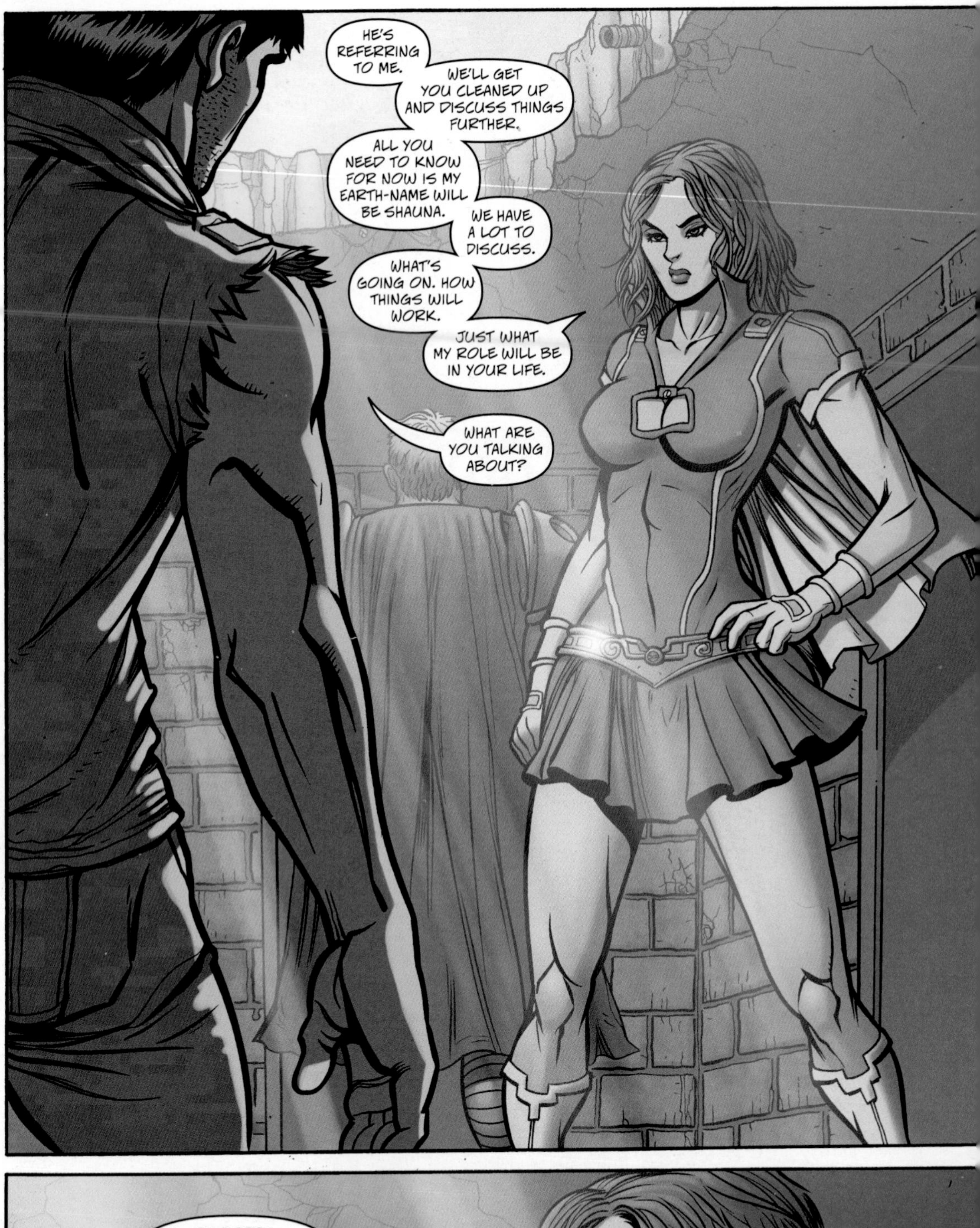
HE'S REFERRING TO ME.
WE'LL GET YOU CLEANED UP AND DISCUSS THINGS FURTHER.
ALL YOU NEED TO KNOW FOR NOW IS MY EARTH-NAME WILL BE SHAUNA.
WE HAVE A LOT TO DISCUSS.
WHAT'S GOING ON. HOW THINGS WILL WORK.
JUST WHAT MY ROLE WILL BE IN YOUR LIFE.
WHAT ARE YOU TALKING ABOUT?

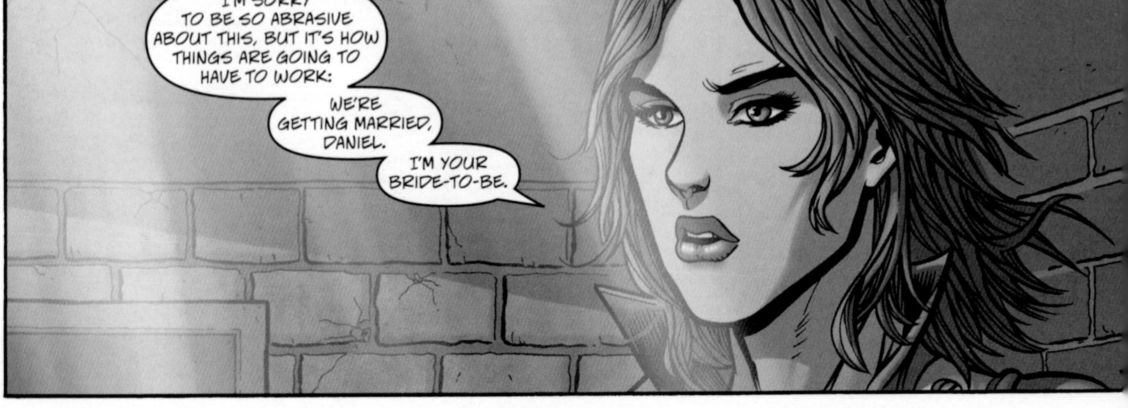
I'M SORRY TO BE SO ABRASIVE ABOUT THIS, BUT IT'S HOW THINGS ARE GOING TO HAVE TO WORK:
WE'RE GETTING MARRIED, DANIEL.
I'M YOUR BRIDE-TO-BE.

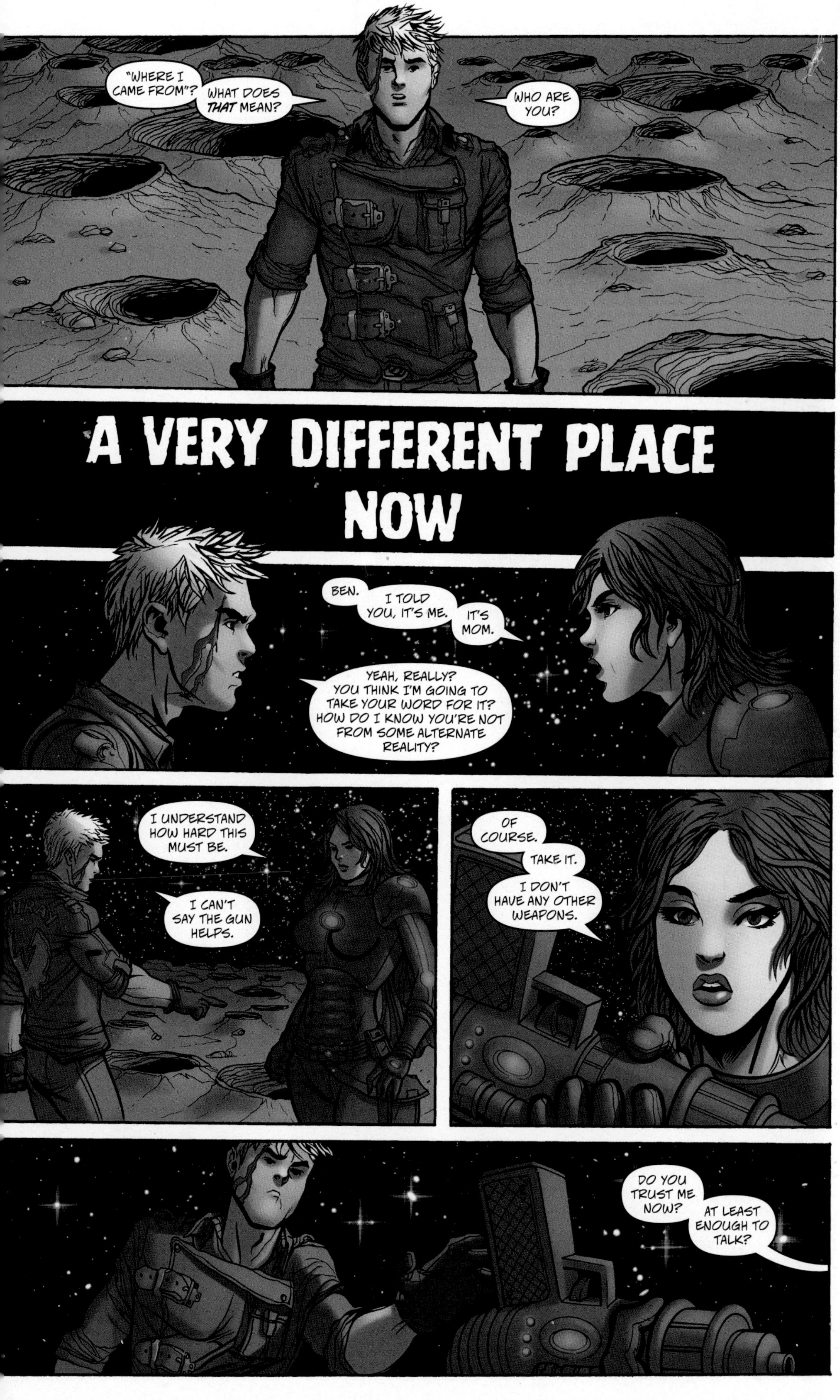
"WHERE I CAME FROM"?
WHAT DOES *THAT* MEAN?
WHO ARE YOU?
A VERY DIFFERENT PLACE NOW
BEN.
I TOLD YOU, IT'S ME.
IT'S MOM.
YEAH, REALLY? YOU THINK I'M GOING TO TAKE YOUR WORD FOR IT? HOW DO I KNOW YOU'RE NOT FROM SOME ALTERNATE REALITY?
I UNDERSTAND HOW HARD THIS MUST BE.
I CAN'T SAY THE GUN HELPS.
OF COURSE.
TAKE IT.
I DON'T HAVE ANY OTHER WEAPONS.
DO YOU TRUST ME NOW?
AT LEAST ENOUGH TO TALK?

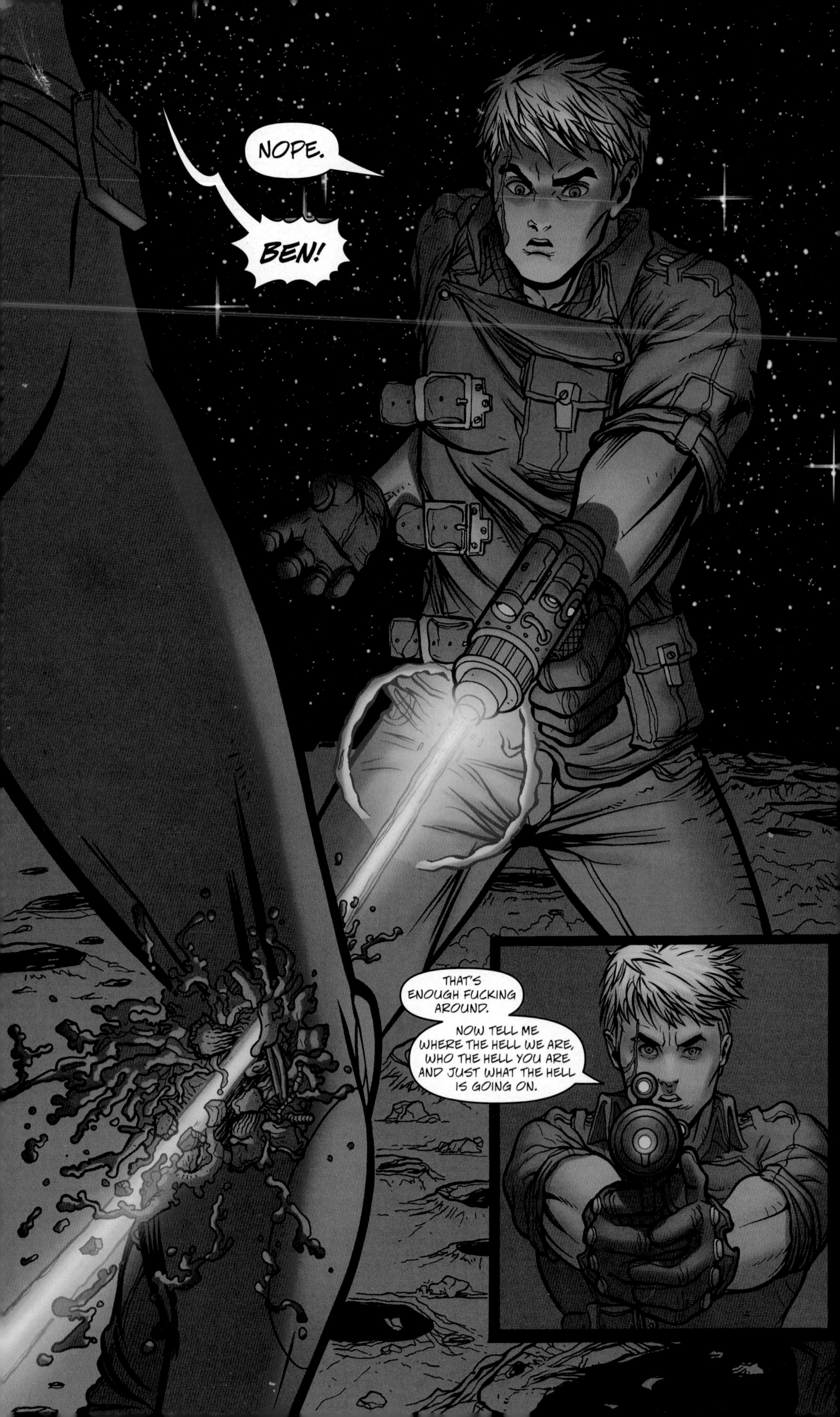
NOPE.
BEN!
THAT'S ENOUGH FUCKING AROUND.
NOW TELL ME WHERE THE HELL WE ARE, WHO THE HELL YOU ARE AND JUST WHAT THE HELL IS GOING ON.

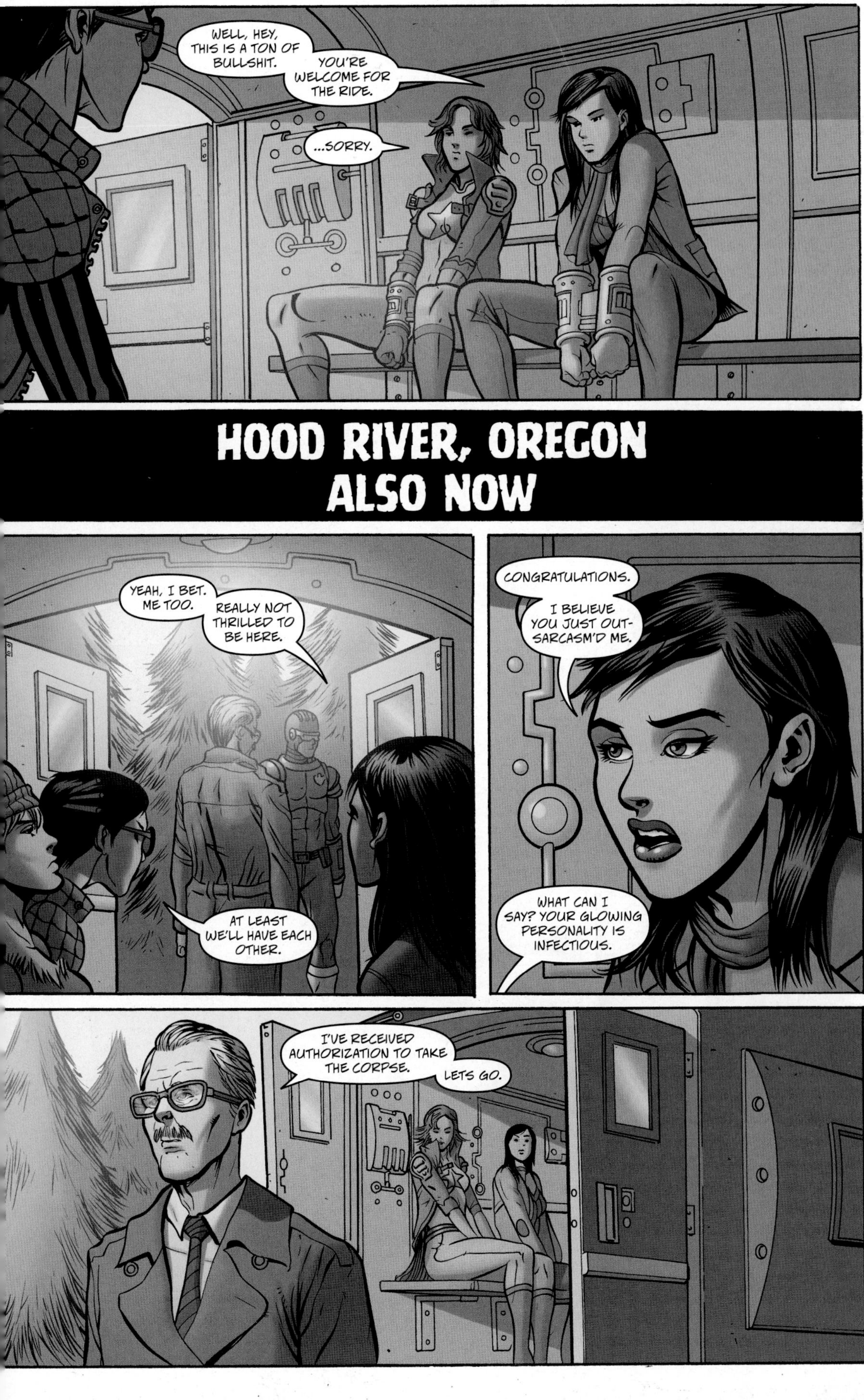
WELL, HEY, THIS IS A TON OF BULLSHIT.
YOU'RE WELCOME FOR THE RIDE.
...SORRY.
HOOD RIVER, OREGON
ALSO NOW
YEAH, I BET. ME TOO.
REALLY NOT THRILLED TO BE HERE.
AT LEAST WE'LL HAVE EACH OTHER.
CONGRATULATIONS.
I BELIEVE YOU JUST OUT-SARCASM'D ME.
WHAT CAN I SAY? YOUR GLOWING PERSONALITY IS INFECTIOUS.
I'VE RECEIVED AUTHORIZATION TO TAKE THE CORPSE.
LETS GO.

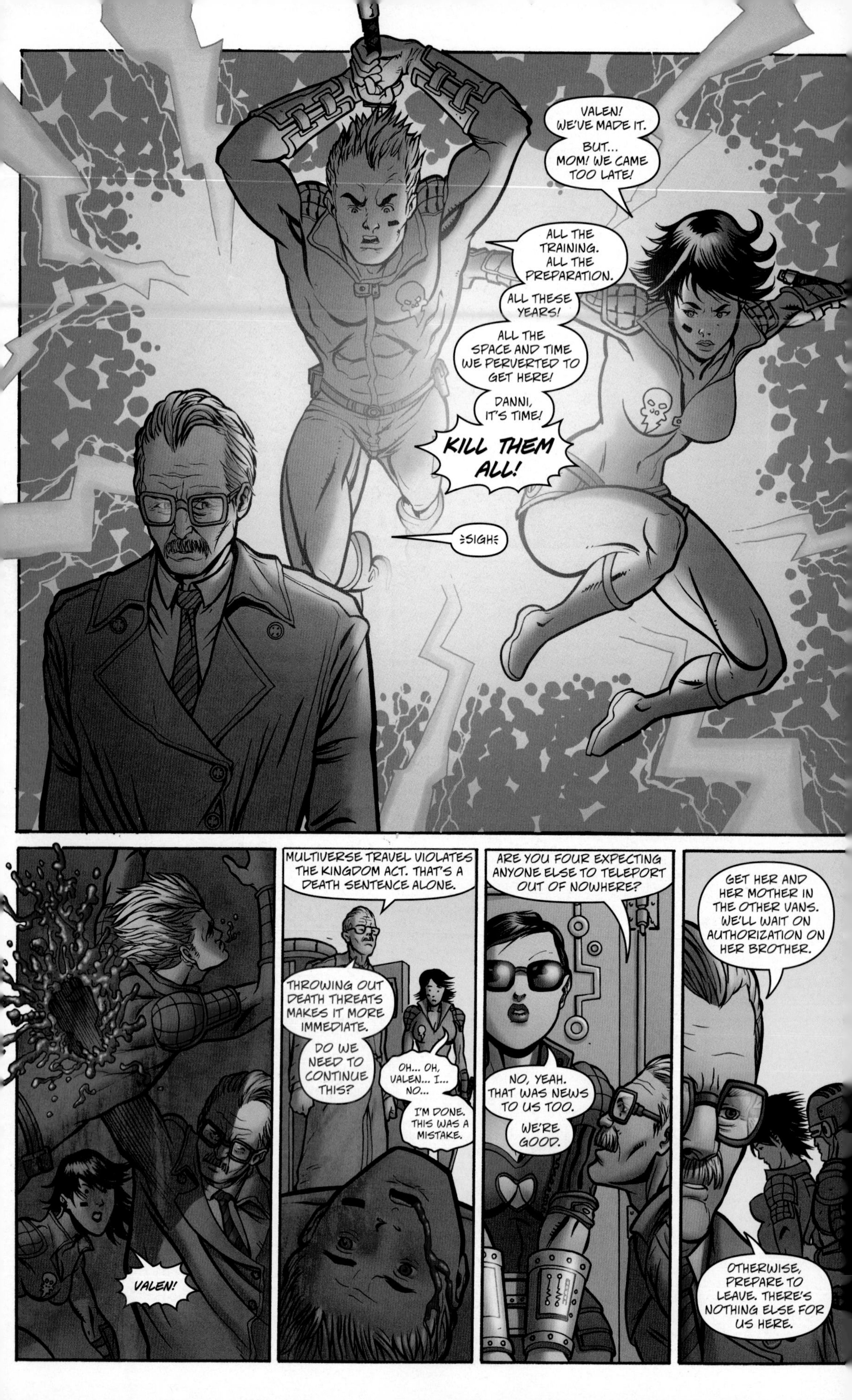
VALEN! WE'VE MADE IT.
BUT... MOM! WE CAME TOO LATE!
ALL THE TRAINING. ALL THE PREPARATION.
ALL THESE YEARS!
ALL THE SPACE AND TIME WE PERVERTED TO GET HERE!
DANNI, IT'S TIME!
KILL THEM ALL!
SIGH
VALEN!
MULTIVERSE TRAVEL VIOLATES THE KINGDOM ACT. THAT'S A DEATH SENTENCE ALONE.
THROWING OUT DEATH THREATS MAKES IT MORE IMMEDIATE.
DO WE NEED TO CONTINUE THIS?
OH... OH, VALEN... I... NO...
I'M DONE. THIS WAS A MISTAKE.
ARE YOU FOUR EXPECTING ANYONE ELSE TO TELEPORT OUT OF NOWHERE?
NO, YEAH. THAT WAS NEWS TO US TOO.
WE'RE GOOD.
GET HER AND HER MOTHER IN THE OTHER VANS. WE'LL WAIT ON AUTHORIZATION ON HER BROTHER.
OTHERWISE, PREPARE TO LEAVE. THERE'S NOTHING ELSE FOR US HERE.

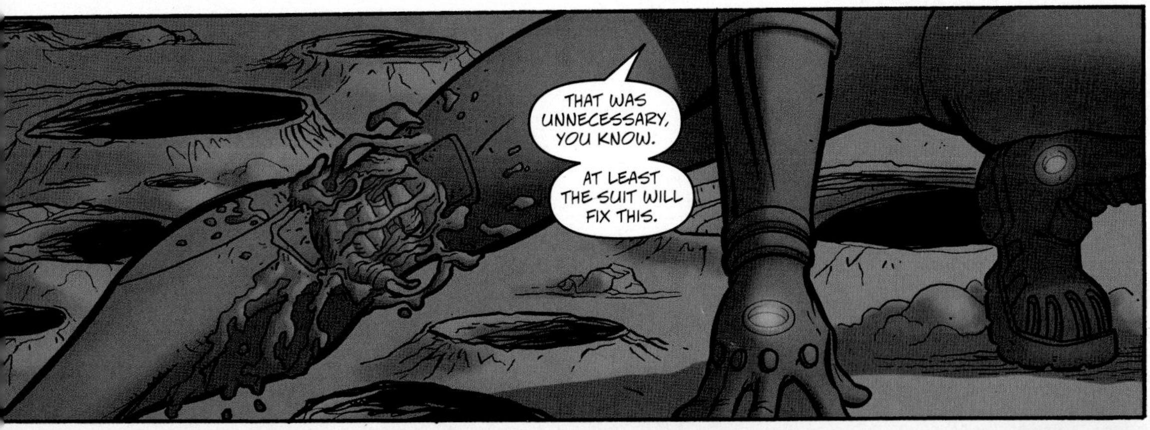
THAT WAS UNNECESSARY, YOU KNOW.
AT LEAST THE SUIT WILL FIX THIS.

IMAGE COMICS PRESENTS

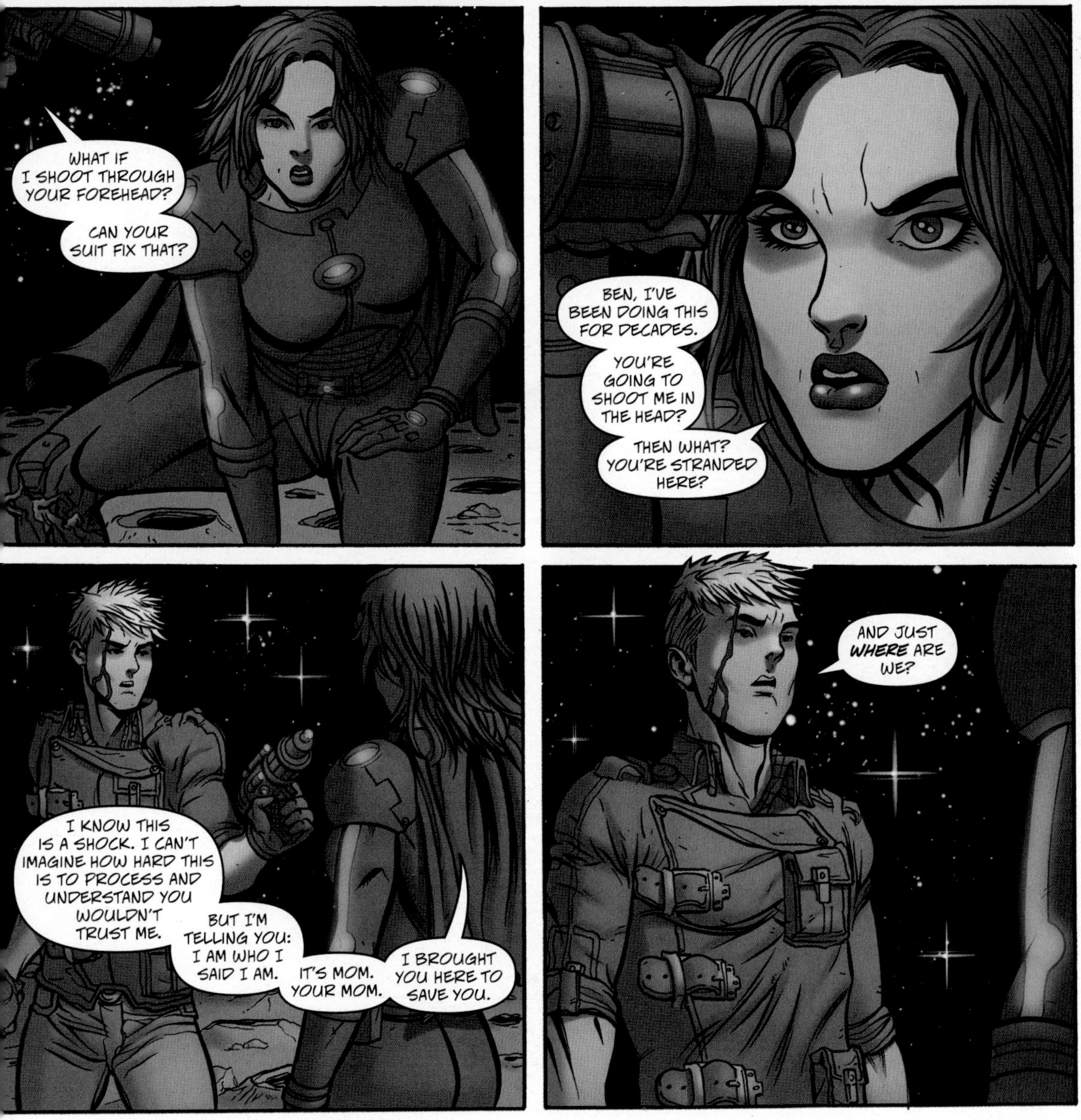
WHAT IF I SHOOT THROUGH YOUR FOREHEAD?
CAN YOUR SUIT FIX THAT?
BEN, I'VE BEEN DOING THIS FOR DECADES.
YOU'RE GOING TO SHOOT ME IN THE HEAD?
THEN WHAT? YOU'RE STRANDED HERE?
I KNOW THIS IS A SHOCK. I CAN'T IMAGINE HOW HARD THIS IS TO PROCESS AND UNDERSTAND YOU WOULDN'T TRUST ME.
BUT I'M TELLING YOU: I AM WHO I SAID I AM.
IT'S MOM. YOUR MOM.
I BROUGHT YOU HERE TO SAVE YOU.
AND JUST WHERE ARE WE?

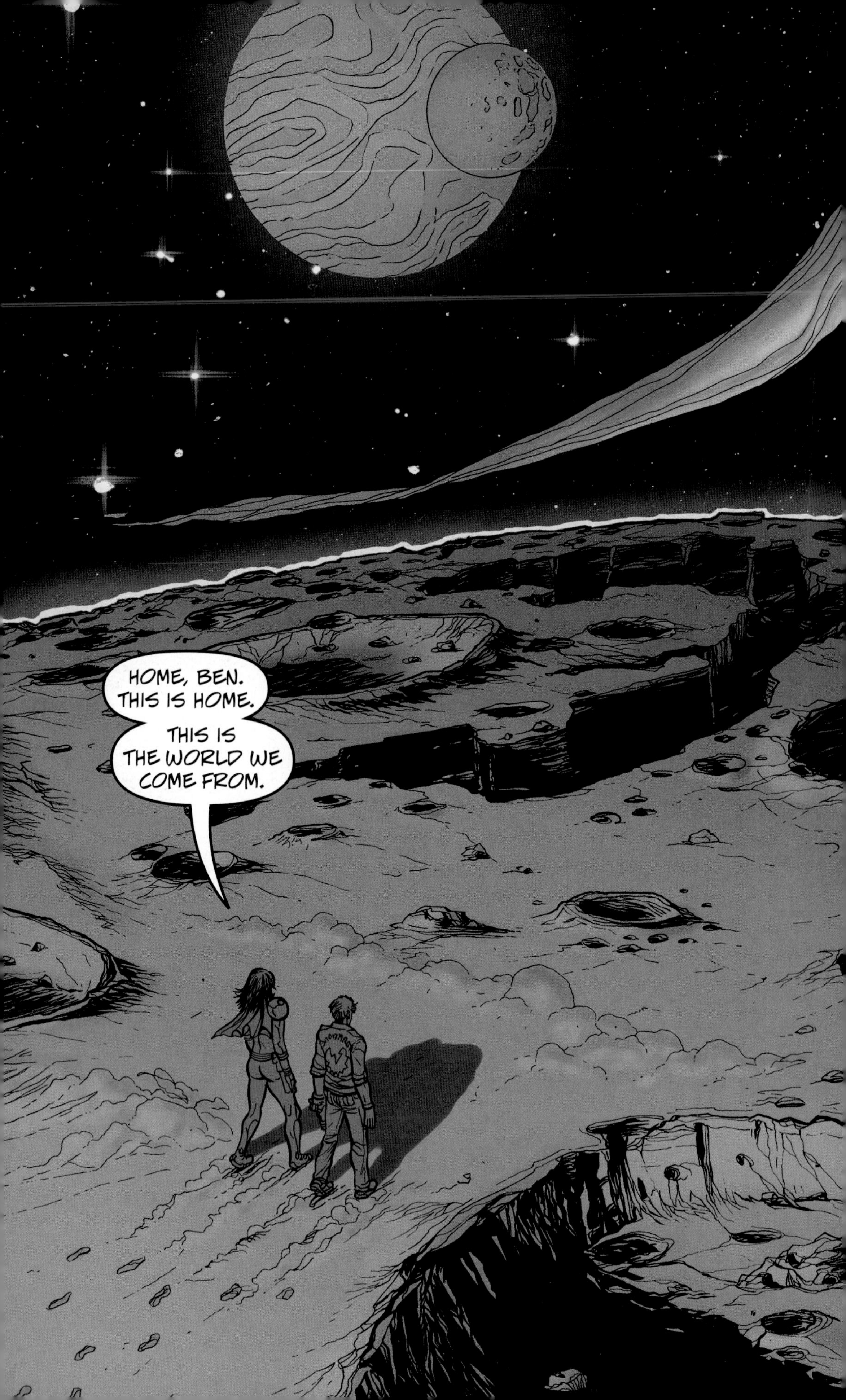
HOME, BEN. THIS IS HOME.
THIS IS THE WORLD WE COME FROM.

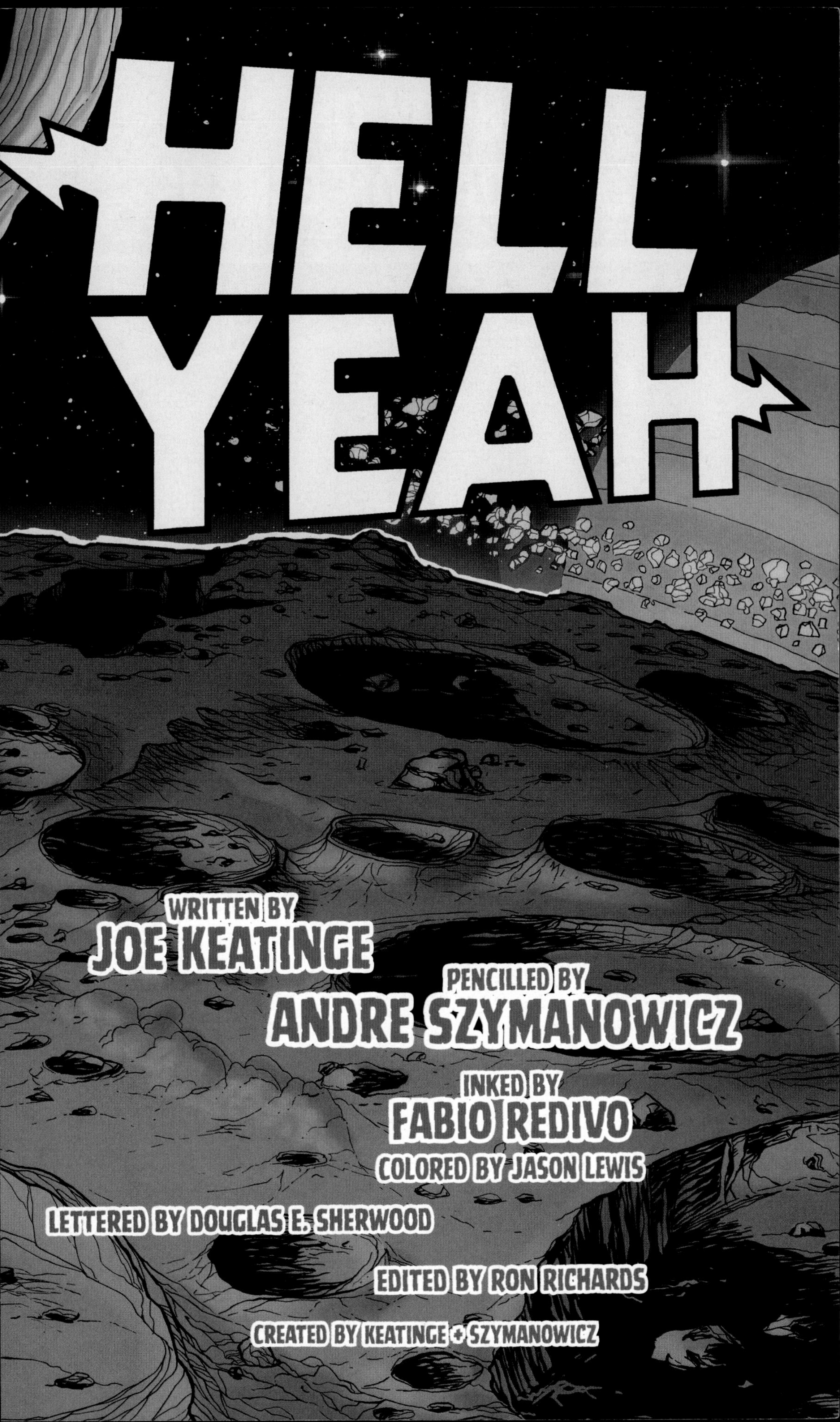
HELL YEAH
WRITTEN BY
JOE KEATINGE
PENCILLED BY
ANDRE SZYMANOWICZ
INKED BY
FABIO REDIVO
COLORED BY JASON LEWIS
LETTERED BY DOUGLAS E. SHERWOOD
EDITED BY RON RICHARDS
CREATED BY KEATINGE + SZYMANOWICZ

BOOK ONE
LAST DAY ON EARTHS

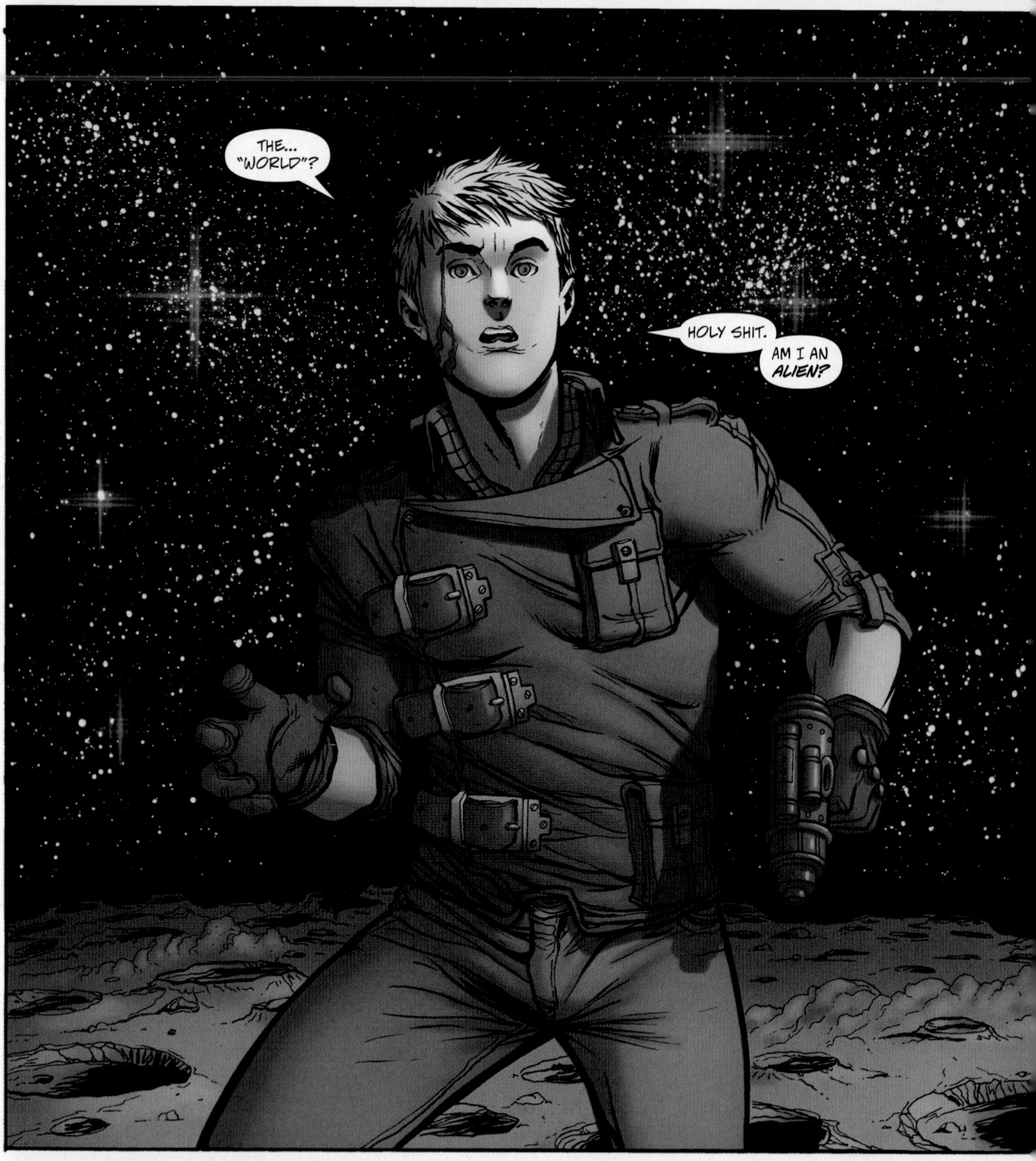
THE... "WORLD"?
HOLY SHIT.
AM I AN ALIEN?

CHAPTER FIVE
THE WORLD THEY LEFT

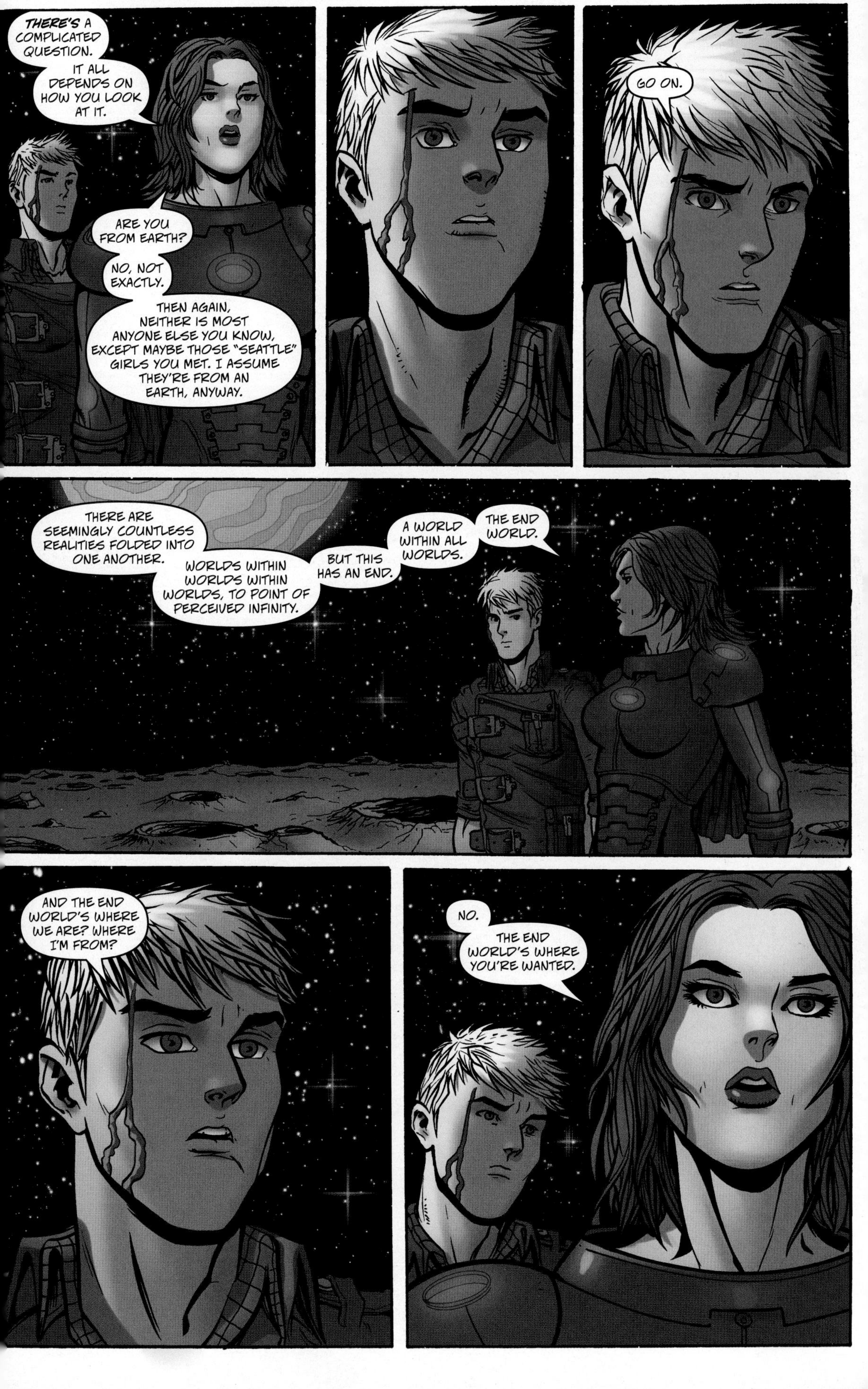
THERE'S A COMPLICATED QUESTION.
IT ALL DEPENDS ON HOW YOU LOOK AT IT.
ARE YOU FROM EARTH?
NO, NOT EXACTLY.
THEN AGAIN, NEITHER IS MOST ANYONE ELSE YOU KNOW, EXCEPT MAYBE THOSE "SEATTLE" GIRLS YOU MET. I ASSUME THEY'RE FROM AN EARTH, ANYWAY.
GO ON.
THERE ARE SEEMINGLY COUNTLESS REALITIES FOLDED INTO ONE ANOTHER.
WORLDS WITHIN WORLDS WITHIN WORLDS, TO POINT OF PERCEIVED INFINITY.
BUT THIS HAS AN END.
A WORLD WITHIN ALL WORLDS.
THE END WORLD.
AND THE END WORLD'S WHERE WE ARE? WHERE I'M FROM?
NO.
THE END WORLD'S WHERE YOU'RE WANTED.

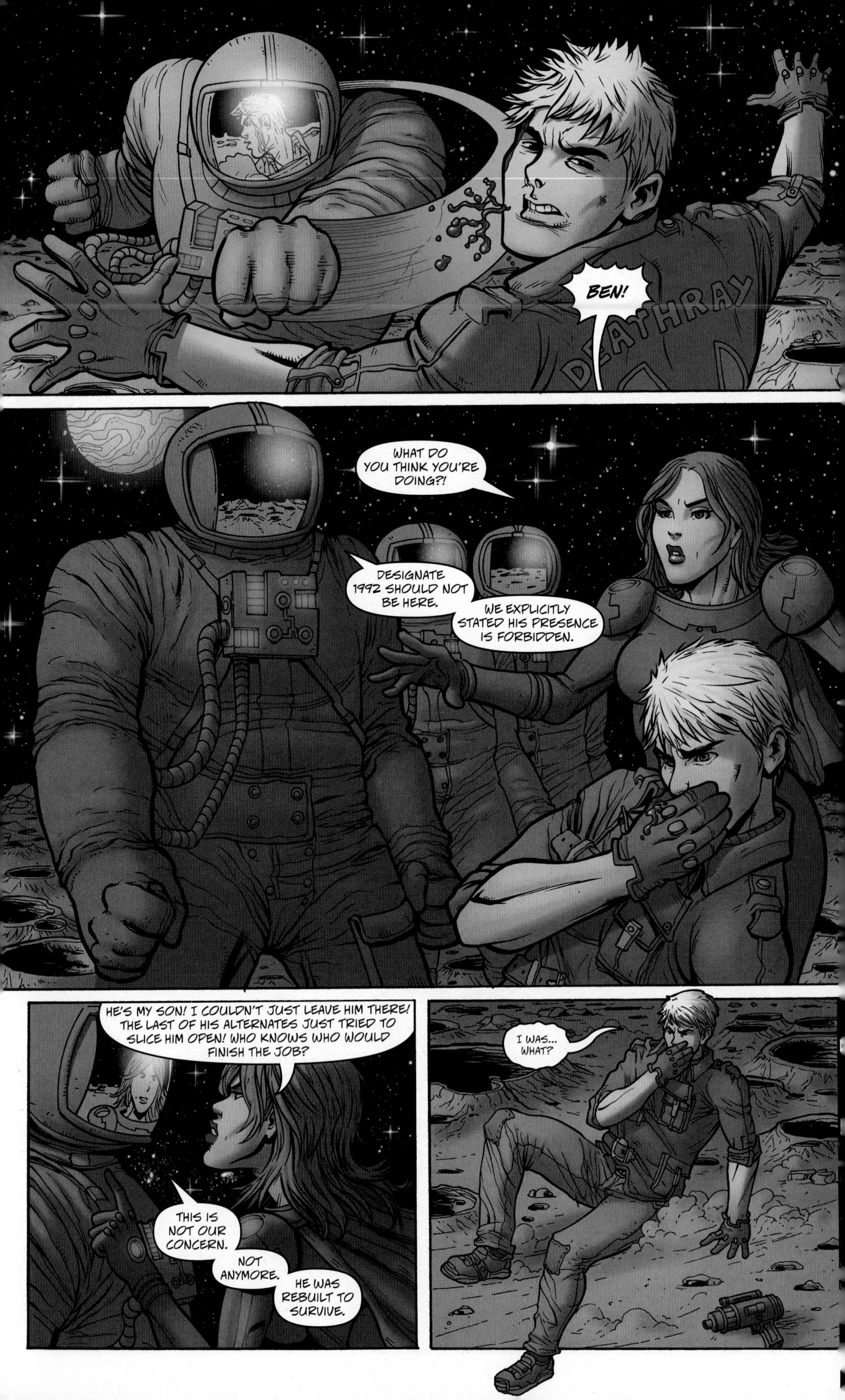
BEN!
WHAT DO YOU THINK YOU'RE DOING?!
DESIGNATE 1992 SHOULD NOT BE HERE.
WE EXPLICITLY STATED HIS PRESENCE IS FORBIDDEN.
HE'S MY SON! I COULDN'T JUST LEAVE HIM THERE! THE LAST OF HIS ALTERNATES JUST TRIED TO SLICE HIM OPEN! WHO KNOWS WHO WOULD FINISH THE JOB?
THIS IS NOT OUR CONCERN.
NOT ANYMORE.
HE WAS REBUILT TO SURVIVE.
I WAS... WHAT?

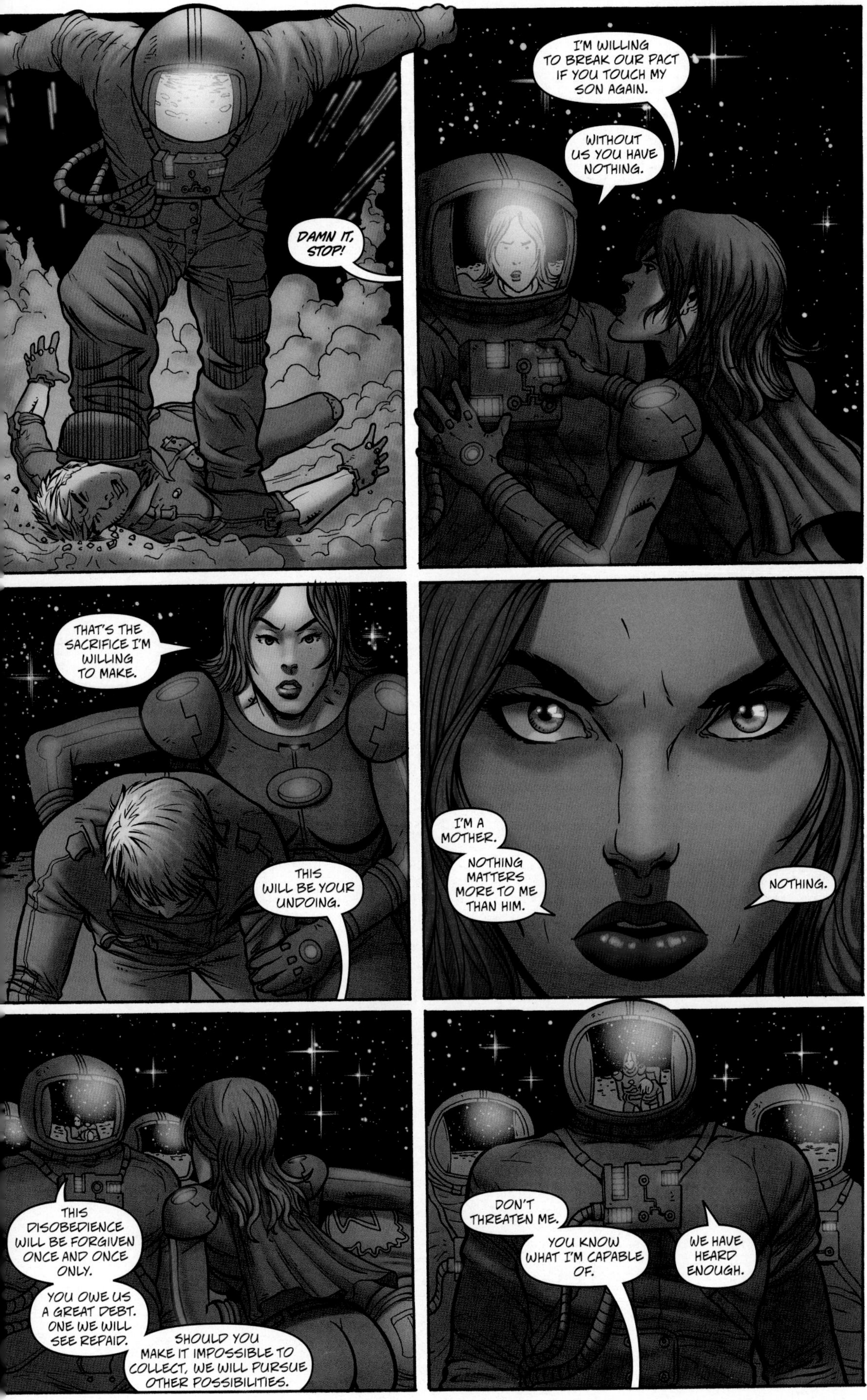
DAMN IT, STOP!
I'M WILLING TO BREAK OUR PACT IF YOU TOUCH MY SON AGAIN.
WITHOUT US YOU HAVE NOTHING.
THAT'S THE SACRIFICE I'M WILLING TO MAKE.
THIS WILL BE YOUR UNDOING.
I'M A MOTHER.
NOTHING MATTERS MORE TO ME THAN HIM.
NOTHING.
THIS DISOBEDIENCE WILL BE FORGIVEN ONCE AND ONCE ONLY.
YOU OWE US A GREAT DEBT. ONE WE WILL SEE REPAID.
SHOULD YOU MAKE IT IMPOSSIBLE TO COLLECT, WE WILL PURSUE OTHER POSSIBILITIES.
DON'T THREATEN ME.
YOU KNOW WHAT I'M CAPABLE OF.
WE HAVE HEARD ENOUGH.

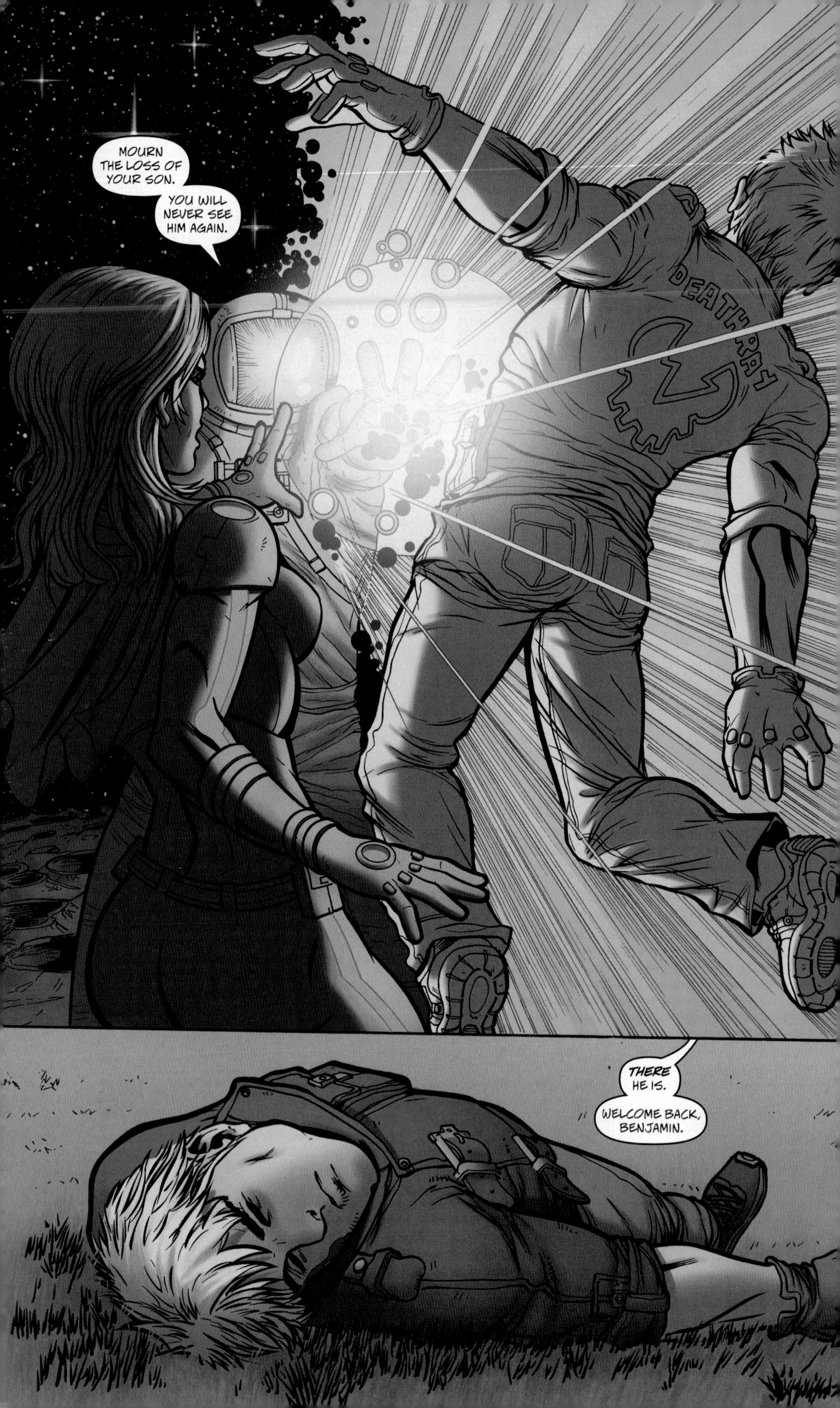
MOURN THE LOSS OF YOUR SON.
YOU WILL NEVER SEE HIM AGAIN.
DEATH RAY
THERE HE IS.
WELCOME BACK, BENJAMIN.

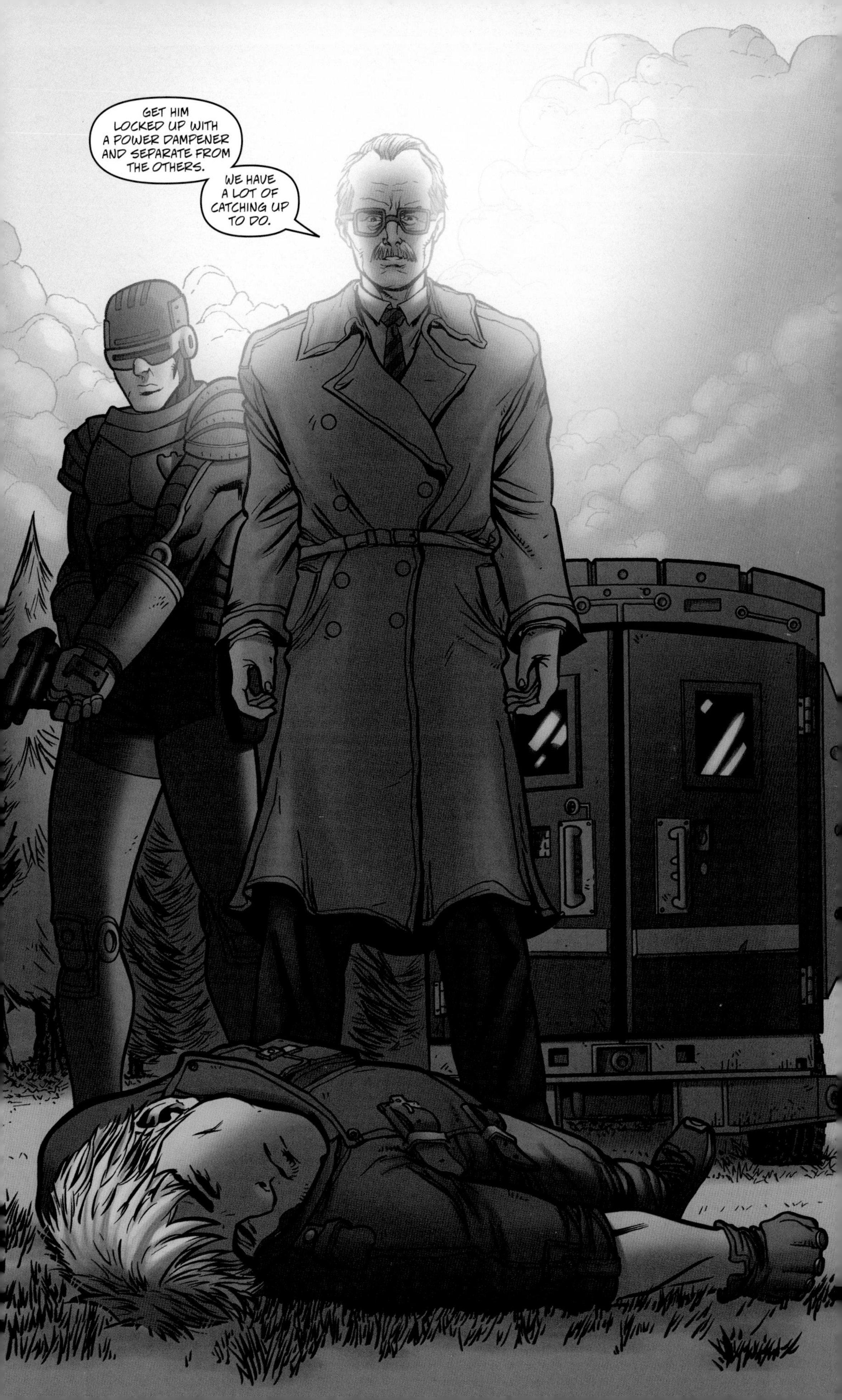
GET HIM LOCKED UP WITH A POWER DAMPENER AND SEPARATE FROM THE OTHERS.
WE HAVE A LOT OF CATCHING UP TO DO.

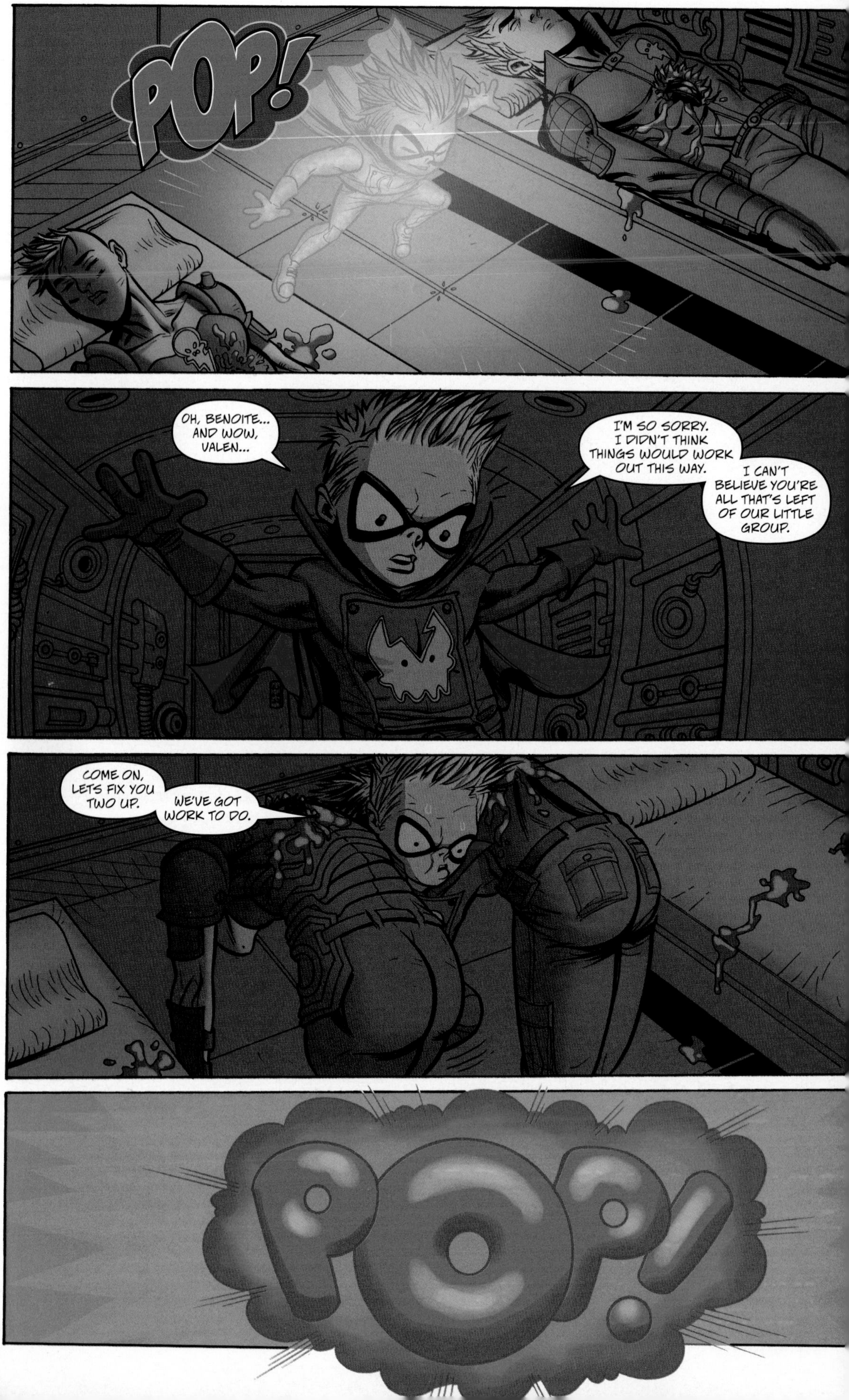
POP!
OH, BENOITE... AND WOW, VALEN...
I'M SO SORRY. I DIDN'T THINK THINGS WOULD WORK OUT THIS WAY.
I CAN'T BELIEVE YOU'RE ALL THAT'S LEFT OF OUR LITTLE GROUP.
COME ON, LETS FIX YOU TWO UP.
WE'VE GOT WORK TO DO.
POP!

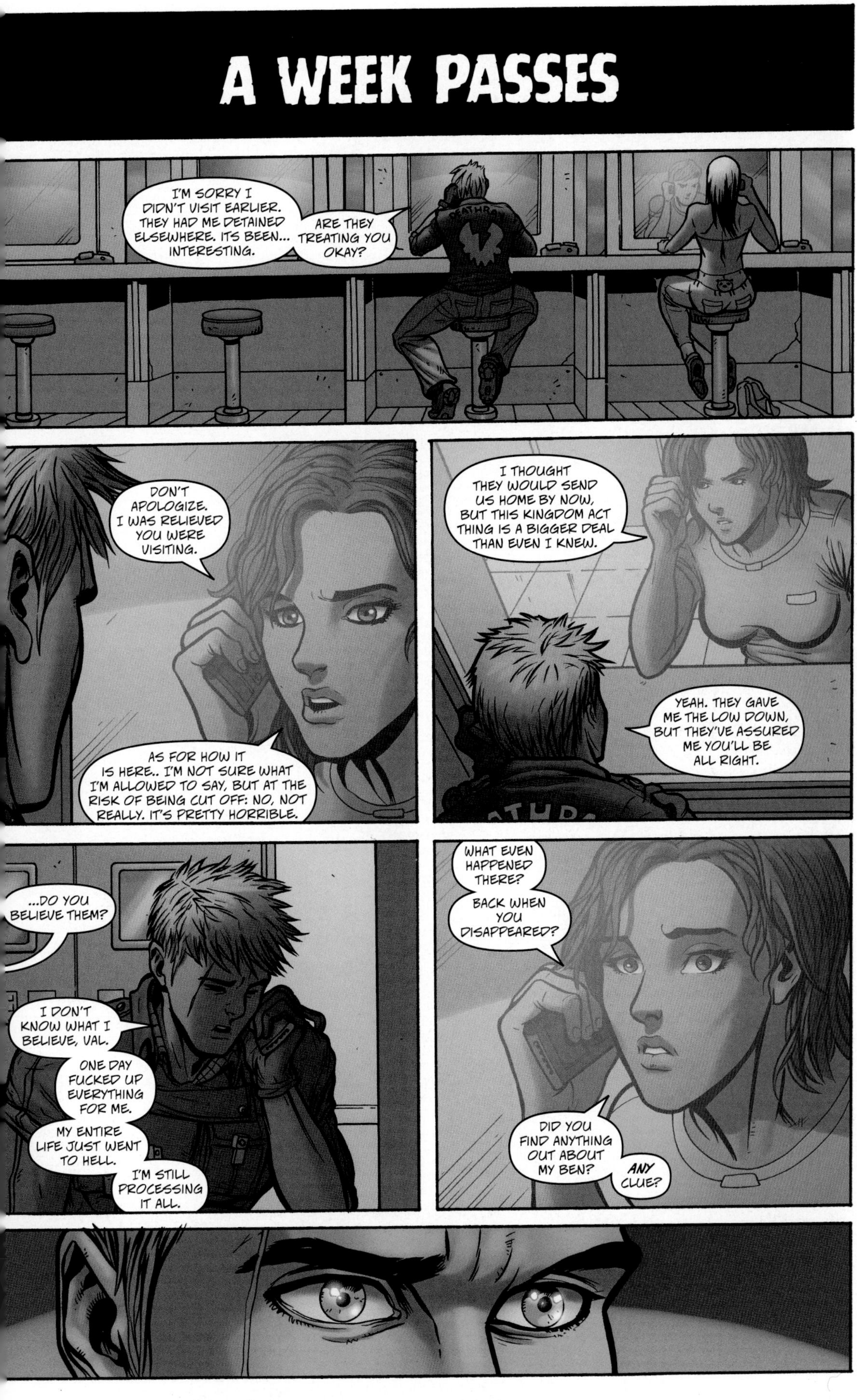
A WEEK PASSES
I'M SORRY I DIDN'T VISIT EARLIER. THEY HAD ME DETAINED ELSEWHERE. ITS BEEN... INTERESTING.
ARE THEY TREATING YOU OKAY?
DEATHRA
DON'T APOLOGIZE. I WAS RELIEVED YOU WERE VISITING.
AS FOR HOW IT IS HERE.. I'M NOT SURE WHAT I'M ALLOWED TO SAY, BUT AT THE RISK OF BEING CUT OFF: NO, NOT REALLY. IT'S PRETTY HORRIBLE.
I THOUGHT THEY WOULD SEND US HOME BY NOW, BUT THIS KINGDOM ACT THING IS A BIGGER DEAL THAN EVEN I KNEW.
YEAH. THEY GAVE ME THE LOW DOWN, BUT THEY'VE ASSURED ME YOU'LL BE ALL RIGHT.
...DO YOU BELIEVE THEM?
I DON'T KNOW WHAT I BELIEVE, VAL.
ONE DAY FUCKED UP EVERYTHING FOR ME.
MY ENTIRE LIFE JUST WENT TO HELL.
I'M STILL PROCESSING IT ALL.
WHAT EVEN HAPPENED THERE?
BACK WHEN YOU DISAPPEARED?
DID YOU FIND ANYTHING OUT ABOUT MY BEN?
ANY CLUE?

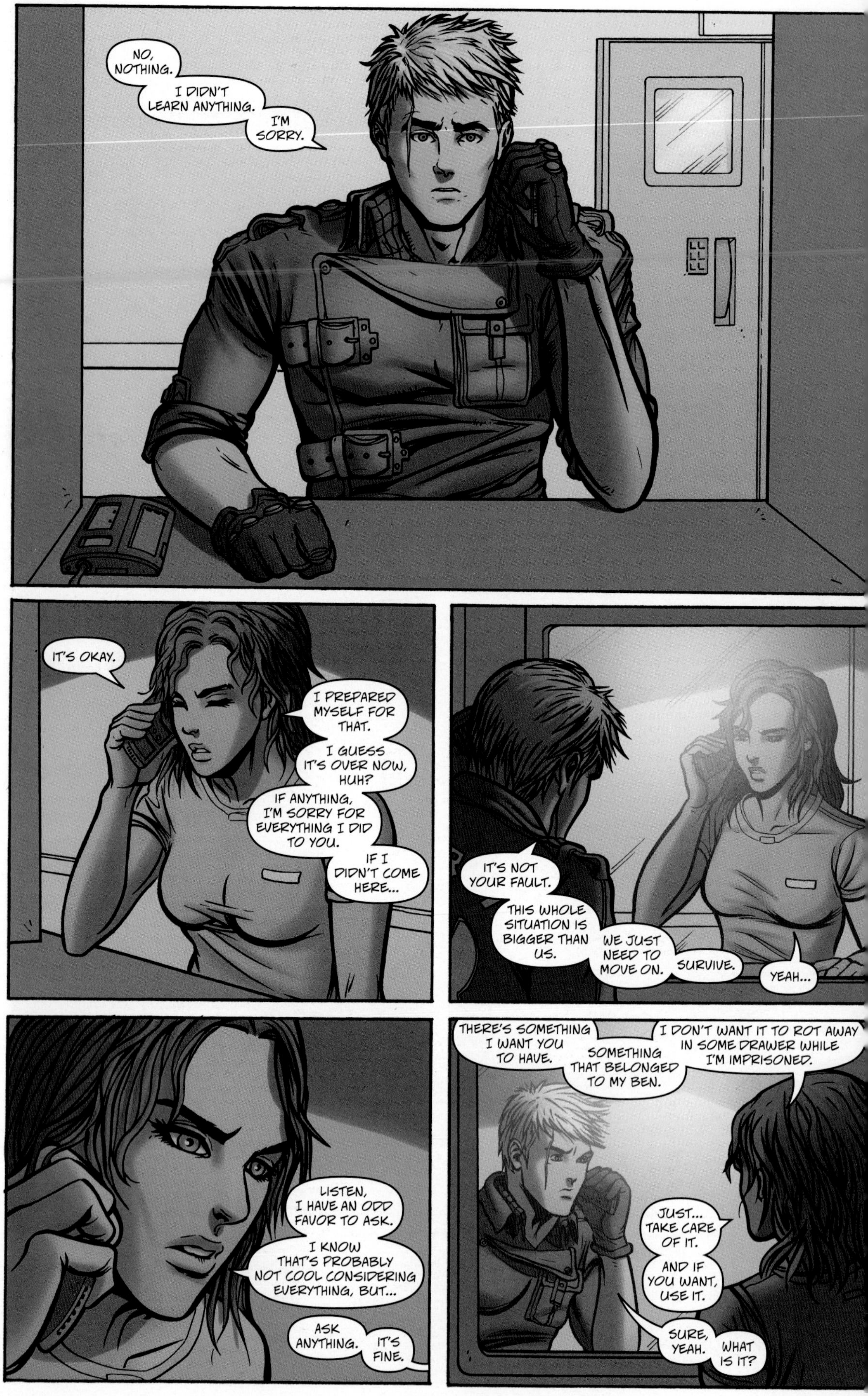
NO, NOTHING.
I DIDN'T LEARN ANYTHING.
I'M SORRY.
IT'S OKAY.
I PREPARED MYSELF FOR THAT.
I GUESS IT'S OVER NOW, HUH?
IF ANYTHING, I'M SORRY FOR EVERYTHING I DID TO YOU.
IF I DIDN'T COME HERE...
IT'S NOT YOUR FAULT.
THIS WHOLE SITUATION IS BIGGER THAN US.
WE JUST NEED TO MOVE ON.
SURVIVE.
YEAH...
LISTEN, I HAVE AN ODD FAVOR TO ASK.
I KNOW THAT'S PROBABLY NOT COOL CONSIDERING EVERYTHING, BUT...
ASK ANYTHING.
IT'S FINE.
SURE, YEAH.
WHAT IS IT?
THERE'S SOMETHING I WANT YOU TO HAVE.
SOMETHING THAT BELONGED TO MY BEN.
I DON'T WANT IT TO ROT AWAY IN SOME DRAWER WHILE I'M IMPRISONED.
JUST... TAKE CARE OF IT.
AND IF YOU WANT, USE IT.

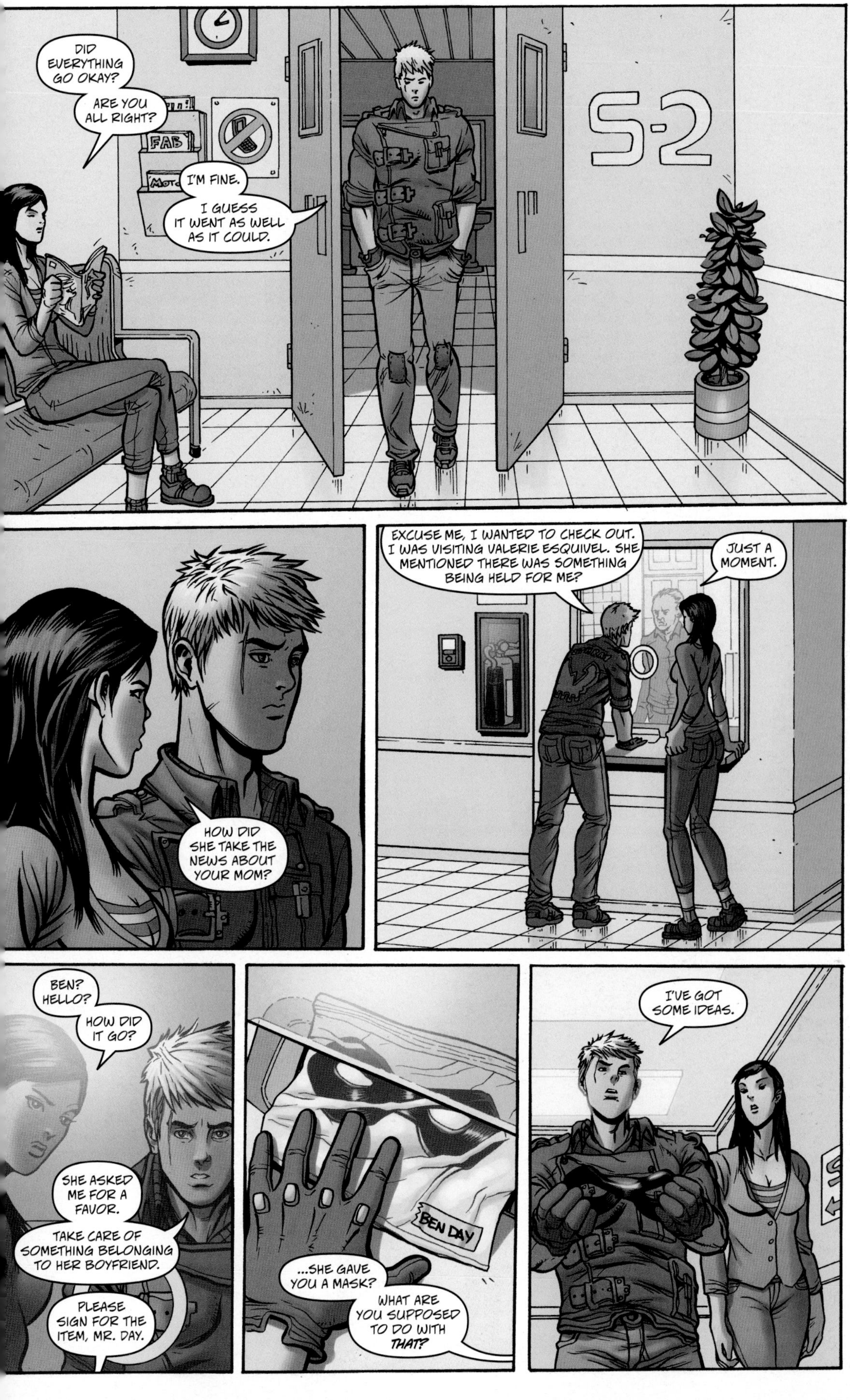
DID EVERYTHING GO OKAY?
ARE YOU ALL RIGHT?
FAB
I'M FINE.
I GUESS IT WENT AS WELL AS IT COULD.
S-2
HOW DID SHE TAKE THE NEWS ABOUT YOUR MOM?
EXCUSE ME, I WANTED TO CHECK OUT. I WAS VISITING VALERIE ESQUIVEL. SHE MENTIONED THERE WAS SOMETHING BEING HELD FOR ME?
JUST A MOMENT.
BEN? HELLO?
HOW DID IT GO?
SHE ASKED ME FOR A FAVOR.
TAKE CARE OF SOMETHING BELONGING TO HER BOYFRIEND.
PLEASE SIGN FOR THE ITEM, MR. DAY.
BEN DAY
...SHE GAVE YOU A MASK?
WHAT ARE YOU SUPPOSED TO DO WITH THAT?
I'VE GOT SOME IDEAS.

FIVE YEARS LATER

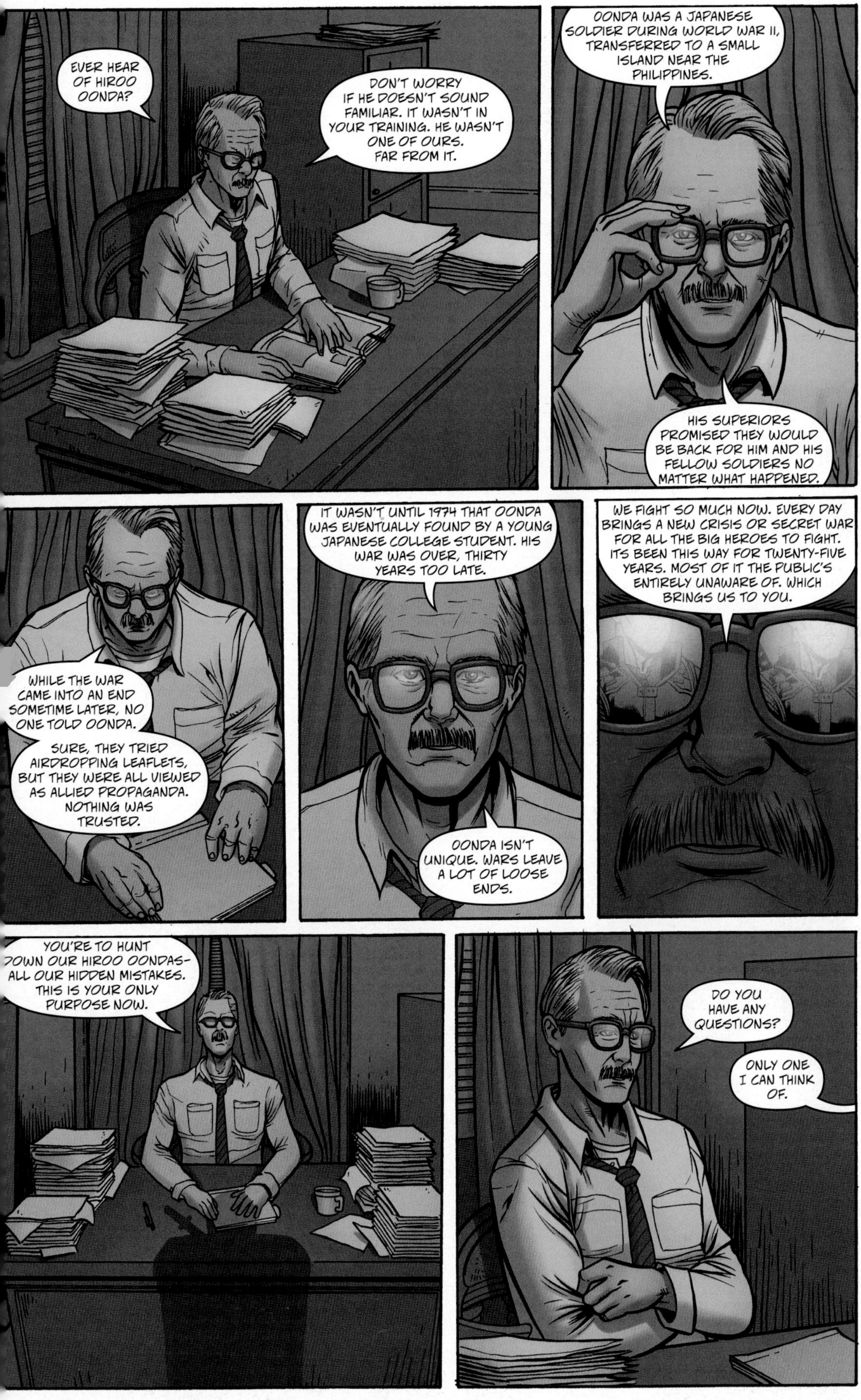
EVER HEAR OF HIROO OONDA?
DON'T WORRY IF HE DOESN'T SOUND FAMILIAR. IT WASN'T IN YOUR TRAINING. HE WASN'T ONE OF OURS. FAR FROM IT.
OONDA WAS A JAPANESE SOLDIER DURING WORLD WAR II, TRANSFERRED TO A SMALL ISLAND NEAR THE PHILIPPINES.
HIS SUPERIORS PROMISED THEY WOULD BE BACK FOR HIM AND HIS FELLOW SOLDIERS NO MATTER WHAT HAPPENED.
WHILE THE WAR CAME INTO AN END SOMETIME LATER, NO ONE TOLD OONDA.
SURE, THEY TRIED AIRDROPPING LEAFLETS, BUT THEY WERE ALL VIEWED AS ALLIED PROPAGANDA. NOTHING WAS TRUSTED.
IT WASN'T UNTIL 1974 THAT OONDA WAS EVENTUALLY FOUND BY A YOUNG JAPANESE COLLEGE STUDENT. HIS WAR WAS OVER, THIRTY YEARS TOO LATE.
OONDA ISN'T UNIQUE. WARS LEAVE A LOT OF LOOSE ENDS.
WE FIGHT SO MUCH NOW. EVERY DAY BRINGS A NEW CRISIS OR SECRET WAR FOR ALL THE BIG HEROES TO FIGHT. ITS BEEN THIS WAY FOR TWENTY-FIVE YEARS. MOST OF IT THE PUBLIC'S ENTIRELY UNAWARE OF. WHICH BRINGS US TO YOU.
YOU'RE TO HUNT DOWN OUR HIROO OONDAS- ALL OUR HIDDEN MISTAKES. THIS IS YOUR ONLY PURPOSE NOW.
DO YOU HAVE ANY QUESTIONS?
ONLY ONE I CAN THINK OF.

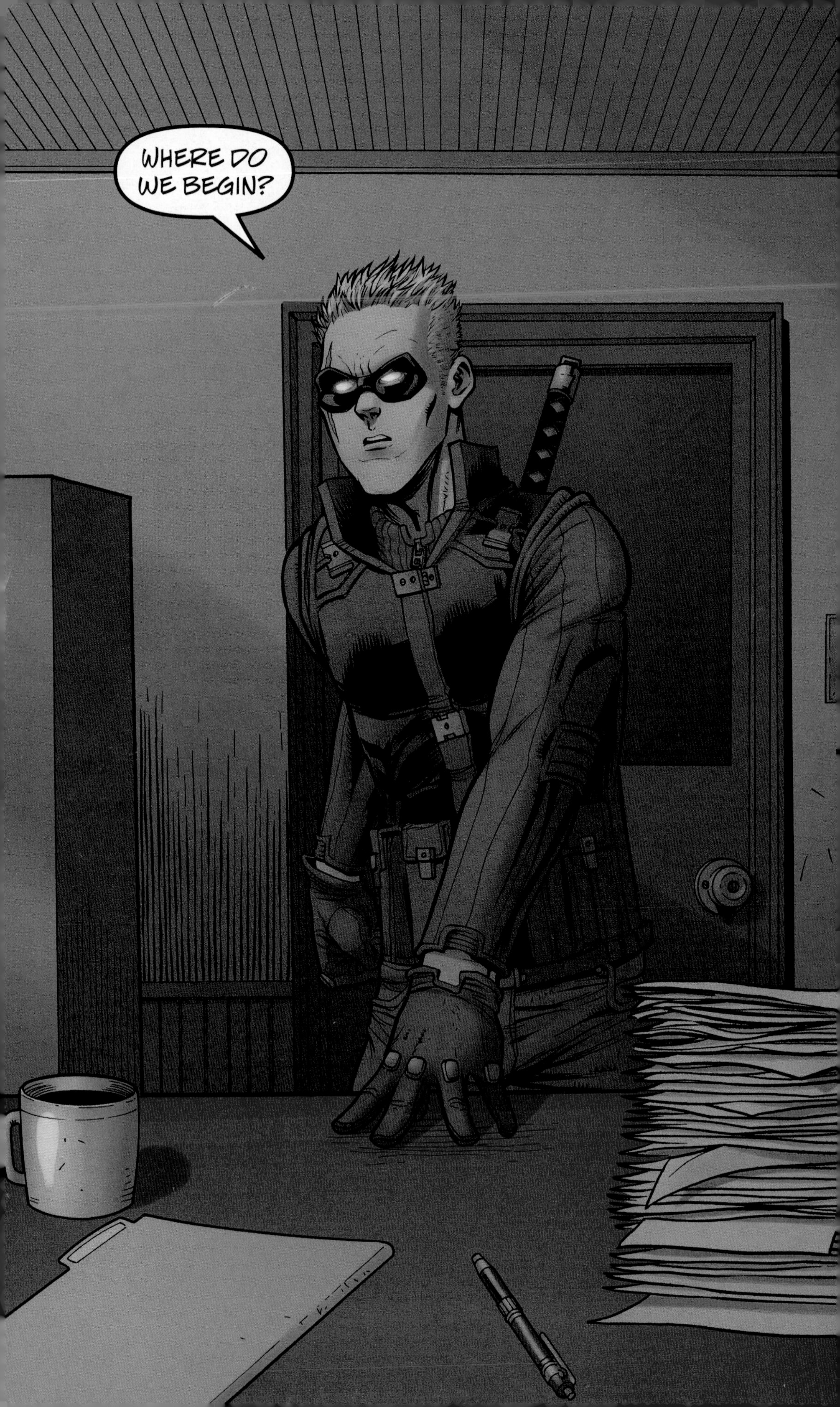
WHERE DO WE BEGIN?

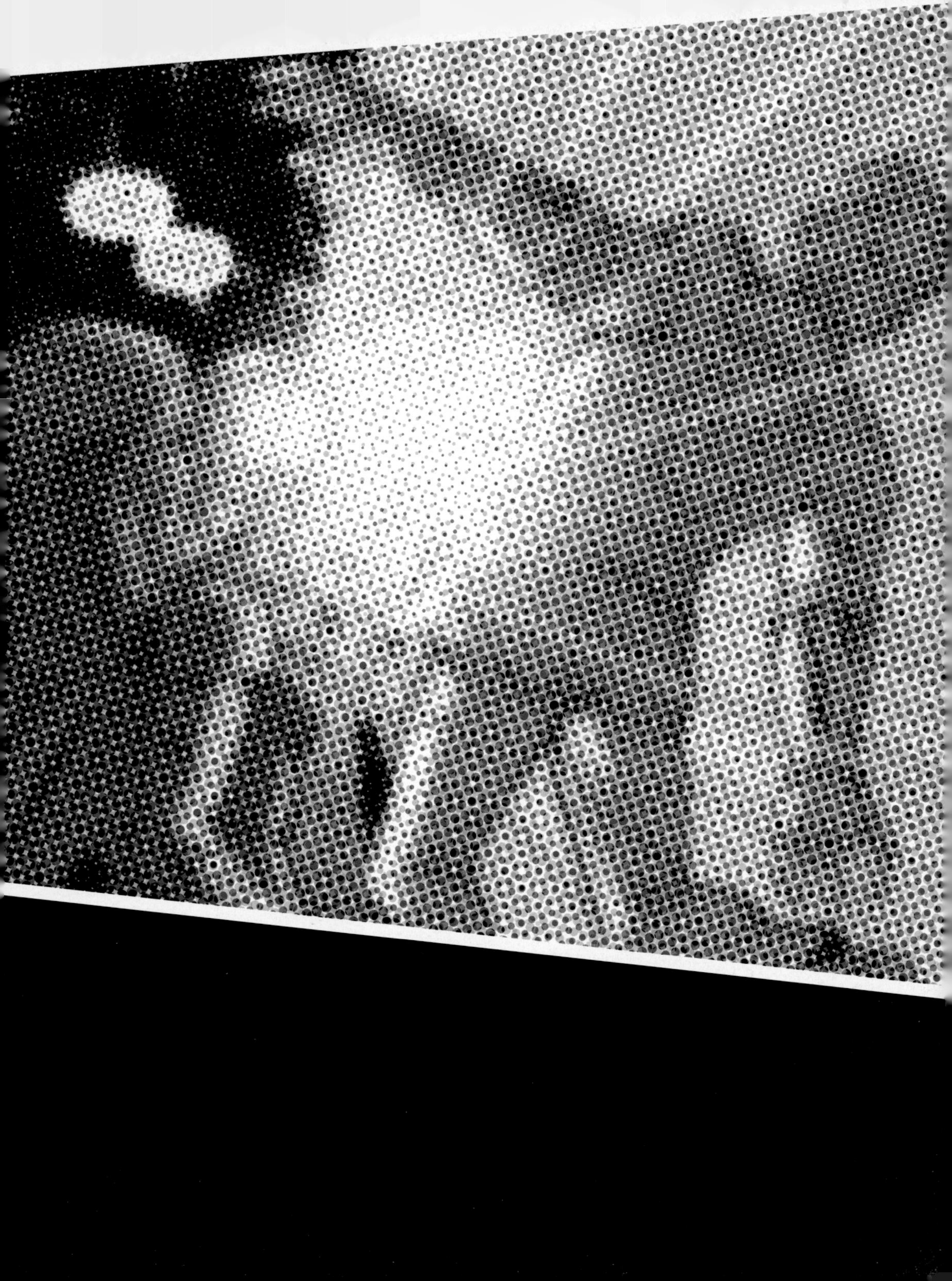

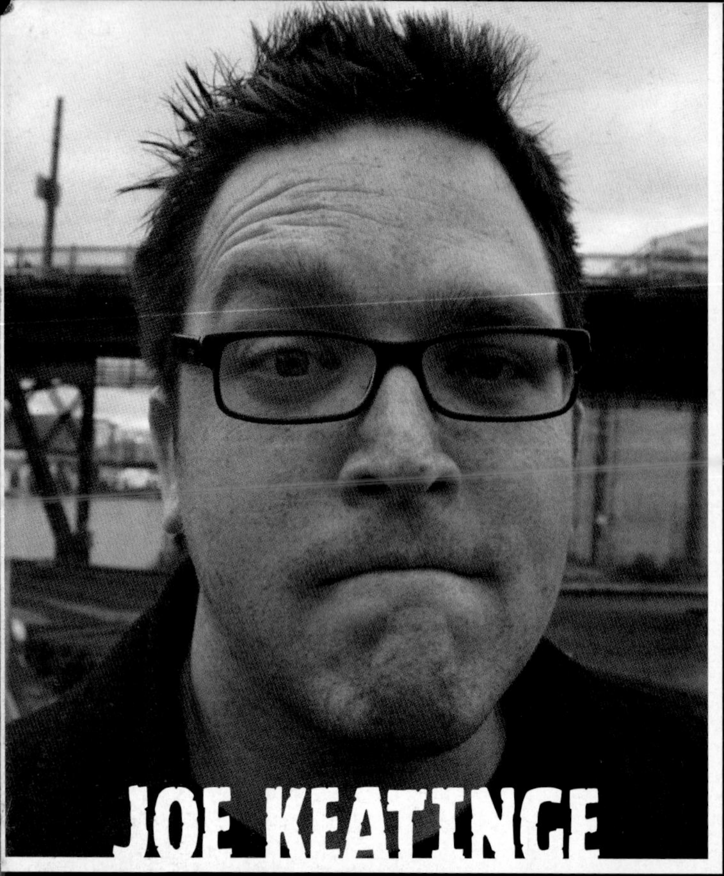
JOE KEATINGE

Eisner & Harvey award-winning comic book writer and editor of Image, Marvel and DC Comics titles including **HELL YEAH, GLORY, MORBIUS: THE LIVING VAMPIRE, INTERGALACTIC, POPGUN, ONE MODEL NATION** and an issue of **AMAZING SPIDER-MAN**. He also writes for the premiere French-language magazine on American comics, **COMIC BOX**. This all goes down at the World's Greatest Comics Studio, Tranquility Base, Portland, OR.

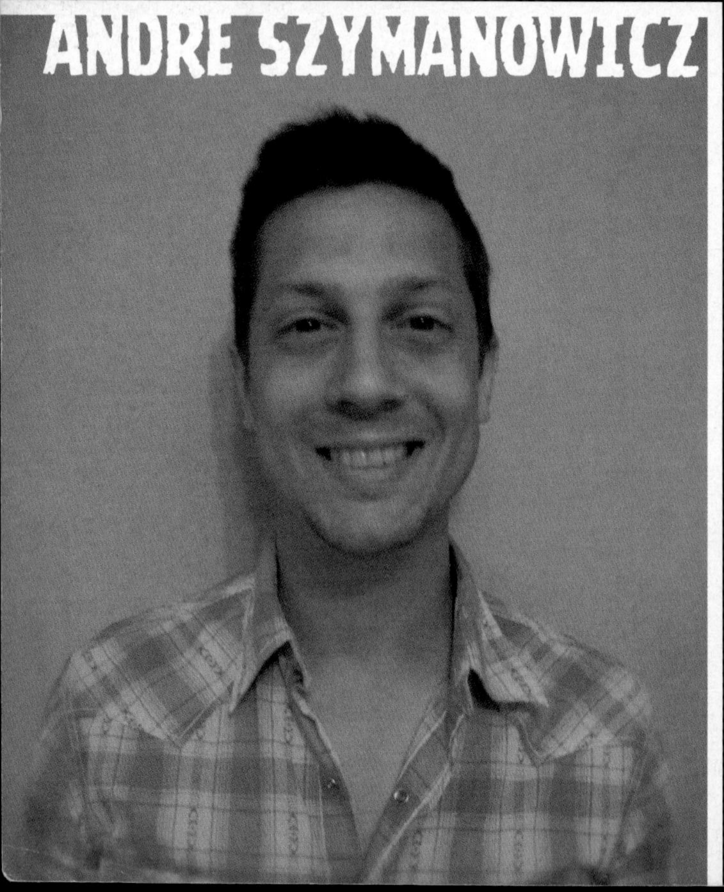
ANDRE SZYMANOWICZ

Joe Kubert School alumni artist and colorist on DC and Image Comics titles including **HELL YEAH, ELEPHANTMEN, ALL-STAR WESTERN & THE SPIRIT** with contributions to the Eisner award-winning anthologies **COMIC BOOK TATTOO** and **POPGUN**. He has a love/hate relationship with ice cream and lives in New Jersey with his wife and kids.

ason Lewis is a professional comic book colorist living in Portland, OR. In his burgeoning
career he has worked for most of the major publishers as well as painting the occasional heavy
metal album cover.

FABIO REDIVO
INKER (ISSUE 5)

Fabio Redivo earned a degree from the University of Fine Arts of Sao Paulo in Graphic Design
and later graduated from The Kubert School. Through A Wave Blue World Inc., he was invited
to work at Tell-A-Graphics, where he was involved in Joe Kubert projects and PS Magazine.
He has worked at Archie Comics and lots of indie publishers and is currently contracted as an
instructor for The Kubert School.

DOUGLAS E. SHERWOOD
LETTERER

Douglas E. Sherwood was born on the planet hVADOXe in 1984. He has done many things, and
now he is here. But you already know this.

RON RICHARDS
EDITOR

Hailing from the mean streets of Long Island, NY, Ron Richards has been reading comics for
two-thirds of his life. This passion lead to his co-founding of the leading comics community
website iFanboy.com in 2001, where he co-hosts one of the top comics audio podcasts. In
addition to his work as a critic, he also works at the digital distributor Graphicly. Currently
residing in San Francisco, most importantly his heart will go on.

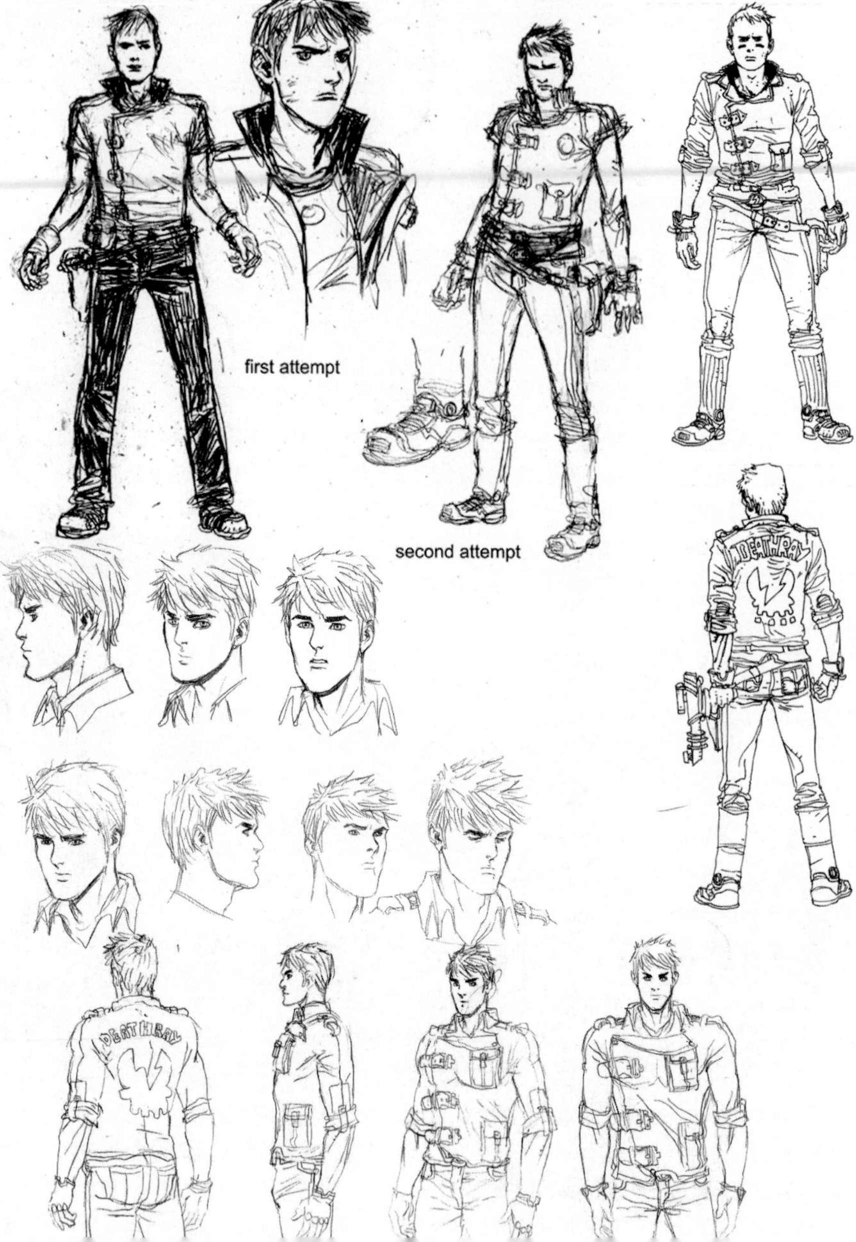
first attempt
second attempt

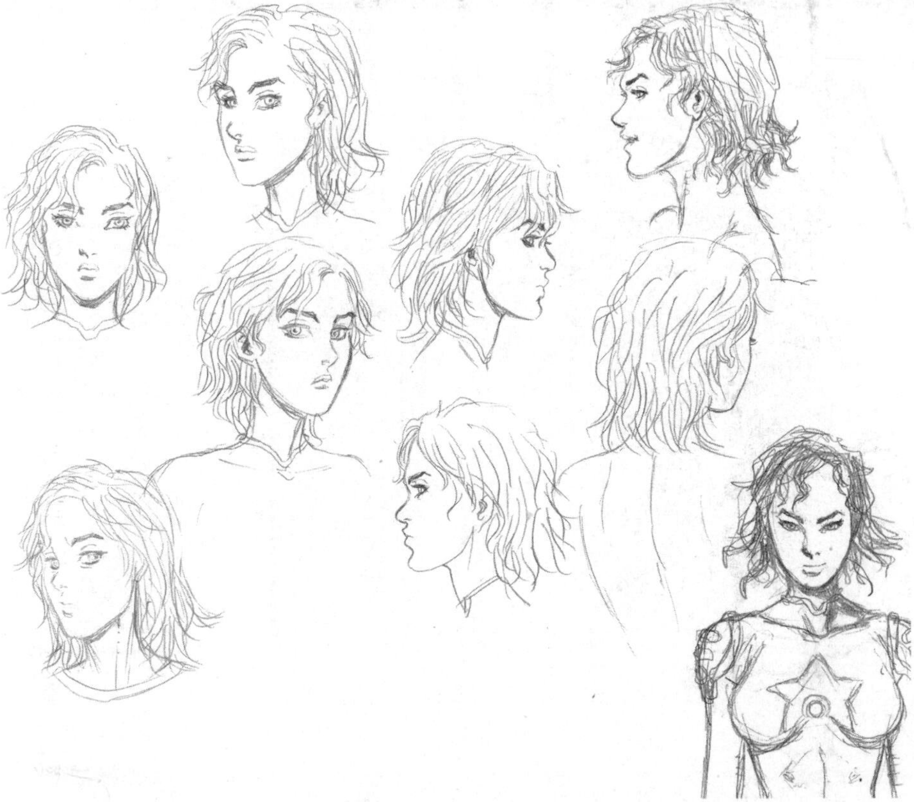

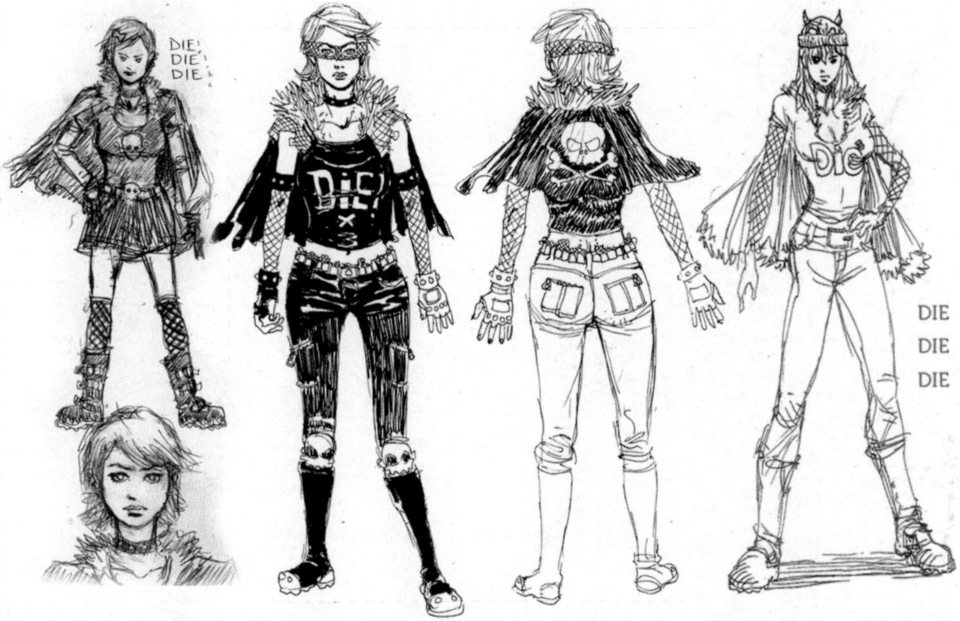
DIE!
DIE!
DIE!
DIE
DIE
DIE

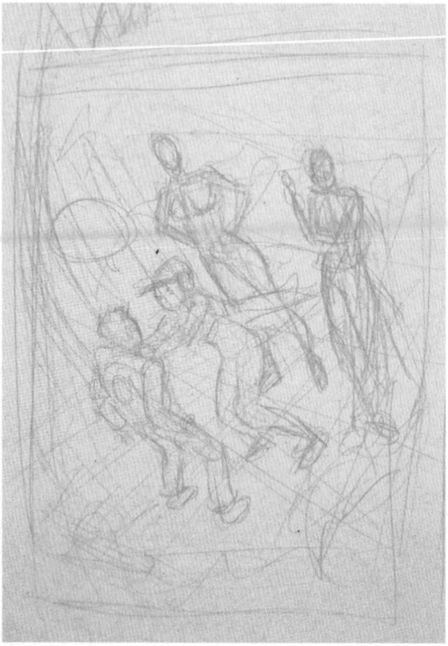

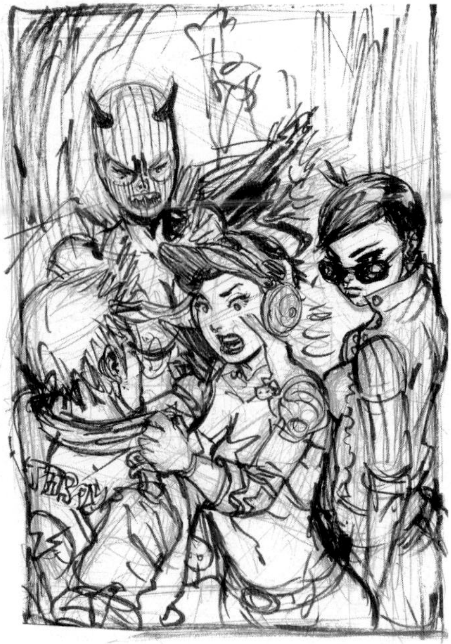

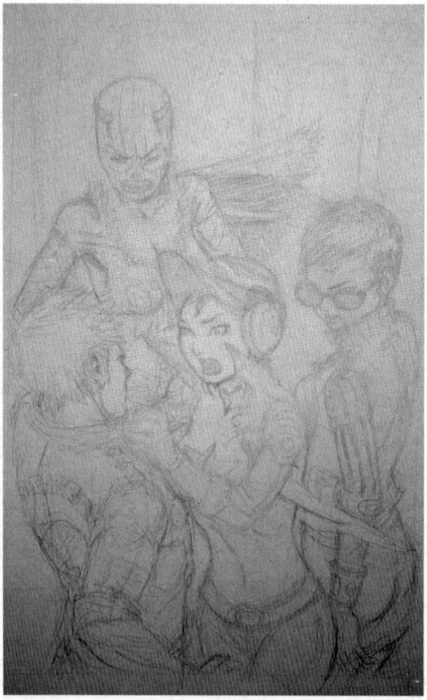

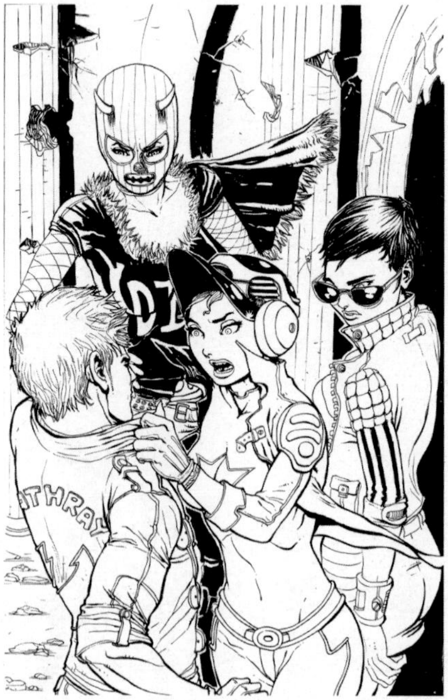